Kirtlington
An Oxfordshire Village

Kirtlington
An Oxfordshire Village

Vanadia Humphries

Phillimore

1986

Published by
PHILLIMORE & CO. LTD.
Shopwyke Hall, Chichester, Sussex, England

ISBN 0 85033 584 1

Printed and bound in Great Britain by
BIDDLES LTD.
Guildford, Surrey

*This book is dedicated to
the late Ernest King and his wife Winifred
whose interest and support has meant so much to me*

Contents

List of plates ix
List of text illustrations xi
Acknowledgements xiii
Introduction xv
 1. The Tun of Cyrtla's People 1
 2. The Church of St Mary the Virgin 5
 3. Virgates and Villeins 12
 4. The Ancient Manor of Northbrook 16
 5. The Ruff and the Wig 24
 6. A State of Emergency 27
 7. An Era of Elegance 30
 8. Cultivation and Conservation 37
 9. A Village at War 43
10. The Struggle for Survival 53
11. The Ways of Village Government 58
12. Farm and Field 63
13. The Horse in the Village 75
14. Money and Muscle: The Oxford Canal 82
15. The Oxford Portland Cement Company 90
16. The Schoolchildren of Kirtlington 98
17. The Days We Remember 106
18. Ernie King: The boy who had room to grow 126
19. 'My Village' by the children of Kirtlington 132
    Appendix One: The Old Folks at Home 135
    Appendix Two: The Folk Tradition in Kirtlington 138
    Bibliography 144
    Index 147

List of Plates

1. Sir Robert Dashwood
2. Miss Muriel Dashwood
3. Kirtlington Park, 1983
4. Christopher Buxton
5. Mrs. Hazel Budgett with 'Pepper', 1983
6. A shooting party, c. 1900
7. The church of St Mary the Virgin, about 1920
8. The Reverend T. K. Chittenden, 1858
9. The Reverend Reginald Ward Bennett, 1929
10. The Reverend George Bennett, 1961
11. Mary and Bob Viner
12. Sophia and Jeremiah Keys, Lilian, Arthur and Bertha, about 1900
13. Mrs. Lilian Wickson, Wilfred and Nora, about 1920
14. Edwell Walter Talbot, with sons Jack and 'Turp'
15. The forge, about 1890
16. Bill Johnson with 'Jolly' at a ploughing match
17. Frederick Blake
18. Workers at Park Farm, c. 1930
19. Percy East, 1914
20. Albert East, 1914
21. 'Prince', 'Jess' and the Kirtland's water cart
22. A concert party, 1911
23. Village children at the turn of the century
24. Kirtlington Football Team, 1908-9
25. Jack Talbot, band leader
26. Miss Ivy Pratt, later Mrs. Charlie King
27. Ernie, Winnie and Ivor King in the early 1940s
28. Marion Kirtland and the Easter lambs, about 1940
29. Victor Tugwood, aged 10, with 'Nellie'
30. Aubrey and Edith Gile with Monty, Stella, Laurie, Bill, Victor and Godfrey
31. Albert and Jessie East with their nephew and the new bread van
32. A 'Number One' boatman on the Oxford Canal
33. Unloading coal at Washford Pits landing stage, c. 1920
34. Cement packers at Washford Pits, about 1920
35. The workforce of the Oxford and Shipton Cement Company Ltd., about 1930
36. Remains of the Kirtlington dinosaur
37. One of the prehistoric mammal teeth found at Washford Pits
38. Erection of the kilns at Washford Pits, 1906-7
39. 'Morston', winner of the 1973 Derby
40. Stirrup cup for the Bicester Hunt, Kirtlington Park, about 1913

41. Ready for the next chukka
42. H.R.H. Prince Charles at the 1983 Varsity Polo match, Kirtlington Park
43. The choir outing, about 1920
44. Colonel Henry Shellard
45. Kirtlington Morris Men, 1980
46. School group, 1908
47. School group, 1984

List of Text Figures

1.	Work begins at Cyrtla's Tun	1
2.	Work begins at Cyrtla's Tun	3
3.	The *Church Monthly*, May 1893	6
4.	Kirtlington Dissenters	10
5.	Charter of Nicholas Jurdan	14
6.	Inventory of Anthony Day, fisherman of Northbrook	18
7.	'The death of ye hare with ye Fleet Hound'	20
8.	The will of Ralph Rawlins, huntsman	21
9.	The Dashwood coat of arms	30
10.	The Agent's notice	37
11.	The 1922 auction	39
12.	The oath of Samuel Hall, Militiaman, 1831	44
13.	The oath of Samuel Hall, Militiaman, 1831	45
14.	Surgeon's certificate for Samuel Hall	45
15.	A Patriotic Meeting, October 1914	48
16.	Apprenticeship indenture for George Smith	54
17.	Settlement certificate for the Spicer family	55
18.	Summons to the Court Baron, 1760	59
19.	The Kirtlington Enclosure Act, 1811	64
20.	Will of Richard Bryon, farmer	65
21.	The Parish allotment agreement	65
22.	The pattern of the plough – Kirtlington farmlands *c.*1805	69
23.	Stock sale at Park Farm, 1870	70
24.	An opportunity for Kirtlington farmers	72
25.	The mad mysterious hare	75
26.	The 'new entry', 1842 print	76
27.	The country mare	78
28.	The new thoroughbred	79
29.	Polo, 1983	80
30.	Osier cutting	84
31.	Osier peeling	84
32.	Canal boy on the tow path	85
33.	A 'fly' boat and passengers, *c.*1810	85
34.	Canal scene, *c.*1870	87
35.	Trade mark of the Oxford Portland Cement Company	90
36.	Plan of the works, 1907-1929	91
37.	Previous and present trademarks	95
38.	The Industrial Exhibition	102
39.	The Diocesan inspection	104
40.	Rabbit	107
41.	Detail from the smock of Charles East, master baker	110
42.	The village shoemaker	113

43. An account from Brackley's stores, 1887 114
44. Off to market 116
45. Laboratory testing equipment 129
46. William Kemp dances to the pipe and tabor 138
47. Morris dancer 140

Acknowledgements

It is difficult to find the right words to express my thanks to David Joliffe, whose valuable sponsorship has enabled my book to be published. I am more than grateful for his help. The Cherwell District Council has contributed generously to my daughter Erica's photographic expenses. My thanks are also due to Mrs. M. G. Buxton of Oxford, for her encouragement and interest during the progress of this book, and her kind donation towards my expenses. The Lord of the Manor of Kirtlington, Mr. Christopher Buxton, O.B.E., M.A., M.B.A., has given me much support, and shown considerable interest in the project. His generous donation was much appreciated, and enabled further research to be carried out.

Mr. K. R. Maltas, Acting Manager of the Blue Circle Group, Shipton-on-Cherwell, introduced me to Ernest King, and I should also like to thank Mr. R. A. Wharam, the Works General Manager at Shipton, and Mr. B. Hedges, of the Group's Public Affairs Department in London, for their help.

The Editor of the *Village News*, Colonel H. M. Shellard, has been a tower of strength, solving many historical queries at short notice, and has filled many gaps in my researches with information from his own notebooks. I should also like to thank the following for specialist information on particular subjects: Mrs. H. M. Budgett and Mr. Alan Budgett (hunting, racing and polo); Mr. Phillip Thorman (Kirtlington Estate) and Mr. J. Eeley of Northbrook Farm (farming and agricultural matters); Mr. and Miss Kirtland (the forge); Mr. and Mrs. Jack Talbot (shepherding); Mr. Sam Miller (sheep in the market place); Mrs. Winifred King (gamekeeping); Mr. and Miss East (bakery); Mr. and Mrs. Len Berry (folklore); Mrs. Edna Edgington (the Lamb Ale); Mr. 'Bill' Wickson, Mr. Brian Keys, Mr. and Mrs. Frank Lawrence (the Oxford Canal and the *Three Pigeons* alehouse); Messrs. Halls' Brewery (pages from a ledger); Mr. 'Vic' Bodsworth (work of a section manager of the Oxford Canal); Mr. Bill Giles (permission to quote from his father's First World War Diary); the Reverend R. George Bennett (history of the church); the Reverend David Wilcox (permission to take photographs); Mr. David Mankelow (use of the old school Log Book); Mrs. Margaret Trafford (information on Mr. Austin, former headmaster); Mr. David Cox (translation of a Latin document); Mr. Eric Freeman and Mr. H. P. Powell, Assistant Curator, University Museum, Oxford (the fossil discoveries at Washford Pits); Mrs. Margaret Trafford, grand-daughter of a 19th-century Kirtlington headmaster (school and village printed ephemera).

I am also most grateful to those villagers whose memories are recorded in the chapter entitled 'The Days We Remember' for sharing their stories with me and with the readers of this book, and to those other villagers whose poems are printed here.

No book on local history would be possible without using research facilities, and my thanks are due to the following persons and institutions: The Bodleian Library; Miss Barnes and Miss Wolgar of the County Record Office, Oxford; Mr. Graham and the staff of the Local History Collection, Central Library, Oxford; Miss Christine

Bloxham of the County Museum, Woodstock; and Mrs. Sarah Gosling of the County Museum, Banbury, for permission to reproduce a painting of Sir Richard Dashwood.

Mrs. Gilly Barnard stepped in at the last moment to type the manuscript for me, for which I am most grateful.

Last but by no means least, I am deeply grateful to my daughter Erica for her careful photography and her endless patience with a difficult project.

Introduction

My first visit to Kirtlington was in 1981. On a mellow September afternoon, as I walked down Mill Lane towards the canal, I passed the entrance to a deserted quarry. A winding footpath led down to its floor. Towering above were its ancient walls, deeply gouged by years of digging and blasting. Suddenly the stillness was broken by a cock-pheasant's harsh call from the nearby spinney, which started a motionless rabbit into sudden flight. I had not felt such intense pleasure in scenery and atmosphere for many years, and knew that I had to discover more about the history of Washford Pits. My enquiries to Blue Circle Industries – who are the present owners, led me to one of their retired employees, who had worked in the quarry as a boy. Ernie King had been born in Kirtlington, and revealed facets of life in the old days that had never appeared in a history book, whilst his wife, Winifred, a gamekeeper's daughter, described her childhood. A few days later I told Ernie that I intended to write a history of Kirtlington. He did not seem in the least surprised, and set about helping me by providing endless notes, old photographs, and arranging for me to meet friends who might have helpful information about the old days. I could not have wished for a better collaborator! Both Ernie and Winnie were anxious to show me Oxfordshire customs: I was a guest at Lamb Ale Feast in 1982, and on Good Friday 1983 I was entertained to a 'bacon clanger' lunch. I had no idea that this was to be my last meeting with Ernie, and the news of his sudden death a few days later was a great sadness. I can only hope that I have portrayed the village and its history as accurately and affectionately as he intended. Unfortunately there are many villagers who I have not been able to include through shortage of time, and I hope they will forgive me.

I have attempted to describe its evolution from a pagan Saxon settlement to the present day, and have supplemented archival material by oral history, which helps to bring sometimes dull historical records to vivid life. I hope my book will give pleasure not only to historians, but to those who work the land, and all who listen and observe, treasuring the atmosphere of the past to be sensed in the fields, lanes and hedgerows of an ancient village. Whatever else has changed, I am certain that the qualities of humour and friendship which were so apparent during the last century, and the determination of so many to make the best of whatever life offered them, remain unchanged today.

VANADIA HUMPHRIES

Oxford
1986

CHAPTER ONE

The Tun of Cyrtla's People

There are no written records from the earliest days of Kirtlington's history, but archaeology may still have some information to reveal. The fertile soil, extensive forestland, streams, brooks, as well as the River Cherwell itself, would have provided good conditions for Neolithic and Bronze Age settlers, whilst excavations carried out in 1973 have proved that people of the Iron Age from the sixth century B.C., who had buried their dead in fields close to the junction where the Romans later built their roads – Akeman Street and the Portway. There may be even earlier remains from the Neolithic or Bronze Age to be found in nearby Hoar Stone Spinney.

The forging of tools and implements was a skill which had made the cultivation of land an easier task for the men of the Iron Age, but their survival still depended on good crops of wheat and barley, and the well-being of their livestock, which were mainly sheep, cattle and pigs. Their homes were of stone, or of wattle and daub with a conical thatched roof, and they produced well-made pottery, bowls of a gritty orange-brown clay, and jars of grey and brown. These people were probably still in the village when the Romans arrived soon after the year A.D. 47. The villagers continued to work the land, although those who had previously owned it may have found themselves displaced by new Roman owners.

Fig. 1. Work begins at Cyrtla's Tun.

It was thought by one researcher in the early 1900s (Mr. Tindall Wildridge) that the first name for the village was 'Cansum', meaning the rivered or watered height, and this seemed to be borne out by two ancient enclosures on the hill plateau which had the name 'Kensome'. Another one close by was called 'Oldbury', and both are shown on a map of the manor of Kirtlington dated 1750.

The Romans quickly set about building roads so that troops and supplies could be moved quickly and efficiently from the nearest port to their garrisons at Alchester and Bicester, known to them as *Berncestre*. Akeman Street, which crosses north Oxfordshire from east to west, was the vital link between London and Cirencester (the Roman *Corinium*). In some places it was 25 feet wide, and the brushwood foundation was paved with slabs of local stone and gravel, bound with clay. In other parts of the Street, there was a firm foundation of beaten earth, layered with stones embedded in mortar, followed by smaller stones, lime, chalk and powdered brick. The final surface was then paved. The Portway seems to have been a less important road, which incorporated part of an ancient trackway. It was only partially paved and led eventually to Portchester and Southampton.

The Roman settlement at Alchester probably served as a market centre for the neighbourhood, as well as a Roman garrison town and supply depot. From a drawing by Stukeley in 1776, it appears to have been situated close to Akeman Street, with Chesterton to the north, and Wendlebury on its western boundary. Founded about A.D. 50, it was a garrison town and supply depot, and also in all probability a market centre for its neighbourhood. Another feature of the town was a building with mosaic floors, brick pavements and walls some four feet thick. Recent excavations have demonstrated that this was a bath house. Alchester was also the administrative centre for the district, collecting taxes and maintaining law and order. In all, the town covered about 25 acres, and was surrounded by a ditch and rampart, 'with four towers to defend the city'. The mysterious Aves Ditch, also known as Ash Bank or Wattle Bank, may have formed part of the defences. Medieval charters also refer to Aves Ditch Way, a lane which used to run parallel with the Ditch. This lane was also known as 'Brackley Road'. The discovery of pottery in a ditch filling and under the bank during excavations in 1963 proved that Aves Ditch was not part of another old road, but a dyke (a ditch and bank), and thus a Romano-British earthwork.

Although this was the main local centre of Roman activity, it is possible that Blacklands Field, east of Slade Farm, was the site of a Roman villa. In 1895 Roman coins were discovered here, and on an allotment in Crowcastle Lane, where coins of the emperors Domitian and Lucius Verus were discovered. Hardley Farm may also have been a Roman site. The name 'Hardley' is thought to mean 'treasure wood or clearing', and could refer to the burial of a hoard here in the fourth century.

Roman coinage has also been unearthed in a cottage garden in the Heyford Road. These dated from the third century, while a Kirtlington resident digging muddy waste ground in the vicinity of Station Road came across a coin from the time of Nero (A.D. 54-68), which is now in the Ashmolean Museum at Oxford.

With the departure of the Romans in the late fourth century, Alchester fell into decay. The later Saxon settlers, who called it 'Old Town', had no use for it, and probably took stone from it for their own buildings. A 16th-century verse mourns its fate:

> In Oxfordshire near Craven Hill Wood
> Stood Alchester so fair and good,
> Allectus walls are brought full low
> Where once they stood, now corn doth grow.

The last years of Roman Britain saw a series of increasingly fierce attacks by the Pictish and Scottish peoples to the north, and from the fierce seafaring peoples from the Continent known most usually as Saxons. The Britons bought the services of groups of the latter as mercenaries to help fight off these opponents, but these mercenaries then seized power for themselves and gradually established permanent settlements in Britain. They came from northern Europe, from the areas which we now know as the Netherlands, Germany, and Scandinavia. In their homelands good land was scarce, and the trickle of settlement became a flood. The native British resisted and even temporarily halted Saxon expansion westwards from their original settlements in the south-eastern corner of England, but eventually they were defeated. Roman Britain had become Saxon England.

Fig. 2. Work begins at Cyrtla's Tun.

The settlement which was to become the home of the Saxon Cyrtla and his people lay within the kingdom of Mercia, one of the most powerful Saxon kingdoms, which straddled the Midlands and for a long time challenged the kingdom of Wessex for the dominance of all England. Cyrtla's party would have been looking for a site with wood for fuel and building, a good supply of water, and grazing for the livestock. They were probably still worshippers of the pagan Saxon gods, rather than Christians, and would have wanted a secluded spot for a temple where animal sacrifices could be made. The long house, or chieftain's hall, where Cyrtla and his immediate family lived also served as a meeting place for the community. No doubt when this building was finally completed there would have been a special celebration, with the women in their best gowns and perhaps displaying the beautiful and intricate jewellery which Anglo-Saxon craftsmen produced, examples of which can be seen in the Ashmolean Museum. Brooches or *fibulae* were often buried with their owners, like those which were found in 1873 where the Portway crosses Akeman Street.

Cyrtla's settlement was not an isolated one. Nearby were the homesteads of Blaecca and Taecca (Bletchingdon and Tackley) – perhaps the men of these settlements fought for the old Mercian king Ethelbald, who was defeated at Burford by the West Saxon monarch Cuthred in 726.

We cannot be certain that Kirtlington was in fact named after a person called Cyrtla, for many theories have been put forward to explain the origin of this place-name. Could it mean 'the church village', or 'church meadow enclosure', the 'township of the Kirtlings'? Two medieval references to the name 'Cyrtla', however, suggest that 'the tun of Cyrtla's people' may be the true answer. In the 10th century a land charter referred to 'Cyrtlan's geat' (Cyrtla's gate) and in the 13th century another one to 'Curtleford Broke' (Cyrtla's Brook). This would seem to suggest that there was a minor chieftain of this name whose name was applied to important features of the area.

Although we may never discover how the villages of Kirtlington, Bletchingdon and Takeley came to be founded, we can be sure that Saxons formed them, and left long-lasting influences behind them. Bill Wickson, who grew up in Kirtlington during the 1920s and 1930s, believes that his family name derived from the Saxon Hwiccae people, and recalls several village dialect words used in his boyhood which seem to derive from Saxon originals – someone with a white, pale face was described as 'schitten', while football teams were urged on with shouts of 'Acol!' or 'Occle!', while something bright and gleaming was known as 'schir' or 'shier'. It is fascinating to think that these words, after so many centuries, may have first reached Kirtlington in the mouths of Cyrtla's people.

Breaking the ground.

CHAPTER TWO

The Church of St Mary the Virgin

The earliest group of missionaries to visit the tun of Cyrtlas's people may have been led by Birinus, the first bishop of Dorchester on Thames, about A.D. 640. Before leaving his Italian homeland, Birinus had promised Pope Honorius that he would 'seek out places where no other missionaries had been, and sow the seeds of the Holy Faith'. Very little personal detail is known about him, although according to the great Saxon ecclesiastical historian Bede, he was a 'dark-skinned stocky little man'. His magnetic personality, and tremendous faith in God resulted in many conversions in the kingdom of Wessex and the Thames valley.

In the beginning, there would have been mutual suspicion. The missionaries, having endured long journeys by sea to reach Britain, were now at the mercy of savage heathens; Cyrtla and his neighbours may have feared that bad luck would follow the abandonment of their old gods.

Whatever the true story, there is still sufficient evidence in the architecture of the present church of St Mary the Virgin in Kirtlington to prove that it was built on a Saxon site. There are the foundations of the apse under the chancel floor, and stones in the eastern arch of the tower have the zig-zag carving which is a characteristic feature of Saxon architecture. There is also a Saxon carving of the 'Tree of Life' over the priest's typically narrow door. Some years ago when workmen were excavating for heating pipes, the skeleton of a horse was found: is it too fanciful to wonder whether this was a last sacrifice to the old gods, placed under the site of the new church to appease their wrath?

The earliest church would have been a stone building of the simplest kind, with a thatched roof and a rush-strewn stone floor, but it is possible that a more imposing structure was built to coincide with the important *Witanagemot* or king's council which took place in 'Cherielintone' just after Easter in 977. This assembly of church dignatories and lay officials had met to discuss matters of importance to the local people, under the leadership of King Edward and Archbishop Dunstan. On this occasion it was decided to allow the people to go on pilgrimage to Abingdon. However, the gathering was thrown into confusion by the sudden death of Bishop Sideman, whose last wish to be buried at Crediton in his Devonshire see was duly honoured.

While Kirtlington was under Norman rule, a chancel and tower were added to the church. In the 12th century, the lord and lady of the manor were Jordan de Gay and his wife Lucy de Aulnay, whose daughter, Agnes, married Richard de Humez, Constable of Normandy. In 1157 the church of Kirtlington was given as a gift to the French Abbey of Aulnay which de Humez had founded, on condition that they provided a priest and were responsible for the church services in Kirtlington.

On a tablet inside the church the names of all the priests and vicars are recorded. In 1086, the year of the Domesday Survey, Osmund the Priest held 'of the King, one

THE

KIRTLINGTON

CHURCH

MONTHLY.

MAY, 1893.

30 & 31, NEW BRIDGE STREET,
✝
Price
One
Penny.
✝
E.C.

Fig. 3. The *Church Monthly*, May 1893.

hide in Cherielintone' valued at 20 shillings. He was succeeded by one Geoffrey in 1150, and then by Mauser in 1210, but there was a scandal when Jordan took office in 1214, as he 'defamed a woman'. When the Black Death swept the country in 1349, the priest of Kirtlington, William Serch, became a victim. It is said that a certain part of the churchyard where plants and trees are reluctant to grow is the site of a mass grave made at this time.

In 1391 there was serious trouble when a certain 'William Grene' was outlawed for killing a man at Kirtlington. The village priest at that time was also called William Grene, and it is possible, since he was replaced in his first year of office by Robert Mareschall, that it was the same man.

The year 1420 brought further changes to St Mary's, when the priors of St Anne's replaced the Abbey of Aulnay as patrons, and William Reve was appointed priest. It was probably during his term of office that the stone seats were built in the porch, so that baptisms could be held there rather than in the church, which only had a bare floor. There were, however, two altars and a rood screen painted in bright colours. The services, conducted in Latin, might not have been understood by many villagers, but the miracle plays which were probably performed from time to time were doubtless more appreciated.

During morning services light would stream in through the four new clerestory windows and through another which had been constructed in the chancel, perhaps for the benefit of lepers, unable to join the rest of the congregation, so that they could see the elevation of the Host during Mass. At evening services, the guttering candles or rush lighting would throw mysterious shadows on the walls, or catch a gleam of gold from the new paintings of St George and the Dragon and St Christopher in the north aisle. These were rediscovered under whitewash when workmen were carrying out repairs in 1905 and have since been restored. The piscina in the Lady Chapel is of 13th-century origin, and was used by the priest to wash his hands before and after celebrating Mass.

Between 1422 and 1508, eight different priests succeeded William Reve, of whom we can say little, though poor Gilbert Fowler (in office 1512-18) was 'attacked', perhaps by some irate farmer protesting against the payment of tithes. This was the unpopular system whereby the priest received part of his income in the form of animals and produce: each parishioner had to give up a set proportion of his livestock and crop to the priest. Hay, corn, wool, pigs, eggs, poultry, honey, fruit and vegetables were all liable to tithe. In addition, fees were payable for the priest's services in special circumstances, for instance at baptisms or burials. Alive or dead, you had to pay!

However, the perennial grumbles about tithes must have seemed of small concern during the turmoil of the Reformation, when the priest and people of Kirtlington must have heard of the deaths of the martyrs Latimer, Ridley and Archbishop Thomas Cramner himself in nearby Oxford in 1556. Kirtlington church itself did not escape unscathed in these years of confusion and vandalism, and the mark of an axe can still be seen on a surviving fragment of the rood screen, now incorporated into the roof timbers. We have no way of knowing what statues or carvings may have been destroyed at this time in Kirtlington.

For 40 years after the reformation, the church had various lay 'patrons' or owners. In 1587 it came into the possession of St John's College, Oxford, who retain the position today although the appointment of the incumbent is no longer their responsibility. In 1558 the vicar (Richard Briggs) acquired a new duty, that of keeping a register of births, deaths and marriages, a document which is a vital part of Kirtlington's history. No doubt the priests of Kirtlington through the ages have always tried to relieve the suffering which was so often the lot of the poor, but they were to have special reason to be grateful for the appointment of Adrian Whicker as their minister in 1596, as it was his son John who left £100 in his will which after investment, would produce an annual sum of £6 to be given to those who were not 'drunkards' or 'Prophaners of the Lords Day'. Although England's national church became Protestant in the 16th century, there were those who refused to join it and remained loyal to Roman Catholicism. These 'recusants', as they were called from their refusal to attend their parish churches, included Christian Treadwell, Margaret Woodward, Margaret Hedges, Ann Owen, and Justinian Walker of Kirtlington. In 1610, a member of the Roman Catholic Order of Jesuits, George Napper or Napier, was captured in Kirtlington and removed to Oxford jail, where he was later executed: it was a capital crime to be a Catholic minister of religion at this time.

Kirtlington's religious life appears to have been peaceful until the Civil War broke out in 1642. Its vicar at that time was Lawrence Brewer, who must have had a difficult time watching lead stripped from the roof and valuables confiscated, and being unable to protest. There was also the unpleasant task of burying the unfortunate Matthew Weatherby, a soldier who had come to a violent end at the *Dolphin*.

In spite of war and upheavals, many of the church's treasures remain intact, like the pulpit, which, although it has a modern base and steps, is Jacobean in origin. Nearby, a beautiful small baroque cartouche records the name of James of 'Jacobi' Evans, a royal escort, sergeant or trumpeter, who died in 1702. He was no doubt related to Abel Evans, vicar of Kirtlington between 1700 and 1707.

The year 1702 saw an unusual appointment as parish clerk: James Sandford, who was only 11 years old, was elected to the office by the vicar and '38 principal householders'. It was during his tenure that the new lord of the manor, Sir Robert Dashwood, presented the Communion plate. Sir Robert also had a gallery erected across the west end of the church, which was later removed. His successor, Sir James, was a generous contributor to church expenses, for painting, repairs, and even for new pews. He also left a legacy of £300 to replace the tower, which had been pulled down, and £30 for a clock, provided that the local farmers would arrange for the haulage involved in erecting the structure. However, they refused to do this, and the tower was not replaced until 1852. The work undertaken at this time included alterations and improvements to the 'ruinous' condition of certain parts of the church, and the installation of new seating to accommodate 320 persons. The estimate for the work amounted to nearly £800. The Dashwood family's involvement with the church continued into the late 19th century, with Sir Henry becoming the first lay rector in 1876.

A 'Curious List' of 1789-91 compiled by the then vicar (Ashton Thorpe) and his churchwardens tells us exactly who attended the morning and evening services. On Christmas Day 1789, for instance, the congregation included 'Hall's wife, Thomas Scarsbrook, Thos. Good and J. Walker's wife, J. Boffin – Boffin's wife, Widow Walton, Widow Horwood, Widow Good, J. Walker's daughter, Widow Phillips, Rich. Allen's wife and Wm. Busby'. Attendances varied in number between 15 and 89 at morning services, and in the evenings between five and thirty.

Although by 1676 there was apparently only one recusant remaining in the village, another category of worshipper appeared in the late 16th and early 17th centuries – the Protestant Nonconformists or 'Dissenters'. Their early meetings were held in such unlikely places as barns, kitchens or outhouses. Amongst the earliest groups to emerge were the Baptists, the Independents or Congregationalists, and in the late 17th century the Quakers. In the 18th century John Wesley and his brother Charles were chiefly instrumental in the emergence of another new group – the Methodists. All these different groups had their followers even in Kirtlington.

In 1821, when James Saunders was the vicar, the Methodist Dissenters at last obtained permission to have their own permanent chapel. One John Morris of Kirtlington was given permission on 7 April by the registrar of the court of the Bishop of Oxford to use 'a certain building as a place of religious worship'. The Ecclesiastical Census of 1851 made of church and chapel congregations showed that Kirtlington had 102 Methodists. They had built their own new chapel in 1830, and the year after the census erected a replacement for it. It may still be seen at the southern end of the village, although no services have been held there for nearly 30 years.

The 1850s was a difficult period for Kirtlington's vicar, the Reverend Thomas Chittenden. The recently-formed local branch of the National Agricultural Labourers Union, which was fighting for better conditions and pay for farmworkers, boycotted church services, regarding the Church as being primarily on the side of their employers. 'The parish has never recovered from the effects of the N.A.L.U.' Mr. Chittenden reported in his diocesan returns. Some employers brought pressure to bear on their workers and issued an ultimatum – 'Go to church, leave the union – or get out of my cottage'.

The effect of music on a church's congregation is considerable. The church had a fine set of bells dating from 1718, most of them bearing the Dashwood arms. Not a great deal is known about the early ringers, but during the 1920s they included Chris Lambourne, Bert Collett, George 'Smoker' Edgington, and one of Ernie King's brothers. The ropes were quite expensive to replace, and cost 16 shillings in 1924.

In the early 19th century, St Mary's had a 'band', consisting of a clarinet and a bassoon, but this was replaced by a barrel-organ in 1839. When the west gallery was removed in 1852, the choir no longer had anywhere to sit, and they had to sing without accompaniment until the gift of an organ in 1877. This was placed in the Dashwood Chapel at first, but was resited to its present position a few years ago. From the evidence of the Reverend Deane's diary, it would seem that there was a fine choir in 1890, with strong support in particular from the men of the village – amongst its members were Mr. Hawkes the tailor and postmaster, Mr. Austin the schoolmaster, Mr. Walklett the butcher, Mr. Pearman (a gardener), Mr. Enser the miller, Mr. Wakefield the baker, and several agricultural labourers, like the Norridge and Edgington families. Amongst the boys in the choir were Peter Scarsbrook, Fred Enser, John and George Bunker, Harry Pearman and Gerald Herbert. Their wage was usually one halfpenny for each church service, and a farthing for attendance at practices!

The choirmaster and parish clerk, Arthur Lambourne, who died in 1913, had a great influence on the choir's development. He was also a composer of hymns and chants; his book of compositions is amongst the documents held in the parish chest.

To the Right Reverend the Lord Bishop of Oxford.
and to his Registrar.

I John Morris *of* Kirtlington in the County of Oxfordshire *do hereby certify, that* a certain Building situated in the Parish of Kirtlington and in the County aforesaid *is intended forthwith to be used as a place of religious worship by an Assembly or Congregation of Protestants; and I do hereby require you to register and record the same according to the provisions of the Act passed in the 52d year of the reign of his Majesty King George the Third, intituled "An Act to repeal certain Acts, and amend other Acts, relating to Religious Worship, and Assemblies, and persons teaching or preaching therein;" and hereby request a certificate thereof. Witness my hand this* First *day of* April 1821.

John Morris
Richard Young [illegible]
[illegible]

I, Robert Morrell Dep. *Registrar of the Court of the Bishop of* Oxford *do hereby certify that a Certificate, of which the above is a true copy, was this day delivered to me, to be registered and recorded pursuant to the Act of Parliament therein mentioned. Dated this* 7th *day of* April 1821

Robert Morrell
Deputy *Registrar.*

Datum April 7th
1821

London: printed by T. CORDEUX.

Fig. 4. Kirtlington Dissenters.

The ladies of the parish have also made their contribution to the church over the years. In 1902, for instance, Lady Mary Dashwood presented a white altar cloth and frontal, Miss Orchard gave some white alms bags, and a pulpit hanging was received from Mrs. Edginton and Mrs. Buckley. Dorothy Castleman and other ladies gave white book-markers, and all these gifts together must have considerably enhanced the Easter celebrations for that year.

In spite of these and many other generous gifts to the church, there are always considerable expenses to be met. In 1903, the collection for the whole year amounted to only £30 4s 6¼d. Bills had to be met for coal, oil, faggots, new bell ropes, cleaning, surplice washing, and even for someone to cut back the ivy in the churchyard, besides the salaries of the organist, the organ blower, the clerk and the sexton. It was fortunate that the chancel cleaning at least was the responsibility of the lord of the manor, who either sent down one of his servants to do it, or gave money in lieu.

The history of the church and its beautiful possessions can be even better appreciated when there is a chance to talk to its incumbent, and I was fortunate to have the opportunity of several conversations with the Reverend Reginald George Bennett, vicar since 1961, before his retirement in 1982. His father, Reginald Ward Bennett, was vicar before him from 1929 to 1944, and a memorial tablet in his memory can be seen in the church.

The church of St Mary's, Kirtlington, has a long history, some of which remains unknown to us. Like the village it serves, however, it has survived wars, disasters and poverty. Its monuments and relics are treasured and preserved for posterity; whilst outside the graveyard, with its well-kept gravestones and immaculate grass, offers a serene and lovely resting-place.

Roach and Dace.

CHAPTER THREE

Virgates and Villeins

When the massive Domesday Survey was undertaken by the Normans in 1086, Kirtlington was by no means an obscure village or unknown hamlet, but a place of some importance with royal connections. Its situation at the junction of Akeman Street simplified communication with the outside world, and gave it trading opportunities. In 1086 the king held 'Cherielintone': 'there are 11½ hides. In lordship 10 ploughs. 42 villagers with 24 smallholders and 2 slaves have 21 ploughs. 2 mills at 35s; from the meadows and pastures and pig-pasturage and other customary dues £8; from the year's corn £20. The Jurisdiction of two and a half Hundreds belongs to this manor, less 2½ hides in Launton which formerly lay there. These King Edward gave to St Peter's of Westminster and his "godson" Baldwin. In total, it pays £52 a year at face value'.

Full use had been made of the good natural resources of the village – the river Cherwell, the streams and brooks, the light cornbrash soil and forest land. The changes which had taken place in clearance and cultivation since Cyrtla's time had obviously been successful, and the total land measurement was substantially the same as it is today, a little over 3,580 acres. Originally, the amount of land which could be worked in a year by one plough, and be sufficient to support a family, was calculated by the *hide*, a unit which varied between 60 and 180 acres according to the quality of the soil in different parts of the country. Hides were subdivided into *virgates* or *yardlands* of between 15 and 60 acres.

The villagers or *villeins* were obliged to perform certain services and pay set taxes and fines to the lord of the manor in return for their virgate shares – long narrow strips of land which were the most convenient shape for cultivation by the cumbersome ox-drawn plough. The cottagers or *bordars* had smaller portions of land, and more menial tasks were required of them, whilst the poor slaves or *serfs* had no land and scarcely any rights at all. At Northbrook, which was part of the manor of Kirtlington, the villagers paid rents of 2s 6d a year for each half-virgate that they held. The lord's permission was required if a man sought to leave his native village to make a new life elsewhere; a villager or cottager might be able to obtain it on payment of a fee, but a slave was most unlikely to be allowed to go. The only chance of freedom was to manage to remain undetected during residence for 'a year and a day' in a town.

Another type of landholder, higher in the social scale, was the knights, who held their land in return for providing military services when called upon to do so by their lords. William de Humez was one 13th-century Kirtlington knight; he was lord of the manor in 1203 and held two *carucates* or hides, amounting to about 200 or 240 acres, as his 'knight's fee'. During the reign of Henry III two fees of the d'Oilly family passed to the de Plesly family until 1364, whilst in 1545 the church living acquired ownership of one-fortieth of a knight's fee. The de Gay family of Northbrook Manor also held one-quarter of a knight's fee. This kind of confused situation arose when a knight who might himself not be resident in the village sub-let or even sold portions of his fee to others, creating endless complications over who was actually liable to military service, and who had responsibilities towards the local people who were the tenants of the fee.

The alienation of land by a lord of the manor could lead to the formation of small new manors, like 'Bowelles', which was owned in the 13th century by Henry and Alice de Beules. In 1461 Sir Edmund Hampden was its lord, and it was worth 60 shillings. The owners of Bowelles had become tenants-in-chief of the crown in their own right, and were entitled to hold their own manor courts.

Between 1130 and 1203, Jordan de Gay, Richard de Humez (his son-in-law) and then William de Humez held the manor. They were followed by Geoffrey le Sauvage, John Fitzhugh, a royal minister, Ralph de Montibus and William de Breaute. After 1224, Thomas Bassett, baron of Headington, and his descendants were in almost continuous occupation of the manor until 1271. They were succeeded by the first recorded lady of the manor – Ela, the dowager countess of Warwick. During her residence, a new wood was planted, using part of the east field.

No doubt all the daily troubles and squabbles over land ownership and the payment of services were forgotten during the colour and excitement of a tournament, like the ones which took place at Middleton Stoney, where they were held in the grounds of the castle owned by Gerard de Camville until forbidden by law in 1250. A special area would be marked out, flanked by seating galleries. Each competitor would have his own special tent, flying his banner, with his coat of arms displayed outside. Some jousts were between individual knights, and others, almost like mock battles, between whole teams.

Another important part of local administration, covering a wider area than that of the parish, was the hundred and its hundred court, which met at set intervals during the year at a convenient landmark. Kirtlington is in Ploughley Hundred, with a meeting-place at Ploughley Hill, a former Saxon barrow in Fritwell parish. Stukeley described this barrow in 1776 as 'curious ... neatly turned like a bell, small and high, it lay by the Portway'. By 1845, however, the barrow had been levelled. The records of the hundred court (kept on long rolls of parchment) tell us that in 1279 Kirtlington had 'one manor, 4 lesser estates, 36 free tenants, 40 *nativi*, 2 *cottars* and no serfs' – an improvement on Domesday times. By 1316 there were 41 taxpayers in the village.

We know something of the buildings in the village during the Middle Ages. It was not uncommon for a man devoted to the religious life, who wished to spend his life in contemplation, to take up residence in a remote spot as a hermit. One such man, whose life seems to have devoted to caring for the poor and sick, lived in Kirtlington. His name was Nicholas Jurdan. In 1338, 'Nicholas Jurdan of Curtlington, Hermit' relinquished his claim to 'a certain house' together with the 'curtilage [grounds] adjacent to the same house' which was to revert to the 'Reverend and noble monks ... the Lord Abbott and the monastery of Aulnay'. As we have already seen, this French monastery owned the living of Kirtlington for a considerable period, and it is possible that Jurdan's house was the vicarage.

After leaving Kirtlington, Jurdan is next heard of in Bicester, where he became the hermit and warden of the chapel of St John the Baptist. In 1355 he was granted a royal licence by Edward III to re-found a hospital 'for the reception of poor and sick persons'. The hospital was endowed with land, and rents to the value of 40 shillings

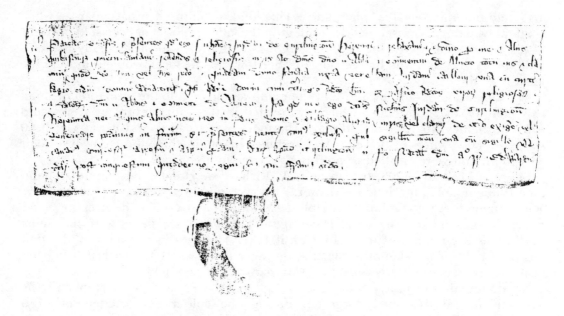

Fig. 5.   Charter of Nicholas Jurdan, 1338.

a year. It was a long, low building, situated in fields which had once been quarried, and from it a path led to the famous healing waters of the Crockwell. In 1536 Bicester Priory was dissolved by the officials of Henry VIII, and the hospital went with it.

Perhaps the building with the most turbulent history in Kirtlington was the manor house, with its great variety of owners and tenants – some rebellious barons, others hard-working yeomen intent on bringing order to often neglected lands and decaying buildings. The present Manor House, on South Green, with its distinctive tower and chimney piece, was built in 1585. The original manor, which is said to have had a triangular moat, could have been on this site, or perhaps on another behind Kytes Pond, near Portway House. In 1297 the manor house was attacked when the unpopular royal minister Hugh Despenser was its lord, and during his exile abroad in 1321, the house was pillaged.

In 1327 Thomas of Brotherton moved in. He was Edward III's uncle, and was succeeded by the de Bohun family in 1332, who also had royal connections. Humphrey and Joan de Bohun's daughter Mary had married Henry IV, the son of John of Gaunt, second son of Edward III. John of Gaunt was apparently a regular visitor to Kirtlington, and doubtless stayed at the manor. It may have been from here that he made visits to Oxford, where the religious reforming group known as the Lollards was based, with which he is known to have been sympathetic.

In 1390 £9 12s 2d was spent on building works at the Manor House, and it was then leased out for a number of years, one of the tenants being Anne, countess of Stafford. When Lady Joan de Bohun died in 1421, however, the property came into the hands of the duchy of Lancaster and became part of the holding of the queens of England. It was then described as 'in good order' and valued at £131 6s 8d with seven oxen. In 1422 a Keeper of the Park, one Thomas Brokenton, was appointed, and Thomas Granger rented the manor for 3s 4d a year.

Between 1444 and 1467 Margaret of Anjou, the beautiful but unscrupulous wife of Henry VI, held the manor, and she was succeeded by Elizabeth Woodville, wife of Henry's successor and enemy, Edward IV. During the latter half of the 15th century the property seems to have been neglected; by 1471 the hall was roofless, and when Thomas Lovell took it over in 1517, its condition was most depressing, the Manor House being merely 'a barne or shepe house, standing on the syght'.

The changes which had taken place in Kirtlington up to the end of the 15th century were not only the result of the actions of man. The devastation of the Black Death, which came to England in 1348, brought by the fleas which black rats harboured, spread to virtually every town and village. There are few Kirtlington records for the period, although it is known that its then vicar, William Serch, did not survive the epidemic, and we have already mentioned the reputed mass grave in the churchyard, which may house the remains of other victims.

The depopulation which resulted from the Black Death meant that labour was in short supply, and lords could no longer enforce their demands for services from their tenants and serfs as they had in the past. In future, they would have to pay for the services they required on their land, and accept money rent for the lands the villagers held from them. Gradually the new village society of farmers, who worked their own land and whose contact with the landowner was solely through the payment of rent, and of labourers, who owned no land themselves and worked the landowner's property for wages, was emerging. Kirtlington now had a number of free tenants such as Thomas de la Haye, Walter Ingeramm and Adam de Marigny. The shortage of labour also meant that there was much unfarmed land; a good deal of this was now converted to sheep pasture, which needed little maintenance. Many Kirtlington farmers prospered in this way.

It was also hard for lords to prevent their villagers leaving the manor, if they thought they could get better conditions elsewhere. Sometimes too they went to the towns, where a man could make his own career and rise to much greater heights than were possible in his native village. The settled pattern of village life was changing, and the old days of servitude would never return.

CHAPTER FOUR

The Ancient Manor of Northbrook

The hamlet of Northbrook was known as 'Norbroc' in 1086. Its principal tenant was Rainald, who held the manor from Robert of Stafford. On the manor there was land for two ploughs, one on the lord's own land and the other farmed by two villagers. There were four acres of meadow. The value remained 25s, as it had been in 1066. Rainald also held two smaller manors (one also in Northbrook and one in Brookhampton) from Roger d'Ivry, amounting to four hides, with land for four and a half ploughs. The one in Brookhampton was valued at 60 shillings, and thus was obviously a more valuable property than the Northbrook manors.

In 1279 the hundred rolls recorded Northbrook as consisting of a single manor, with six free tenants, nine 'nativi' and one cottager. In 1334 the Lay Subsidy valued it at £1 4s 2d. The hamlet consisted principally of two large open fields, the management of which was controlled by the manor court of Kirtlington.

Towards the end of the 12th century, the family which was to exert *de facto* control of the manor for the next 400 years made its first appearance in the shape of Hilda de Gay, who is described as owning property at Northbrook, and there is mention of a chapel. However, in the next century the Gay family sank to the level of tenants and the abbey of Westminster became the property's feudal overlord. The Gay family were obliged to pay a rent of three shillings a year, and to appear both at the manor court of Kirtlington and at the abbot's own court of Islip: these requirements were enforced until well after the Reformation. As late as 1540, John de Gay was paying the king (who had by then adopted the position of supreme head of the English church) 13s 5d a year in rent. By the late 16th century, however, the Gays felt secure enough of their ownership to end their long connection with it. Thomas Gay sold it to a Devonshire man, William Arscote, as a result of a marriage agreement between the two families which did not materialise.

A further marriage settlement in 1575 resulted in the ownership passing to John Fox, a Kirtlington yeoman. His 18-year-old daughter Frises was to marry a certain William Holleyman, but she chose John Lake instead! John Fox, and the rejected suitor, later sold Northbrook to John Hollins of Oxford University in 1619. The deed describing this sale – in spite of damage which has rendered some portions illegible – still gives perhaps the most detailed account of 17th-century Northbrook available. It was described as a 'capital messuage called the farm house of Northbroke' and the sale included 'all houses, edifices, buildings, barns, stables, dovecotes, pigeon houses, structures, orchards, gardens, courts, yards, back sides, hop yards and ponds'. Also included was 'the one moyety of all fishing in the Rivers of Thames and Cherwell, and all other fishing, waters, watercourses, etc., which belonged to the Manor ...'.

The various tenants of the land, and field-names, are also included in detail. The latter included 'Northbrook Close', which was about seven acres, and divided 'with hedge and ditch' from 'the other part occupied by Wm. Holleyman and Sibell

Bennett, widow'. There was also a hemp plot of a quarter yardland (about seven and a half acres). This lay 'without the great gate of the Messuage, along by the Orchard Way'. The nearby 'Kitchen Piece' was bordered in willow 'down to Deddington Way'. Near the hemp plot, Stephen Smyth and George Elymot were the owners of a 'gutter or watercourse'. Long Briton Mead was then occupied by Thomas Hall, and contained a small plot known as 'Harepipe Acre', whilst James Chamberlain had a ley next to furze land in Long Goldwell. The best meadows were allocated by yearly 'lottes', and appear to have included 'Long Briton', 'Northam Mead', 'Hill Mead' and 'Pittyardes'.

On the common land '16 milch kine' or other beasts and 'one hundred, three score and fifteen' [175] sheep were allowed to graze, 'when the West Field of Northbrook and Kirtlington lyeth open'. When the East Field was in use, the numbers were 16 'milch kine' or other beasts, and 218 sheep. The total acreage covered by the deed seems to have been '3 yard lands, and three quarters of a yard land' – which had not altered very much since the Domesday Survey of 1086!

The several changes of ownership after the Gay family's departure probably had some effect on the people living and working on the estate. In 1631 there were ten houses in Northbrook 'where poor people lived', and they were left sixpence each in the will of John Facer, who may have been one of their neighbours. Dr. John Hawley of the University was now the owner, but in 1641 his son Edmund sold the manor to Sir Thomas Chamberlain of Wickham Park near Banbury. A new manor house had been built towards the end of the 16th century to replace the old farmhouse, and there was now an 'Ox-house' and a 'malt-house' at Northbrook, with 'common land for 240 sheep and 30 young beasts'.

We can discover a little more about the villagers of Northbrook in the 17th century from entries in the parish register and various surviving wills. For instance, Sibell Bennett, mentioned in the deed cited above, was probably the widow of the yeoman Rowland Bennett. In 1643 the register recorded the death of William Hickman 'a servant to Esq. Chamberlayne – once being an honest well disposed young man', whilst in 1679 James Hatton, Sir Thomas's butler, was buried. Perhaps the most interesting family were the Kings, as descendants of 'Eduard Kinge of Norbroke' were living and working in the village up until the 1920s.

For a young man with a fishing-boat and tackle, and some land and livestock, there was quite a good living to be made in the 1690s, as the will of Anthony Day shows. The inventory of his possessions, which was made by his neighbours Humphrey Rayer and John Cozier, included:

	£	s	d
His Wearing apparall and money in purfe	3.	0.	0.
His fishing tackell	2.	10.	0.
Chamber over the buttery [contents worth]	3.	0.	0.
In the hall, brafs and Puter			
one table and 2 chares	3.	0.	0.
One gelding	2.	0.	0.
Two cows and one Pige	4.	0.	0.
A crop of corne growing upon the ground	5.	0.	0.
One fishing boate	1.	0.	0.

He left £10 to his father, William Day, and also 'all nets and rods, and all such things as belong to my calling' and five pounds apiece to his brother and sister. His 'house

A True and Perfect Inventorie of all the
Goods Cattells Chattells and Creditts of
Anthony Day deceased In the Parish of
Kirtlington In the County of oxon taken
the 12 day of Agust 1698 according to the
Custom of the Church of England And
Prised and valued by Humphrey Rayer
and John Cyser

Imprs	His Wearing Apparrell and mony In Purse	05 — 00 — 0
	His ffishing tackll value 3ll	02 — 10 — 0
	In the Chamber over the Buttery two bedsted and bed belonging to the same and linen with other Lumber	03 — 00 — 0
	In the Chamber over the Hall one bed And bedsted and bed in theirento belonging with other small things	01 — 00 — 0
	In the Buttery Barrills and tubs	00 — 10 — 0
	In the Hall Brass and Puter one table and Chares	03 — 00 — 0
	one Gelding	02 — 00 — 0
	two Cows and one Pige	04 — 00 — 0
	one litle Cole of Hay In the Barejard	01 — 00 — 0
	wood In the Barejard	01 — 00 — 0
	A Crope of Corne Growin upon the Ground	05 — 00 — 0
	fishing Boate	01 — 00 — 0
		27 — 00 — 3

Humphrey Rayer

John Cyser

Exhibit & apud oxon 13 August 1698
Per Annam Relict et Extricem digno
vero & que hactenus & fideliplicarit
& addendo & L &

Geo: Cooper Noew Publicus

and close' were left to Ann Day 'if she be alive', or to his nephew John, who was also
a fisherman.

Sir Thomas Chamberlain, the new lord of the manor, had a beautiful daughter,
Penelope, who in due course became engaged to a young man of 21, whose family
had an estate in Somerset. His name was Robert Dashwood. The very generous
marriage settlement which Sir Thomas made on his daughter included the manors
of Kirtlington and Northbrook. After their marriage in 1682, Robert and Penelope
Dashwood lived at Northbrook. Only two years later they had an important change
of status, as in 1684 Robert was knighted. His father George had apparently owned
a patent of baronetcy which he had not taken out, and so his son was granted it
instead. Their crest was a griffin's head, erased, per fess erminous and gu, with the
family motto '*VIRTUTI NIHIL INVIUM*' - 'nothing is inaccessible to virtue'.

Sir Robert appears to have been a very capable lord of the manor, taking a keen
interest in the running of the estate, and also in the well-being of his less fortunate
farm-workers. He was a methodical man, and extracts from his many account books
make interesting reading, especially those entries relating to his children. In 1720 he
paid six shillings 'for bleeding George Dashwood' (a common medical treatment at
the time). Between 1713 and 1726, Robert Dashwood paid various school fees for his
sons – sums of £31 and £46 – and in 1725 he equipped them with 'drugget suites,
great Coates and a Periwigg for Bobb, which all cost £8 15s 1d'. The school fees at
'Eaton' amounted to £61 4s 6d in one year for 'Bobby and Jemmy', and there were
regular visits to Abingdon to buy 'Wiggs' or to undertake such household tasks as
ordering 'Ten chaldern of Coales' from Mr. Tomkins.

Sir Robert was a keen businessman, who regularly bought property to add to his
already large estates. In 1695 he purchased 'the mannour of Yarnton' from the heirs
and executors of Sir Thomas Spencer, for which he paid £31,000, and in 1695 he
bought the *George Inn*, a Kirtlington alehouse, from Margaret Napier, the only child
of Henry Arden, a former lord of the manor. However, a more modest sum was
needed in 1684, when he obtained a lease for one year of '3 acres of land covered with
water, extending from Catsham Ford (otherwise Catsham Planque) to Bacon's Wyer,
free and several fishing ...' for which he paid one penny a year plus a down-payment
of five shillings to the Bletchingdon miller, William Hall.

Sir Robert and Lady Penelope had nine children, but memorial tablets in
Kirtlington Church and entries in the parish register show that 'Love' died when she
was only ten, and 'Robertos' when he was fourteen. George died at the age of 20 of
a fever in Rome, where he was probably undertaking the fashionable Grand Tour of
Europe. Perhaps their saddest loss was Robert, their eldest son and heir, who died
at forty-one.

There was one rather exotic member of the Dashwood household of whom little
is known apart from the information on his memorial plaque on the church wall.
Thomas the Blackamoor died on 23 March 1691, when he was 23 years old. At this
period it was fashionable in wealthy households to have young black boys as pages,
dressed in colourful costumes. Thomas's origin is a mystery. Was he perhaps bought
from a consignment of slaves that had arrived from North Africa? Whatever the true
story, the Dashwood family obviously thought a good deal of him, and treated him
well.

Fig. 7. 'The death of ye hare with ye Fleet Hound'.

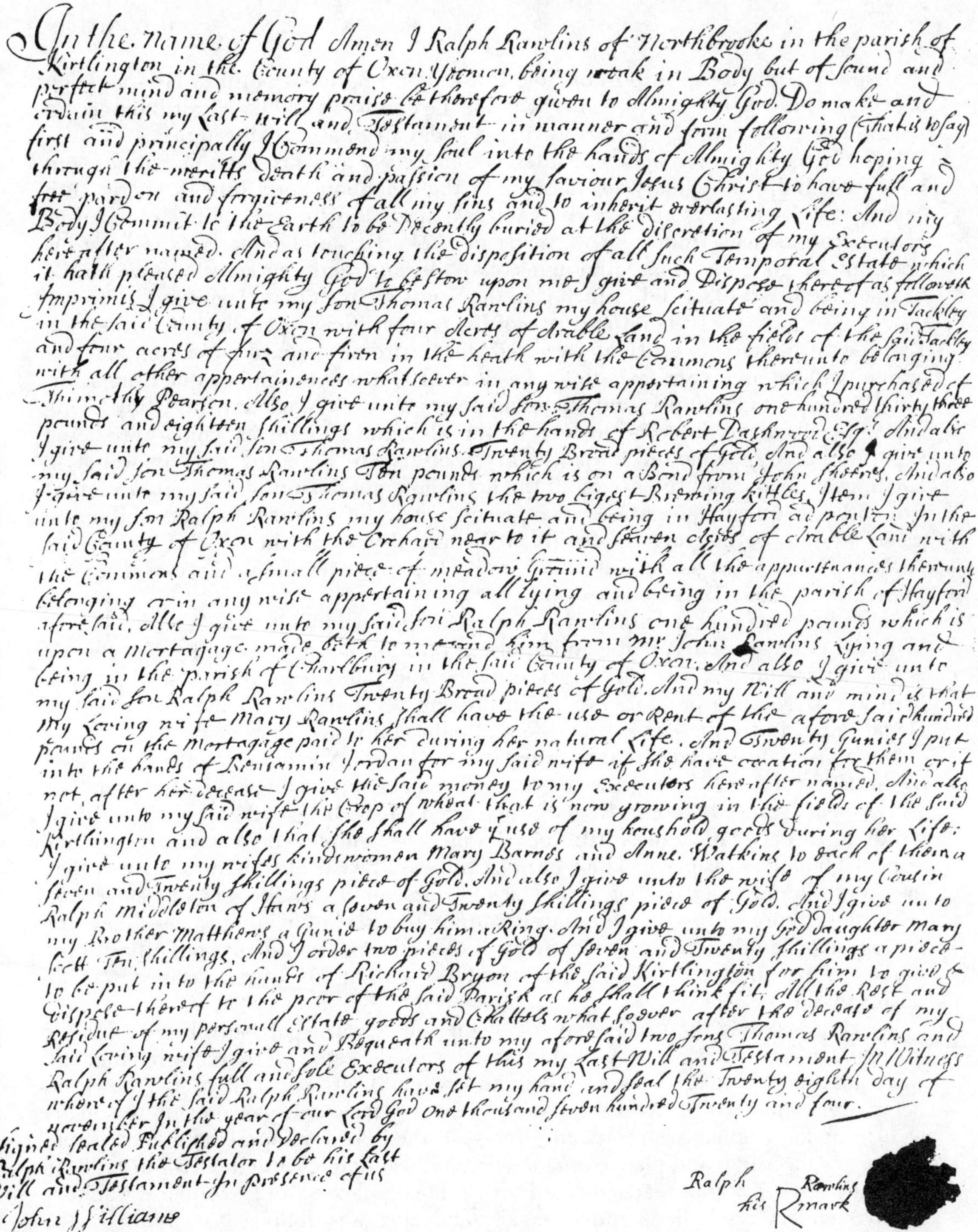

In the name of God Amen I Ralph Rawlins of Northbrooke in the parish of
Kirtlington in the County of Oxon Yeoman, being weak in Body but of sound and
perfect mind and memory praise be therefore given to Almighty God. Do make and
ordain this my Last will and Testament in manner and form following (that is to say)
first and principally I Commend my soul into the hands of Almighty God hoping
through the merits death and passion of my Saviour Jesus Christ to have full and
free pardon and forgiveness of all my sins and to inherit everlasting Life: And my
Body I Commit to the Earth to be Decently buried at the discretion of my Executors
hereafter named. And as touching the disposition of all such Temporal Estate which
it hath pleased Almighty God to bestow upon me I give and Dispose thereof as followeth
Imprimis I give unto my son Thomas Rawlins my house scituate and being in Tackley
in the said County of Oxen with four acres of arable Land in the fields of the said Tackley
and four acres of furz and firen in the heath with the Commons thereunto belonging
with all other appertainances whatsoever in any wise appertaining which I purchased of
Thimothy Pearson. Also I give unto my said son Thomas Rawlins one hundred thirty three
pounds and eighteen shillings which is in the hands of Robert Dashwood Esq. And also
I give unto my said son Thomas Rawlins Twenty Broad pieces of Gold. And also I give unto
my said son Thomas Rawlins Ten pounds which is on a Bond from John Shotes, And also
I give unto my said son Thomas Rawlins the two biggest Brewing kittles Item I give
unto my son Ralph Rawlins my house scituate and being in Hayford aforesaid In the
said County of Oxen with the Orchard near to it and Seaven closes of arable Land with
the Commons and a small piece of meadow Ground with all the appurtenances thereunto
belonging or in any wise appertaining all lying and being in the parish of Hayford
aforesaid. Also I give unto my said son Ralph Rawlins one hundred pounds which is
upon a Mortagage made both to me and him from Mr John Rawlins lying and
being in the parish of Charlbury in the said County of Oxen. And also I give unto
my said son Ralph Rawlins Twenty Broad pieces of Gold. And my Will and mind is that
my Loving wife Mary Rawlins shall have the use or Rent of the aforesaid hundred
pounds on the Mortagage paid to her during her natural Life. And Twenty Guinies I put
into the hands of Benjamin Jordan for my said wife if she have occation for them or if
not, after her decease I give the said money to my Executors hereafter named. And also
I give unto my said wife the Crop of wheat that is now growing in the fields of the said
Kirtlington and also that she shall have y use of my houshold goods during her Life:
I give unto my wifes kinswomen Mary Barnes and Anne Watkins to each of them a
seven and Twenty shillings piece of Gold. And also I give unto the wife of my Cousin
Ralph Middleton of Staws a seven and Twenty shillings piece of Gold. And I give unto
my Brother Matthews a Guini to buy him a Ring. And I give unto my God daughter Mary
Sott Ten shillings. And I order two pieces of Gold of seven and Twenty shillings a piece
to be put into the hands of Richard Bryon of the said Kirtlington for him to give &
dispose thereof to the poor of the said Parish as he shall think fit. All the Rest and
Residue of my personall Estate goods and Chattels whatsoever after the decease of my
said Loving wife I give and Bequeath unto my aforsaid two sons Thomas Rawlins and
Ralph Rawlins full and sole Executors of this my Last Will and Testament In Witness
whereof I the said Ralph Rawlins have set my hand and Seal this Twenty eighth day of
November In the year of our Lord God One thousand seven hundred Twenty and four.

Signed Sealed Published and Declared by
Ralph Rawlins the Testator to be his Last
Will and Testament In presence of us

John Williams

William Grantham

Tho: Grantham

Ralph   Rawlins
his   R mark

Fig. 8.   The will of Ralph Rawlins, huntsman.

Sir Robert played an important role in local and national politics. He was High Sheriff of Oxfordshire in 1683, and M.P. for the county in 1699, and for Banbury on several other occasions. His portrait hangs today in Banbury Museum.

He still had time for sporting interests, however, and his pack of hounds and huntsman Ralph Rawlins were familiar in the neighbourhood into the early 18th century as they hunted 'ye hare with ye fleet hound'. Rawlins was quite a prosperous man as can be seen from his will, made in 1724. His son Thomas was to have his house in Tackley, which had four acres of arable land, and four acres of furze on the heath, as well as £133 1s 0d, 'which is in the hands of Sir Robert Dashwood'. Thomas was also to have a £10 bond and two of his biggest brewing kettles! His other son Ralph was to have his other house in Heyford, with an orchard and seven acres of arable land, common and meadow, as well as £100 mortgage money due from a Mr. John Rawlins of Charlbury, and '20 broad pieces of gold'. Mary Rawlins – 'my loving wife' – was to have the 'rent' or 'use' of the £100 and 20 guineas which were being kept for her by Benjamin Jordan. Mary was also to have the crop of wheat in Kirtlington fields, and the use of all the household goods during her lifetime. Apart from other bequests to relations, two pieces of gold 'of seven and twenty shillings a piece' were to be put into the hands of Richard Bryon for 'the poor of Kirtlington parish'. Ralph Rawlins actually died in 1751 at the age of 83, 17 years after his master, Sir Robert Dashwood.

Sir Robert was succeeded in his estate and baronetcy by his grandson, Sir James. With the family now occupying an important position in the county, they felt the old house of Northbrook was no longer suitable, and plans were drawn up for a new mansion at Kirtlington. In 1746 these dreams became reality, and a new era of elegance began for Sir James, his wife and baby son at Kirtlington Park.

Not a great deal is known about the later tenants of Northbrook until the middle of the 19th century, although we do know it remained a Dashwood possession. The 1851 census showed George Rogers, then aged 34, with his wife Hannah and four children, in occupation of Northbrook Farm. They employed 24 labourers to look after the 600-acre property. Their farm bailiff was 22-year-old Thomas Rogers; they had two general servants and a 15-year-old nursemaid. Mr. Rogers was clearly an important figure in the parish administration: at a vestry meeting in the 1850s the point was raised that 'persons occupying outlying farms should not hold office in the parish of Kirtlington' – but it was resolved that in his case 'distance was no disadvantage'!

We do not know the precise layout of the 'model farm' at Northbrook, but the ancient Tudor brick walls remained intact, the ponds were still there for fishing, and the good rich soil was still used for fruit and vegetable growing. There had, however, been other changes at Northbrook. Sir James Dashwood was one of the many well-to-do landowners who took an interest in the new developments in agriculture and animal feeding, and planted the new crop of sainfoin on Ramley Hill in 1738. In 1787 the Oxford Canal reached Northbrook, making access to Oxford and Banbury for passengers and goods much easier, and this was followed in 1800 by the construction of Northbrook Bridge over the canal. The gradual spread of enclosure affected the Hunt Races, which had been held at Northbrook since 1809, and in 1811 their site was moved to Bicester.

In 1881 Thomas and Priscilla Edgington were living at Northbrook Farm, with Priscilla's mother Elizabeth King, aged seventy. The residence was shared with

William Canning, who worked as a gardener at the farm, and his wife Elizabeth. The other families of Northbrook were mostly agricultural labourers and their wives, like the Scarsbrooks, Catos, Siggars and Smiths, and the shepherd William Purbrick.

As the 19th century drew to a close, there was probably no indication to the villagers of Kirtlington and Northbrook of the changes which were to take place within the next few years. In 1909, the Dashwood family reluctantly decided to sell Kirtlington Park and move away from the village. Heavy taxation, a large family, and the maintenance of such a large house had proved too much of a burden for Sir George and Lady Dashwood. The new lord of the manor was the earl of Leven and Melville, but the lordship was to change ownership twice more before 1922.

A new tenant was now occupying Northbrook Farm at a rent of £550 per year, one Kirby. A keen horseman, he had suffered a number of serious falls over the years, some resulting in concussion. Unfortunately, he was also a heavy drinker, and this combination led to some rather eccentric behaviour. Coming home one day after he had been drinking, he noticed his men at work with the heavy-horse team. Telling them to unharness the animals, he made them go to the nearby quarry. There they were to move away some heavy stones, as he had 'seen the Devil hiding behind them, and he wanted to catch him'. The place is still known as Devil's Bank. On another occasion he set fire to two oat ricks on the side of Northbrook Road. It was 5 November, and he said he didn't have to go into Kirtlington to see a bonfire – he would have his own!

In 1922 Mr. and Mrs. Hubert Budgett became the new owners of the Kirtlington estate. They had retained the mansion house, two farms and some land, but a large number of farms and cottages were now available to buy, if their tenants could afford them. As a result, in the same year the Eeley family arrived from Bletchingdon and established themselves at Northbrook. The family tradition is continued by Mr. and Mrs. Jim Eeley and their son and daughter-in-law.

The lovely old dovecot with its 18 rows of nests inside is still a dominant feature, but it has been newly roofed. An even older, if humbler, treasure of Northbrook is the clay loomweight found near the bridle-path to Kirtlington, which may date from early medieval times. The ancient garden walls of the farmhouse still overlook the fish ponds and fruit trees, and there are traces of an old tennis court. In the farmyard, gnarled beams support a roof and and door; an unusually-shaped window speaks of centuries past; whilst the fields have seen more oxen and horses than tractors. Perhaps the only grumble Jim Eeley has at the moment concerns the size and headroom of the old buildings. They were not meant to fit a modern tractor, but to cope with a horse-drawn wagon, or a man carrying a sack. In spite of this, it seems unlikely that there will be drastic changes made. A modern farm might be easier to run, but 'Norbroc' has an atmosphere and character that have taken almost 900 years to achieve.

CHAPTER FIVE

The Ruff and the Wig

The Elizabethan village of Kirtlington was a vigorous and enterprising community, whose people were in a much stronger position than their medieval ancestors to withstand the effects of war, disease and economic disaster – like the influenza epidemics and poor harvests which affected most of England between 1556 and 1558. Amongst the 240 or so inhabitants in 1523, there were 57 taxpayers, liable to pay the lay subsidy levied in that year, the total of their payments amounting to £7 17s 0d. In 1562 a special royal charter removed some of the financial burdens from the villagers – 'toll, pannage, passage, lastage, tallage, tollage, carriage, pesage, picage, and terrage' throughout the whole of the kingdom, with the exception of the purely local fairs and markets. There had been gradual changes in the social structure, and a new 'middle class' had emerged since feudal times. These were the more prosperous husbandmen and yeomen farmers – men like Hugh Keate, who farmed the manor land in 1622. In 1665 the wheelwright Henry Ebborne was providing a vital service and prospering in so doing, like his father Thomas before him.

The villagers had now made themselves and their stock more secure by a system of gates which enclosed the village greens at night. Their names were Hatch, Fox, Woodstock, Cockenbread, Brokesgrene and Basset Gates. Sheep farming had become a profitable occupation, which required a smaller labour force. It also attracted the dealer or middleman, like John Cockes, who acted as bailiff for the Kirtlington and Tackley manors, as well as caring for his own flocks. There were times when John Cockes' 'deals' proved too enterprising and he found himself facing various charges in the manor court; but his grand-daughter and heiress eventually married Anthony Arden, who had acquired the manor of Kirtlington in 1568.

With wool in plentiful supply but strict laws governing its distribution, there had also been plenty of work for the village fuller since the middle of the 15th century. After extracting the fibre from the flax straw, which had been steeped in a retting pond, the woven cloth was 'fulled' by being trodden under water, or using a drop hammer, operated by the mill waterwheel turning a camshaft. This part of the work was no doubt undertaken at one or both of the two mills still in existence in 1568, when Bicester Priory had sold them with some land to the Ardens. When the wet cloth was taken to the tenting fields, it was attached by the selvedge to a number of 'tenterhooks', fastened to long stakes, and then stretched out to dry. By 1656 the English cloth trade was so important that laws were passed forbidding the export of materials for fulling, such as 'fuller's earth', used for absorbing fats from wool, and the teasels for raising the nap on the finished cloth.

Thomas Harres, who in 1543 obtained a licence from the manor court to erect a 'teynter' on the Green, was one of the many fullers in the village. In 1619 Thomas Bull paid 2s 6d a year for the use of the 'fuller's rack' in Oldburie Field, close to the church. He also leased the valuable Washford Pits quarry, which at one time had a

24

lime kiln, built by the previous owners, Bicester Priory. A certain strata of the rockface here could have provided him with the fuller's earth he needed, whilst teasels still grow here plentifully in the autumn. Bull had married Margaret Myles in 1577, and she or another lady of the family may have given the name to 'Betty Bull's Lane'. When Thomas Bull made his will in 1632, he bequeathed five pounds apiece to his grandchildren, Henry, John, Elizabeth, Margaret and Christian, which they were to have on reaching the age of twenty-one. He left 10s apiece to the church and the poor of the village, and the rest of his estate to his son Henry. This will shows the prosperity which could be made in the cloth trade.

The women of the village were no doubt adept at dying wool or cloth, using dyes like madder, woad, saffron, lichen, or even bee gum from the hives for a certain yellow. Amongst the village's weavers in the 16th century were Thomas Tolly and Richard Jobon, whose wills reveal that their estates were worth £4 11s 2d and £13 4s 2d respectively. In 1625 John Bartlett was one of the village tailors.

The preparation of leather was another important village industry. The curriers or leatherworkers first obtained shredded oak bark from Kirtlington Park to make the special tanning solution in which the leather was immersed after it had been cleaned and had the hair removed from it. Once this soaking had softened the leather, the official 'leather-searcher' had the responsibility of checking it before it could be sold to shoemakers or saddlers by a 'fellmonger' or leather-dealer.

Although it is not known exactly where or when the first slaughterhouses were built, one of them was probably on the same site as that occupied until fairly recently by Mr. Stockford, the butcher on North Green. When this building was being converted to a private house, a torn and faded receipt was found. Although difficult to read, the name on it could be Edward Hall, who had apparently paid three pounds towards the sum of £8 6s 0d, being the sum 'due to the King'. This may be the record of market tolls collected by the Clerk of the Market, a post held by a member of the Hall family in 1638. From 1677, Kirtlington had full 'market' status.

There were certainly butchers in the village in Tudor and Stuart times, incuding Robert Arden (1476), John Andrews (1513) and William Davies (1592). They would no doubt all have had combined abbatoir and shop premises, where most of the village cattle would have been killed each autumn as there was often insufficient food available to keep them through the winter.

Amongst the many other village tradesmen there were, of course, bakers, who supplied the villagers with the mainstay of their diet – men like Edmond Copland (who died in 1587) and Richard Jakeman, who was clearly a wealthy man, as he left £53 8s 0d at his death in 1692.

Although there were obviously many hardworking and law-abiding inhabitants, even Kirtlington had its share of troublemakers. The stocks were renewed in 1526 and used until 1601, whilst the ducking stool and pillory were also still in use in the early 16th century. Agnes Johnson was apparently a scold and a thief, but in 1522 she fortunately decided to leave Kirtlington. Joan Brotherton was equally troublesome, being fined fourpence on several occasions for being a scold. Poor John Martyns, a servant, seems to have been the victim of three 16th-century muggers, who pulled him off his horse, dislocated his shoulder and injured his head. For this the offenders were fined fourpence each in the manor court. In 1548 Henry Hogkyns was off work for a week after William Persons had beaten him up with a cudgel. The good strong local ale may have had something to do with these troubles, and perhaps the skilful doctoring of Francis Flight, a miller who owned 'bokes of Churgery' and medical instruments may have been called upon.

Another cause of friction may have been the arrival of 'strangers' with foreign ways to settle in the village. The 'boke of Christenings' records several of these families in the 17th century, like Richard Rayer, a 'Ju', and Martha Wilbore, George Adams and Richard Warren, three babies whose fathers were all 'Londinors'.

While new families arrived in Kirtlington, several young men from the village had decided to seek their fortunes elsewhere. In the early 1600s, Antony Hall went into partnership with his friend John Moreton from Tackley, to run the *Mermaid Tavern* in Oxford. Perhaps a keen token collector somewhere has found one of the special trade tokens he issued in 1674, bearing the inscription 'Antony Hall – at the Mermaid'. The previous year Hall had become mayor of the city, and the occasion was celebrated in great style at *The Bear* in the High Street. Unfortunately it ended in a 'town and gown' riot owing to a rather tactless speech made by the new mayor, alluding to French and Spanish wine, a delicate subject at that time. The scholars began to hiss, whereupon the townsmen turned them out of the inn and fighting broke out. Antony Hall died in the spring of 1675 and was buried in Kirtlington, where a memorial plaque on the outer wall of the church records his achievements. He seems to have died childless, and his property on South Green was left to the Wakefield family, who were the village bakers for many years. It is now a private house.

Another Kirtlington native who left the village was Thomas Rogers, son of Robert Rogers, a farmer, who in 1676 began his apprenticeship with the carpenter Francis Meadows of London, and his name is duly recorded in the Apprentice Entry Books of the Worshipful Company of Carpenters. The statutes ordained that the apprentices were 'not to speak adversely of each other's work' and were to spend Sunday and holy days away from 'ale houses, taverns, plays and unlawful games'. They were also forbidden to run away or to marry during their seven-year apprenticeship. We do not know how Thomas fared, but he was no doubt the envy of many of his former schoolfriends in Kirtlington, since his London qualifications would have made him certain of employment.

It seems that Kirtlington itself could have done with a good carpenter and a good builder, for in the early 17th century squatters had erected ramshackle houses on waste ground. These houses were of poor construction with no window glass or chimneys, and probably had inadequate roofs since a thatcher could ask for fourpence a day in wages. In the 1600s Thomas Tolley, Widow Hawley and Francis Walker all occupied houses like these, and were fined sums of between fourpence and two shillings in the manor court for so doing.

The following century, however, saw the employment of building expertise of a high standard in the construction of a splendid new mansion house, owned by another ambitious young man, who had been inspired by the architecture he had seen on his travels in France and Italy. With the arrival of Sir James Dashwood and his family at their new residence – Kirtlington Park – the age of the ruff gave way to that of the wig, a new and more settled period in national and village history.

CHAPTER SIX

A State of Emergency

In the autumn of 1642, the pressures of the Civil War had reached Oxford, where Charles I had his headquarters until 1646, but the situation also meant difficulties for the nearby villages. The lord of the manor of Kirtlington was Sir John Lenthall. He was in despair at the state both of the manor house and the rectory after troops from both armies had been quartered there, and reported to St John's College (the patron of the living) that it would cost over £200 to have the damage repaired. The money given for the troops' accommodation only totalled £32 2s 0d, which was of little help.

The village had a new vicar, Mr. Laurence Brewer, who had taken office at a most difficult time for the Church of England, and the registers during 1643-4 have very few entries indeed. Although exact figures for the population of Kirtlington at this time are hard to establish, 470 inhabitants can be traced from other records at the end of the 17th century.

It is likely that the church roof was stripped of lead to make bullets, and the whole building was left in a bad state. Repairs were not carried out until some time after 1662, helped by the generosity of Sir Robert Dashwood, then lord of the manor.

Although Kirtlington manor had been in royal ownership until 1604, like most villages and towns, there were bound to be divided loyalties when local residents encountered strange soldiers, whatever the latter's allegiance. The soldiers also fought amongst themselves, as in the incident which took place at the *Dolphin Inn* on a Sunday evening in October 1644, when Matthew Weatherby was shot through the body with a pistol by another soldier. The next day the body of poor Matthew was buried in Kirtlington cemetery.

Problems also arose from the difficulty of identifying soldiers with certainty. Coming home from market, on a dark night with a laden packhorse or wagon, the man who rode out of the shadows to accost you might be wearing the orange scarf of a Parliament man, or the red of King Charles' men. Not all Royalists had long flowing hair and pointed beards, any more than all Parliamentarians had closely-cropped short hair: and uniforms for most of the war were a miscellaneous assortment of styles and colours. A journey to Oxford was fraught with difficulties, even if you had provided yourself with an official pass. One horseman had not mentioned his saddle on the document, so it was taken away, and he rode bareback to his destination – where he was accused of stealing the horse! It was also rumoured that the governor of Oxford had a habit of hanging people for trivial reasons, or at least sentencing them to floggings and imprisonment.

King Charles experienced great difficulties in finding enough food for his garrison, and money was in even shorter supply, but confiscating the university's silver and melting it down was a temporary solution. The Parliamentarian newssheet *Mercurius Aulicus* reported on his plight in its issue of 10 January 1642:

> It is confidently reported and believed in London, that the King's Army in this City of Oxford
> is in as miserable a condition for horse and man as can be imagined...

The newssheet claimed, probably with some truth at least, that 'fat oxen' were intercepted on the roads and other cattle brought in from the countryside, whilst Charles demanded a 'brace of fat bucks' from the keeper of the royal manor of Woodstock. The unfortunate man was threatened 'if you faile to send the bucks, I shal not faile to fetch you, if you dare to lye in your house'.

Arrangements for commandeering corn supplies were a little more orderly. A body of horse under Lieutenant-Colonel Boncle, Waggon-Master General to the king, and led by Captain Henry Stevens, carried away about 40 quarters of corn from Kirtlington on one occasion in 1644. The normal trading system of the Oxford area, centred around markets at Oxford itself, as well as at Banbury, Bicester, and Woodstock, was disrupted by the garrisons of troops stationed there, and their constant and unpredictable requisitioning of goods. If the unfortunate country people were lucky enough to get paid, the money often had to be handed back to one army or another as 'taxes'. Although Kirtlington was not granted market status until 1677, a Clerk of the Market and a Water Bailiff were appointed in 1638, so clearly some unofficial arrangement already existed at the time of the war.

Bletchingdon and Woodstock, as well as Oxford, were both Royalist garrisons, but Banbury was very much a Parliamentarian stronghold. To the bawdy and boisterous, the sober Puritans, with their strict observance of the Sabbath day must have been a source of amusement, and of annoyance on occasion. But their adherence to their cause and their singleness of purpose was admirable. Cromwell's New Model Army (which took the field for the first time in 1645) had officers who were picked for their military ability, their religious beliefs and their sober outlook – thereby setting, it was hoped, an example for other 'honest men' to follow. Ordinary infantrymen on both sides, however, were generally pressed into service rather than volunteers.

Kirtlington's nearest military engagement took place at Tackley Bridge, just across the fields behind Flight's Mill, when the Earl of Essex and his 'Roundhead' soldiers were fought off by Sir Jacob Astley and his forces in June 1644. A relic of this fight – a cannon ball – was discovered near the bridge some years ago.

What was perhaps one of the saddest incidents of the war took place at nearby Bletchingdon on 25 April 1645. The Parliamentary forces, under Cromwell, had just won a skirmish at Islip and were pursuing their opponent, the Earl of Northampton, and his remaining troops, to their garrison at the old manor house of Bletchingdon 'lying in the village strete'. The officer in charge of the garrison was Lieutenant Colonel Francis Windebank, who had recently married. He was now faced with an unenviable choice – should he stay put, defend the garrison, and possibly risk the lives of his wife and house-guests, or surrender and put his own neck in danger? He chose the latter course, and after being imprisoned at Oxford, he was executed there on 3 May. The Royalists considered that a garrison equipped with 200 men, 300 muskets and 'three score and eleven horses more' should have put up a good fight against Cromwell, and thus regarded Windebank as nothing better than a traitor.

The fortunes of the war ultimately turned decisively in Parliament's favour: the position of the Oxford headquarters became increasingly difficult to maintain, and in 1646 it was abandoned. King Charles himself became a prisoner and was beheaded in 1649. There followed more than ten years when England was without a royal government, ruled first as a Commonwealth and then by the Protectorate of Oliver Cromwell. After the latter's death, no-one could be found to take his place. Charles II was restored to his throne in 1660, and after one of the greatest dislocations of daily life in English history, the people of Kirtlington, like their counterparts all over the country, faced the task of picking up the pieces and rebuilding the economy.

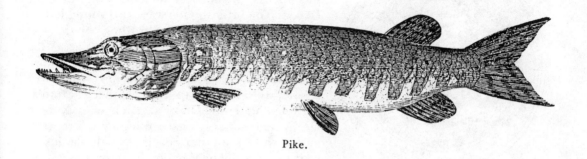

Pike.

CHAPTER SEVEN

An Era of Elegance

Fig. 9. The Dashwood coat of arms.

In the autumn of 1712, Robert, the fifth son of Sir Robert Dashwood of Northbrook Manor, was invited to be best man at a wedding in Devon. The bridesmaids were two young ladies from Hertfordshire, whose brother, the rich Sir John Reade, had died the previous year. After the wedding, the guests made their way home. For the first part of the journey, Dorothea Reade, the heiress to her brother's estates, travelled in Lady Drake's coach with Robert Dashwood, suitably chaperoned by her mother and sister. In another coach were the ladies in waiting. Suddenly the perch or groom's seat broke and the ladies precipitated to the ground, but they sent for the Duke of Beaufort's calash, which carried the party as far as Gloucestershire.

This dramatic incident does not seem to have affected the development of a relationship between the two young people. Only two months later, in December 1712, Robert and Dorothea were married. Part of the marriage settlement included the manor of Duns Tew, to add to the large amount of land and property already in the possession of the Dashwood family. Their son James was born in August 1715 at their London house. He had an expensive education of the kind usual for boys of his background, attending Eton and also a boarding school in Abingdon where the headmaster, a Mr. Thomas Wood, was known as 'Caning Tom'.

In the fashionable manner, James embarked on the Grand Tour of Europe in 1732. He was accompanied by his manservant William and travelled in his own chaise. His luggage included some fine buckskin breeches, as well as such useful domestic items as a tea kettle, a wig stand, and a mousetrap. In France, he attended the academy of Monsieur de Pignerolle, and had tuition in French, drawing and fencing. It was probably here that he first became interested in architecture, visiting many magnificent houses. Their elaborate design, intricate plasterwork, and elegant decor were vastly different from the family mansions at Northbrook and Kirtlington, now falling into decay.

When James returned home he found new responsibilities awaiting him, as he had become the second baronet following the deaths of his grandfather Sir Robert and his father. Although there had probably been discussions about building a new mansion before his grandfather died, there was now even more reason to pursue the idea as James married an heiress, Elizabeth Spencer, in 1738.

The site chosen was part of the Great Wood of Kirtlington, where the heron and spoonbill had nested in years past, and only hunting parties had previously disturbed the green depths. No time was lost in seeking out expert craftsmen, and it appears from Sir James's accounts that payments were made to a Mr. Garrett, a Mr. Gibbs and later to John Sanderson for drawing up plans for the new house. It was to be in the Palladian style and built of local stone. There still seems some uncertainty regarding John Sanderson's partner. Was he Humphrey Smith, renowned for his skill with drainage problems and water supplies? He would no doubt have been on hand to advise when Sir James noted in June 1742 that the workmen had 'begun the water' – this either being the house's own water supply, or work on the creation of the lake. Humphrey Smith is known to have died in 1743, however, and the name of William Smith is found later in Sir James's accounts.

Workmen began to clear the site in readiness for laying the foundations on 5 April 1742, but it is quite likely that tree felling had been taking place for some years beforehand. Oak and Spanish chestnut were the principal indigenous growths, and this timber was used extensively in the new house. On 30 August 1746, Sir James and Lady Dashwood had two events to celebrate. Their son Henry Watkin was one year old, and they had just moved into their beautiful new house – Kirtlington Park. A dream had been realised at the comparatively low cost of £32,541. That evening port, champagne and delicious food were enjoyed in the new house, whilst the villagers of Kirtlington feasted on an ox roasted whole on the Green and washed it down with eight hogsheads of strong beer – gifts from the new lord of the manor.

In 1747 '*Vitruvius Britannicus*' published five plates of the elevations and plans of the house, and described it as 'erected upon an edifice in the middle of a large park, commanding a very extensive prospect over a rich vale bounded by the Chiltern Hills ... the principal front, the centre consisting of a rusticated basement, which supports an Ionic tetrastyle, finished with a pediment. The offices are on each side of this front. The principal entrance is by means of a flight of steps, which leads into a hall, from whence are communications to the chief apartments'. The fifth plate shows the south front, which 'has many decorations, and a flight of steps to descend from the principal floor to the park'. The architects were named as 'J. Saunderson and Smith' in this publication.

In the same year John Loveday of Caversham rode over to Kirtlington Park. He was very impressed with its spaciousness, that was sufficient for 'fourteen lodging rooms, on a floor with a dressing room to each'. Horace Walpole also remarked on the house when he passed by in 1753, describing it as 'a vast new house, situated so high that it seems to stand for the county as well as himself'.

The Dashwood family now owned so much land through marriage settlements and purchase that they could probably have ridden from Kirtlington to Banbury without leaving their own boundaries. The pleasure grounds of Kirtlington Park were mostly the work of the famous Lancelot 'Capability' Brown, who according to his critics, sometimes created 'an artificial form of naturalness'. The charge for his design work amounted to almost £1,000, but he may have adapted an original plan by another landscape gardener named Greenings, whom Sir James had commissioned earlier.

In 1748 the methodical lord of this domain recorded over 150 different varieties of trees, shrubs and sweet-scented flowers in a special notebook. There were ash, oak, fir and spruce trees, almond, sweetbriar, honeysuckle, clematis and tamarisk, mulberry and perfumed cherry, as well as musk, cabbage, large red and double yellow roses, peaches, plum and flowering raspberry. No doubt the garden in full bloom rivalled the dresses of visiting ladies who strolled along a specially designed walk near the house. This was over fourteen feet wide, and allowed two couples walking in opposite directions to pass each other without needing to interrupt their conversations!

With such a valuable house, filled with expensive treasures, it was naturally sensible to take out some form of insurance. A policy was arranged with 'Mr. Drought of Oxford' on 14 December 1767, and the total valuation placed on the house, furniture, contents and stables was £10,500. There was also additional protection in the form of a fire engine.

When the delights of the pleasure grounds and magnificent lake had been sampled by visitors and admiring friends, there was more to feast the eye inside the house, although it had not been finally completed. There was the alcove in the entrance hall, with its ornate pedimented doorway, and the fireplace with its grey stone chimneypiece, and the carved wooded overmantel, the work of Grinling Gibbons, which depicted game and fish and may have come from the old manor of Northbrook. Even the elaborate and formal 'French-style' library, with its rococo ornamentation, busts and 'Aesop medallions' cannot have prepared visitors adequately for the dazzling ceiling of the Monkey Room, which had been painted by the French artist Clermont for a fee of £70. This unusual work of art depicted monkeys dressed for the chase and riding on the backs of hounds, in pursuit of the stag, fox, bear and hare.

Some confusion exists over the identity of the artist or artists responsible for the plasterwork and medallions. They were probably the work of the Anglo-Dane Charles Stanley, although Mr. Rogers of Oxford was no doubt responsible for some of the decoration. This matter has been discussed at some length in an issue of *Country Life*. Sir James Dashwood's guests would also have seen the elegant dining room, the interior of which was sold to an American museum a few years ago.

In 1778 Mrs. Lybbe Powys visited Kirtlington Park with a small party, and was most impressed with Lady Dashwood's 'china room': 'the most elegant I ever saw, 'tis under the flight of stairs going into the garden, it's ornamented with the finest pieces of the oldest china, and the recesses and shelves painted pea-green and white, the edges being green, in a mosaic pattern'. Mrs. Powys was fortunate enough to meet Sir James himself during her visit: 'We could not help saying, at our return, that he was, at sixty-three, one of the finest men we ever saw'. Like many large men (Sir James weighed 17 stone at the age of 35), he must have had considerable presence and an air of authority, having been a successful politician and High Sheriff of Oxfordshire.

Even for a man of his wealth, politics was an expensive business, and he had been a M. P. since 1741. The most notorious election in which he took part occurred in 1754. The campaign opened in 1752 with a fete in Kirtlington Park, and this elegant preliminary must have been in great contrast with the later events nearer polling day, when the 'Mob' were often 'tumultuous and indecent in their support of the New Interest, entering churches, and blaspheming from the pulpit'.

The candidates concerned were Sir James himself and Viscount Wenman, a school friend from Abingdon days, standing for the 'Old Interest' (the 'Blues' or Jacobites), against Sir Edward Turner and Viscount Parker, who represented the 'New Interest', 'Yellows' or 'Hanover Rats', who were in favour of the reigning monarch, George II.

'Old England, Old Interests and Christianity for ever – down with the New Interest!' cried Sir James's supporters.

William Jackson first printed his *Oxford Flying Weekly Journal* in 1746, partly as a politicial broadsheet, and introduced his second publication *Jackson's Oxford Journal* in May 1753. This was full of poems, articles, letters and political satires on the two parties. One of the letters it contained was addressed to 'Friend James' and purported to come from 'thy friend Obadiah', one of the Yellows. In the first issue of the *Journal* a satire appeared, based on the manufacture of 'shag' in various parts of Oxfordshire. This claimed that 'the American Green is a dirty colour, liable to change, and presently takes spots, but the Kirtleton True blue never stains'. The contest became even more heated when it was alleged that Sir James had not been present in the House when the bill for naturalising the Jews had passed, but was in a tavern instead, although his vote was recorded.

Although politics occupied a good deal of his life, Sir James still found time to enjoy his farm and livestock, horsebreeding, racing, lotteries and card-playing. His interest in music, and the contents of his well-stocked library (containing almost 2,500 books) no doubt also gave pleasure to him and his family. He was generous to his tenants, as we have seen in the previous chapter, arranging special dinners for them on rent days, and held ox-roasts on occasions of celebration, with home-brewed ale.

His account books show the payment of a stream of taxes, for possessing 'a coach, chariot and chaise', a 'watch rate', and 'scavenger's rate'. When we find that the marriage settlements for his three daughters amounted to £34,000, it is not surprising that when he died at the age of 64 in 1779, there were still parts of his mansion house that had not been completed – much to the despair of his descendants.

Henry Watkin Dashwood, his heir, was no help in repairing the family fortunes, as he was a spendthrift. He had married a beautiful young wife, and they were moving in expensive court circles. He sold off valuable parts of the estate and other inherited lands. His wife, the former Mary Helen Graham, born in India, was only 17 when they married in 1780, but she was beautiful and intelligent, endearing herself not only to the famous Dr. Johnson, when she met him at a dinner party, but also to the royal family in her position as lady-in-waiting to the daughters of George III and Queen Charlotte. All who knew her were saddened by her early death at the age of 33, leaving six children. Her husband outlived her by many years, dying aged eighty-three.

In 1803 the family suffered a tragic blow when Sir Henry's eldest son, Henry George Mayne, engaged in a duel with their neighbour Lord Valentia's son. Poor Henry was shot in the head, and his body was carried home in the back of a cart.

The fourth baronet, who succeeded to the title in 1828, was Sir George Dashwood, who also married well, his bride being Marianne, daughter of Sir William Rowley of Suffolk, by whom he had a large family. Their son and heir Henry William was educated at Harrow and Corpus Christi College, Cambridge; he married Sophia Drinkwater, from Warwickshire, in 1845.

The new lord of the manor greatly improved the estates, taking a keen interest in progressive farming methods and land reclamation. Kirtlington Church also benefited from his generosity, which enabled the churchyard to be enlarged. Like Sir James before him, he took an interest in politics, and was appointed as Lord

Lieutenant of the County, a position he held for four years. At a time when the temperance movement was gathering strength, he identified with these reformers. In 1879 Sir Henry chaired a public meeting held in Kirtlington's schoolroom. The object of the meeting was to try and form a club for the working men of the village, where they could meet to chat, smoke and read the papers or weekly magazines. Over thirty villagers put their names forward as prospective members, and they were joined by Sir Henry himself and his brother, Major Frederick Loftus Dashwood, who was acting as the agent to the estate and farmed over 1,000 acres in Kirtlington. The premises for the new reading room were on the top floor of 'West View', next to the village stores. The 'Coffee Tavern' occupied the ground floor for a number of years.

Sir Henry died in 1889, and his successor was Sir George Egerton Dashwood, who had been educated at Eton and later received a commission in the Scots Fusilier Guards. He married Lady Margaret Seymour. Queen Victoria sent her father, the fifth Marquis of Hertford, a shawl as a wedding gift for her, with a personal letter which sent her best wishes. The villagers of Kirtlington celebrated Sir George and Lady Mary's homecoming by arranging to have lights on in every house in the village, shining cheerfully as they drove through.

For an owner with adequate finance, Kirtlington Park was a magnificent home, but for someone with a large family to provide for, heavy taxation, and responsibilities for the village and the county, it was a burden. It was a sad day for Sir George and his family, and for Kirtlington, when it was finally decided that they must leave. The estate was purchased by the earl of Leven and Melville in 1909, but there was one last family celebration at Kirtlington which must have given pleasure to everyone.

On 20 July 1909 Margaret Frances Dashwood married Captain Ronald Henderson, late of the Third Hussars. 'It is only on rare occasions that a marriage excites such interest' wrote a correspondent of *Jackson's Oxford Journal*, and he went on to describe the beautiful flowers, the schoolchildren dressed in white holding shepherd's crooks, Mrs. Norridge at the organ, and the bride herself, dressed in soft white satin, with an heirloom Brussels lace veil, followed by a page and six bridesmaids in Ninon dresses. 'The celebrations of the village were of a particularly enthusiastic and gay character' the *Journal* reported. Practically every cottage had been decorated, and there were Union Jacks, other flags and bunting everywhere. Before the young couple left for their Cornish honeymoon, a reception for 150 guests was held at the manor house in the village, whilst the Oxford Post Office Band played in the garden. The wedding presents included a silver tea set from the estate tenants, and the schoolchildren gave an illustrated hymn book. Among the guests were Viscount and Viscountess Valentia from Bletchingdon, with their daughters Kathleen and Lettice, and Viscount Dillon and his family from Ditchley Park.

As the celebrations drew to a close, and people slowly began to make their way home, one man in Kirtlington still had a delicate task to perform. Mr. Hawkes the postmaster, carefully holding a casket containing an illuminated address and a special letter, was on his way to Kirtlington Park to make a presentation on behalf of the village. Sir George and Lady Mary were no doubt very touched when they read the sentiments expressed in the address:

> The Parish is deeply sensible of the benefit it has received from this connection. It has found in you not only the most considerate of landlords and sincerest of friends, but an example in every department of life, of the truest and kindliest virtues of English country life.

The bellringers of Kirtlington, in their special letter, appreciated Sir George's 'many acts of kindness', and expressed regret that they were losing 'one whom we are proud to think has always been our friend'. Sir George himself, replying to these tributes, hoped that the villagers would understand 'what a trial it is for all my family to sever a connection that has lasted for so many years'.

While her parents were looking back with regret on the end of an era, young Muriel Dashwood was looking forward to a new future, as she boarded the train at Bletchingdon on her way to school at Wycombe Abbey. 'I remember the day after my sister's marriage, in 1909, I put my hair up and let my skirts down – and it was goodbye to Kirtlington Park' she told us, as we sat talking in her comfortable sitting room during an autumn morning in 1982. I had the great pleasure of meeting this delightful lady soon after her 90th birthday, and she was happy to recall the celebrations which had taken place on that occasion at Kirtlington Park through the kindness of its present owner, Christopher Buxton. 'Do you know – the house even smelled right when I walked in, as the housekeeper had found a tin of the polish that mother always used!'

Muriel was the youngest of Sir George and Lady Mary's 11 children, and from all accounts they were as naughty and mischievous as most families – climbing out of the window when they had been locked in the schoolroom by their governess, playing noisy games along the corridors, and in the billiards room. Muriel helped to look after the little Welsh pony Taffy who took her brother hunting. 'We were just a large and happy family in those days – we didn't always do the right thing – perhaps we were a bit unconventional sometimes, but we were far from elegant!'

Among Miss Dashwood's childhood memories was that of the Good Friday mornings when Kirtlington children picked primroses to decorate the church. Obviously unused to the bending and stretching, one older member of the party, tightly corseted, fainted at the church. 'It was the first faint I had ever seen', Miss Dashwood recalled.

In 1892, after Sir George had recovered from an illness brought about by the strain of a long political campaign, the family left Kirtlington Park and moved to Warwick for five years. During this time they travelled to Switzerland a great deal, and Miss Dashwood remembered enjoying tobogganing – 'it was before skiing came in so much'. Then they moved to Brussels for a while, and her two older sisters were presented at the Belgian court.

In the spring of 1899 they returned to Kirtlington. Whilst they had been away, the house had been let to a very pleasant but eccentric family who were great animal-lovers. To their horror they found that pigeons had been nesting over grandfather's picture, goats had eaten the face out of another family picture, and the curtains were a bedraggled mess after unhousetrained cats and dogs had been running amok! Even the mattresses had become homes for colonies of rats and mice.

After the family left Kirtlington, they moved to Abingdon, and then to Oxford. When Muriel Dashwood left school, she took up nursing, and thought of becoming a doctor. In the event she became assistant librarian at Somerville College, Oxford 'for a very happy fifteen years'. 'Now, here I am, living under the umbrella of a hundred unanswered letters', she said cheerfully, pointing to the pile of correspondence on her desk. Sadly, many of these letters were probably never answered, as Miss Muriel Dashwood died on 12 January 1983.

Her memorial service at Kirtlington drew a large number of friends and relations, and for a moment, as we listened to Mr. Bower's address, we had a sudden, vivid picture of her. 'Whenever she came into a room, it somehow became alive – and everyone started to enjoy themselves'. Sir James Dashwood not only left posterity a beautiful house, which is still a source of pride for the village of Kirtlington, but he and his descendants who lived there for so long will never be forgotten either.

Pike.

CHAPTER EIGHT

Cultivation and Conservation

The Later Owners of Kirtlington Park: 1, The Earl of Leven and Melville

In *The Times* of Monday 18 June 1909, an advertisement appeared concerning a large Oxfordshire estate, 'to let, with the shooting'. It was Kirtlington Park. The Dowager Countess of Leven and Melville, who had been widowed in 1906, decided to rent the mansion house with a view to purchase, and in due course her son the earl became the new owner. The Leven family had a seat at Glenferness, Nairnshire, and could trace their ancestry to Sir Alexander Leslie, the first earl of Leven, who had fought in the First Civil War on the Parliamentary side, although his sympathies had later become Royalist after the execution of the king.

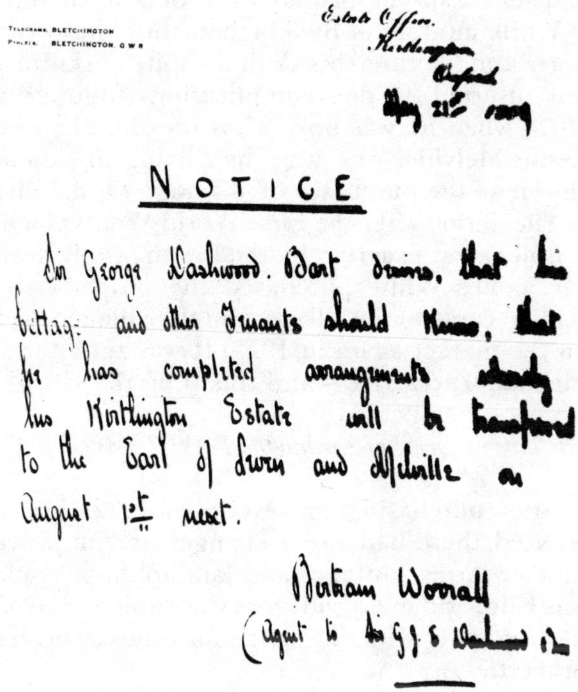

Telegrams. BLETCHINGTON
Parcels. BLETCHINGTON. G W R

Estate Office.
Kirtlington
Oxford
May 21st 1909

NOTICE

Sir George Dashwood. Bart desires, that his Cottage and other Tenants should know, that he has completed arrangements whereby his Kirtlington Estate will be transferred to the Earl of Leven and Melville on August 1st next.

Bertram Worrall
(Agent to Sir G. J. E. Dashwood Bt)

Fig. 10. The Agent's notice.

The arrival of this family must have been a great relief to the villagers of Kirtlington, who had relied for so long on the continuity of the Dashwood family's ownership. It was soon obvious that the young earl was as kind and considerate as Sir George Dashwood before him. If a Kirtlington couple were getting married, they would be offered his open landau, with coachmen and horses, to take them to and from the church in fine style. He charged low rents to his tenants, especially in the case of widows or large families, whilst if the countess heard that any child was ill, hot lunches would be sent down to them from the house until they were better.

We know few details of the daily life led by these new owners of Kirtlington Park, but in 1911, *Jackson's Oxford Journal* reported on the annual Infirmary Ball, which had been held at Oxford Town Hall.

> The music by Archibald Joyce's band was fine and crisp, and the dancing went with great spirit.
> Wallflowers were practically non-existent ... The important persons went into supper at 11 o'clock
> ... and for some time they remained at the chief table in exclusive dignity ... Mr. Horatio Symonds
> took in Lady Leven and Melville.

The *Journal* reported on the same event in the following year:

> The [Dowager] Countess of Leven and Melville from Kirtlington Park was there – wearing a
> becoming gown of black velvet, only open in a small 'V' shape at the neck, a style which looked
> warm and comfortable, and in her dark hair was a row of diamond stars, mounted on a band of
> black velvet. Her son – the Hon. David Leslie Melville – was a steward.

The family were also involved with the Bicester Agricultural and Horticultural Show,
and sent a special display of flowers to the meeting of 1911.

While hunting in Buckinghamshire, however, the young earl was thrown from his
horse and fractured his skull. In spite of skilful surgery in London, when a silver plate
was inserted, further complications followed and he died in the early summer of
1913, when he was only 27 years old. His brother, the Hon. Archibald Alexander
Leslie Melville, who was then living in London, succeeded to the title, and he is
shown as the purchaser of Vicarage Farm, Kirtlington, in 1916.

The period after the First World War was a difficult one for many landowners, but
it is not clear exactly why the Leven family decided to sell the estate and move away.
Mr. James White purchased the property, but to the dismay of Kirtlington, he
seldom came to the village, and the villagers were not surprised when the estate came
on the market again in 1922. It was time for another caring and concerned lord of
the manor to arrive – and this time the villagers were not disappointed.

The Later Owners of Kirtlington Park: 2, Mr. and Mrs. Hubert Budgett

After purchasing the estate in 1922, Mr. Budgett and his wife Hazel quickly
realised there had to be changes and improvements. After deciding which of the
smaller farms, cottages and landholdings could best be dispensed with, an auction
was held, and many villagers were able to buy their previously rented homes, leaving
the Budgetts with the mansion house, the larger farms, and some miscellaneous
properties.

One of the most important contributions made during the Budgetts' residence in
the village was the improvement of the water supply. Although the ground was
prepared for the laying of the water main, in the meantime it still had to be collected
from the village pump or from rainwater barrels outside the cottage doors. Some
were fortunate enough to have wells in their gardens. Here Mr. Budgett's amazing
gifts as a water diviner came in useful: many people found they had water in hitherto
unsuspected sites after a visit from him.

Mrs. Hazel Budgett, who has now passed her ninetieth year, is still full of charm,
energy and determination – qualities which she put to full use as the new lady of the
manor. One of her first public duties after arriving in Kirtlington was to chair a
meeting of the newly-formed Women's Institute. Sixty members were enrolled that
November evening, in the men's Reading Room at 'West View', and it was not long
before the new branch was making a name for itself in various county events and
competitions. However, the Reading Room was not really suitable as a permanent

OXFORDSHIRE

9 miles from Oxford, 6 miles from Bicester;
and one and one half miles from Bletchington Station.

𝔍𝔩𝔩𝔲𝔰𝔱𝔯𝔞𝔱𝔢𝔡 𝔓𝔞𝔯𝔱𝔦𝔠𝔲𝔩𝔞𝔯𝔰 𝔴𝔦𝔱𝔥 ℭ𝔬𝔫𝔡𝔦𝔱𝔦𝔬𝔫𝔰 𝔬𝔣 𝔖𝔞𝔩𝔢
of

The Remaining Portions of
The Agricultural and Sporting Property

KNOWN AS

The Kirtlington Estate

INCLUDING

**RESIDENTIAL HOLDINGS,
AGRICULTURAL PROPERTIES,
PORTLAND CEMENT WORKS, VALUABLE MINERAL RIGHTS,
ACCOMMODATION LANDS & BUILDING SITES,
WAY LEAVE,
BUSINESS PREMISES, NUMEROUS COTTAGES, ETC.,**

comprising nearly the whole Village of Kirtlington,

Extending to about 2,012 acres

To be offered for Sale by Auction in 54 Lots by

Messrs. KNIGHT, FRANK & RUTLEY

*(Sir Howard Frank, Bart, K.C.B.; John Frederick Knight;
Alfred J. Burrows, F.S.I.; and Arthur Horace Knight ;)*

*Having sold the Mansion and Lands adjoining
in conjunction with*

Mr. WILLIAM YOUNG

*at the Clarendon Hotel, Oxford, on Thursday, the 15th day of June, 1922,
at 2.30 precisely (unless previously disposed of)*

Solicitor : O. L. RICHARDSON, Esq., Thanet House, 231-2, Strand, W.C. 2.
Auctioneers : WILLIAM YOUNG, Esq., 4, St. Peter's Street, St. Albans.
Messrs. KNIGHT, FRANK & RUTLEY,
20, Hanover Square, London, W. 1,
41, Bank Street, Ashford, Kent,
90, Princes Street, Edinburgh,
78, St. Vincent Street, Glasgow.

Fig. 11. The 1922 auction.

meeting-place, and Mrs. Budgett put her considerable powers of organisation to good use, as well as some of her personal savings. She chose a suitable site in the Heyford Road, close to the Old Laundry, and arranged for the estate carpenter, Mr. Castle, to erect a new Institute Hall. This was officially opened in February 1925, and after speeches the assembled company of over 150 persons spent a happy social evening with dancing, whist and a concert. This building must have done much to improve the quality of life in Kirtlington, and it is only now that it may be retiring in favour of a new village hall.

In 1923 Mrs. Budgett extended her kindness to the schoolchildren, when she brought a wireless set to the school to enable them to hear King George V's Empire Day speech. The parties she held for the children will be long remembered, with plenty of good things to eat, often a film show, and always a present to take home afterwards.

Mr. Budgett, although a successful businessman with a sharp scientific mind, had a keen sense of humour and organised 'hare coursing' up at the park, where village pets chased a clockwork mouse, wound up by turning a stationary bicycle wheel.

The many ways in which the Budgetts have been involved with the farming and sporting life of the village are described in other chapters. Although the mansion house has now been sold to Mr. Christopher Buxton, Mrs. Budgett's son, grandchildren, and even great-grandchildren are still in the village, all making their special contribution to its working and social life.

The Later Owners of Kirtlington Park: 3, Christopher Buxton, O.B.E., M.A., M.B.A.

The day after Christopher Buxton learnt in 1971 that Kirtlington Park was for sale, he went to see it. 'As I walked round the great rooms, they were almost bare, but I knew at once that I wanted to live here' he says. 'The house was evocative of its past and had a marvellous atmosphere'. Within a week the contract had been drawn up and signed. 'I knew I had done the right thing – I suppose it was just instinct'. Not only had Mr. Buxton found his perfect house, but Kirtlington Park had gained an ideal new owner, with extensive knowledge of the architecture and history of country houses gained through years of restoration work carried out by his specialist company.

The origins of Kirtlington Park have been described above, and I first traced it from manuscript sources, which can sometimes be a little dull. When Christopher Buxton outlined the history of the house (which he considers 'a perfect Palladian composition'), I had the additional pleasure of being able to stroll in the house and grounds themselves as he spoke of the work of their creators, James Gibbs and Capability Brown.

One of the first problems faced by the owner of such a large property is the heating, as it is too expensive to keep all the rooms warm at the same time. This problem has been solved by creating an inner core of essential rooms, and the others are used only if there are a large number of guests in the house. The installation of a lift has also been a help in getting luggage and supplies quickly to and fro, without having to negotiate the 66 stairs from the ground to the bedroom floors.

A beautiful house needs expert care if it is to remain that way, and this is provided by Mrs. Whitley, the housekeeper, who has worked at Kirtlington Park for over 30 years. Her husband Fred, now retired from working on the estate, helps in the house, mows the lawns and marks out the grass tennis courts. They are helped occasionally by their daughter-in-law Marcia, who has learnt the skills of tapestry and repairing gilding from studying books in the house's own library. Harold Ellis, another important member of the staff, has been the gardener for over 25 years. In addition, he skilfully arranges flowers in the house, and acts as major-domo on special occasions.

The lake is still a beautiful feature of the grounds, its loveliness enhanced by some majestic swans. There are some people, however, who cannot see beauty without wishing to destroy it: in 1982 a female swan and her cygnets were found dying near the lake, having been hit about the head, according to the vet's report.

As our conversation progressed from the house to the village, I was interested to discover Christopher Buxton's views on Kirtlington. 'A village is only as effective as the people who live in it, and it depends on the contribution each one makes. We are fortunate here that there are a great number of people who 'do their bit' – and a good deal more, too'. As lord of the manor, he feels strongly about his own commitment to continue the traditions of village life which are now gradually disappearing in many parts of England. Villages like Kirtlington should not be looked upon by people outside as just one of many pleasant backwaters.

One of the traditions which Mr. Buxton is interested in continuing concerns trees. It is recorded in the manor rolls that in 1475 the duke of Gloucester ordered the great oak forest of Kirtlington to be planted. Thus 500 years later, Christopher Buxton proposed a further tree planting, this time to replace the trees on the village green which had been decimated by Dutch Elm disease. After church service, on a bright and sunny morning in November 1977, representatives of various Kirtlington organisations gathered to plant lime trees on South Green. This was follwed by a further ceremony on North Green, where three fine oaks were planted – one each by Christopher Buxton, Mrs. Hazel Budgett, and another on behalf of the parish council.

A further event of great importance involving the lord of the manor took place in 1981, when the ownership of the village greens and Kites Pond was transferred to the people of Kirtlington. This began with a proclamation, read out by Gerald Johnson:

> Know ye, by these presents that I, Christopher Reader Godfrey Buxton, of Kirtlington Park in the County of Oxfordshire, currently holding the Lordship of the Manor of Kirtlington, and I, Richard Alan Budgett of Portway House, Kirtlington in the County of Oxfordshire, have jointly and severally this day presented as a gift to the Kirtlington Parish Council, being the elected representatives of the inhabitants for the time being of Kirtlington, all that land and property known respectively and separately as South Green, North Green and Kites Pond, and all that land described in a deed of conveyance executed this day of May in the year one thousand nine hundred and eighty-one. Such land to be for the enjoyment in perpetuity and for the benefit of the inhabitants for the time being of Kirtlington.

As lord of the manor, Christopher Buxton possesses three qualities essential for success in the role: the ability to negotiate, placate and innovate. These qualities have also been essential for his work as Honorary National Chairman, and now as President, of the Abbeyfield Society for the care of the lonely and elderly. There are now over 500 local Abbeyfield Societies and soon thousand houses will have been opened. Discussions have even begun about the possibility of an Abbeyfield house being opened in Kirtlington. Kirtlington Park had perhaps one of its most exciting evenings in 1978, when the Prince of Wales came to dine on the occasion of the Centenary of the University Polo Match. After the 'Old Blues' match, which was won by Oxford, and the University Match, in which Cambridge were the winners, 80 people sat down to dinner in the hall. Afterwards there was dancing for five hundred! During this visit, the prince was invited to become Royal Patron of the Society. Since then, Prince Charles has made many visits to Abbeyfield houses throughout the country, and has subsequently given them a property in the Duchy of Cornwall. In 1982 the Prince and Princess of Wales attended a Gala Evening of ballet at Covent Garden in aid of the society, an event organised by Christopher Buxton. As a permanent tribute to his dedicated work and to mark his 13 years as National Chairman, the Society commissioned the artist Carlos Sancha to paint his portrait, which now hangs in the dining room at Kirtlington Park.

Mingled impressions of this beautiful mansion house linger in the visitor's mind. The skilful lighting and beautiful flower arrangements enhance not only the graceful curve of an antique chair, and the rich sheen of a polished table, but the beautiful paintings, ranging from a wall-length battlefield scene with Jacobean horsemen, to the gentle romantic portraits of 18th-century beauties. Above are the intricate plasterwork and intricate mouldings on walls and ceilings. It had been easy to dream and reminisce of the past, as I sat talking to Christopher Buxton in his book-lined library, whilst the log fire spluttered and we sipped pale sherry from fragile glasses. It was not until I was leaving that I was brought back to earth as I glanced around at the busy scene of today. There by the hall door was a clutter of hats, tennis racquets and gumboots; in the desk in the library, papers and letters. Kirtlington Park is far from being a museum – it is still very much a home.

Snipe.

CHAPTER NINE

A Village at War

Part One: the Napoleonic Wars

In 1793 the English people, terrified by Napoleon's military successes on the Continent, feared a French invasion at any moment. All sorts of preparations were made. *Jackson's Oxford Journal* advocated food rationing: 'abolish gravy, soups and second courses: destroy useless dogs, don't give human food to dogs'. By 1796 a tax was put on the unfortunate animals for the first time. Humans were of course also affected by wartime. The demand for recruits to the militia spread to every corner of Oxfordshire. As far back as 1777, *Jackson's Oxford Journal* had announced that the militia was short of officers. Traditionally, soldiers were found by ballot, but it was possible to pay a substitute to take your place. In 1798, for instance, Mil. M. Webb took the place of Thomas Haward of Kirtlington.

It was even possible for an enterprising man to become a 'professional' substitute, putting his name forward on more than one occasion, receiving payment from the person whose name had been drawn in the ballot, and then vanishing. One such case is reported some 20 years after the Napoleonic period, when 'Samuel Smith' of Kirtlington proved to be one and the same as 'Samuel Hall' of Banbury, substitute for William Goffe!

There is a sad entry in the Kirtlington churchwarden's book for 1797: 'the village contributed to the widows and orphans of those killed in the French war' but it is not clear whether this referred to local men, or to a general fund. However, money was given generously to some men 'begging their way home', although it was sometimes hard for the parish authorities to distinguish genuine war veterans and enterprising civilian vagrants.

In the same year, it was decided that 398 cavalrymen were to be raised by Ploughley district (in which Kirtlington lay). A meeting was held at the *King's Arms*, Bicester, to discuss the matter, and decisions taken:

> It is the opinion of this Meeting that in all cases where the person providing a mare or gelding shall be entitled to an allowance, it will be expedient for the sub-division meeting to allow such sums as will appear adequate to the value of the horses provided, not exceeding twenty guineas. Also £5 – a proper allowance for providing a substitute if ballotted. The sum of £2.9.6d. would also be allowed for a suitable dress for a private soldier of Cavalry, and £4.16.5d. for a military bridle and saddle complete.

In *The Story of the Oxforshire Yeomanry*, there is a description of their drill and uniform:

> Except during harvesting, haymaking, and sheep shearing, they met for drill once a week, all ranks together, using their own horses. They were only to be called out of the county for 'suppression of riots or tumults' or by Royal Warrant during an invasion. They were to receive

43

No. 12.

43 Geo. III. c. 50, and
57 Geo. III. c. 57.

SCHEDULE B.

MILITIA.
Oath.

I *Samuel Hall* do make Oath, that I am by trade a *labourer* and have been usually resident in the Parish of *Stoke* in the County of *Oxford* that I * *am unmarried*

and that I have no rupture, nor ever was troubled with fits, and am nowise disabled by lameness or otherwise, but have the perfect use of my limbs; that I am not a Seaman or Seafaring Man, or an Apprentice; and that I do not belong to His Majesty's Navy, Army, or Marines, nor to any Corps of Militia. As witness my hand, at *Banbury* the *4th* day of *July* one thousand, eight hundred and *31* Sworn before me, at *Banbury* this *4th* Day of *July* one thousand eight hundred and *thirty one*

Samuel his X Hall Signature.

Mark

Witness present,

Description of the above-named.

Age.	Height.		Hair.	Eyes.	Complexion.
	Ft.	In.			

Fig. 12.   The oath of Samuel Hall, militiaman, 1831.

No. 14.

MILITIA.

Oath prescribed by the Act of the 51st Geo. III. Cap. 118, Sect. 2, to be taken by Substitutes, Hired Men, or Volunteers, or otherwise than by Ballot—for the Militia.

I *Samuel Hall* —————— do sincerely promise and swear that I will be faithful and bear true allegiance to His Majesty King *William* and that I will faithfully serve in the Militia, in any part of the United Kingdom of Great Britain and Ireland, for the defence of the same, during the time of five years, or for such further time as the Militia shall remain embodied, if within the space of five years His Majesty shall order and direct the Militia to be drawn out and embodied, unless I shall sooner be discharged.

his
Samuel + Hall.

Dated this 4 day of *July*

18 31.   *Wright*   Signature.

5,000. Sept. 1826.—Printed by J. Hartnell, Wine-office-court, Fleet-street, for His Majesty's Stationery Office.   4—262:

Fig. 13.   The oath of Samuel Hall, militiaman, 1831.

SURGEON'S CERTIFICATE.

I CERTIFY, that I have this day examined *Samuel Hall* and find him in every respect fit for His Majesty's Service.—Witness my Hand, at *Banbury*, this *Fourth* Day of *July* 18 31

Signature of }
Surgeon.   }   *Jn.º Wise*
                              Surgeon

Fig. 14.   Surgeon's certificate for Samuel Hall.

cavalry pay, and be subject to military law. The uniform was blue, with white facings, white breeches, large white scarves, black leather light cavalry helmet with bearskin crest, and side hackle feather plumes.

The Ploughley or Bicester troop was in the charge of Captain John Harrison, and was disbanded in 1807. In May 1911 a picture in the *Jackson's Oxford Journal Illustrated* showed 'Oxfordshire Yeomanry Officers of Forty Years Ago', amongst whom was Captain Dashwood from Kirtlington and Viscount Valentia from Bletchingdon. These officers were members of the 'South Midland Division' of what was obviously a re-formed version of the Yeomanry.

Charles Dashwood, the third son of Sir Henry Watkin Dashwood, served with distinction in the Peninsular War. He first joined the Navy, and married an admiral's daughter. In the army, he attained the ranks of lieutenant and then captain, 3rd Guards in 1806, and was appointed an extra aide-de-camp to Brigadier the Hon. Charles Stewart during the Corunna campaign of 1808-9. He was only 22 years old! Although severely wounded in the final struggle against Napoleon during the Waterloo campaign, he had nevertheless attained the rank of lieutenant-colonel. In 1824 he became Groom of His Majesty's Most Honourable Privy Chamber in Ordinary, and afterwards served as British Consul in Guatemala. However, on his return home in 1832, he was brought ashore severely ill, and died at Plymouth. The family papers still preserve his 'routes of the campayne, 1808' from his Peninsular days.

Apart from this interesting career, very little can be traced of Kirtlington's involvement with the war, and it is possible that some material dealing with this subject may have been destroyed.

Part Two: 1914-1918

By 1913, the stormclouds of the First World War were gathering, and even in Kirtlington, on 14 November, the school was closed because of 'military manoeuvres near the station'. The imminence of war also affected the lord of the manor, the earl of Leven and Melville. At a vestry meeting in that year, the vicar nominated the earl as his Warden, but he wrote 'regretting that his military duties kept him so much from the Parish that he was unable to accept' and Mr. Austin, the headmaster, was appointed in his place as Warden for 1914.

Between 1914 and 1915, German prisoners of war began to arrive in the village to help with the harvest and potato-picking. One young man was only 13 when he was captured. After the war he stayed on to work at Park Farm, and is still living in the village.

The King family was typical of many others, both in Kirtlington and elsewhere. Harry King, aged 18, joined up in 1914, and Charlie lied about his age in order to join the Oxford and Bucks Light Infantry in May 1916. In the accommodation left vacant, their parents were able to house soldiers from the Pioneer Corps, who were billetted in the village to deal with the hay commandeered from local farmers for army horses.

The East family at the Red House also had sons in the army. Charles was with the Oxford and Bucks Light Infantry, and Robert in the R.A.S.C., where he was promoted to staff sergeant and put in charge of an army bakery in Ipswich. Percy served with the Queen's Own Oxfordshire Hussars Yeomanry: and made regular trips to Ireland to bring back remounts for the army in France. He was renowned in the family for his horsemanship ('he could ride anything bareback' his brother remembers). Albert himself served in the Oxford and Bucks Light Infantry, and remembers that his army service 'was practically a tour of the world, we served in so many parts of the world'. In Bulgaria, he was a mule-handler, and became very fond of his animals. He was not so fond of the local food – the troops once lived for three weeks on dry biscuits! In India they had to wear topees to avoid sunstroke; in Cape Town, they wondered how they were going to cope with the intense heat; in Egypt Albert caught malaria ... it was an extraordinary experience for a Kirtlington lad.

His father, meanwhile, continued to run the bakery, the carriers' business, and the dairy herd, as best he could without the help of the eldest sons. Walter made regular journeys to Oxford to take flowers from the 'Big House' and deliver them to an emergency servicemen's hospital which had been set up in the University Examination Rooms in the High Street. On his return, he would bring clothing from the hospital for alterations at the sewing classes presided over by the Dowager Countess of Leven and Melville. Many of the soldiers had lost limbs and needed their clothes remade in consequence.

Most Kirtlington servicemen returned home: but some did not. Sir George and Lady Dashwood lost three sons – Ernest George, a captain in the Territorials, who was killed in the trenches near Ploegsteert Wood by a rifle grenade; Wilfred James, who died from wounds in 1917, whilst serving with the 1st Battalion the Grenadier Guards; and Lionel Albert, who enlisted in the Royal Engineers, was killed in 1915 at Festubert after receiving a temporary commission in the Oxford and Bucks Light Infantry. Their names, along with those of Sergeant L. A. Pratt, Sergeant T. F. Simmons, Corporal A. Edgington (who died from influenza in the epidemic of 1918), Corporal R. Mosto, Private W. Edgington, Private C. Giles, Private J. Hayward, Private S. Hayward, Private G. Herbert, Private W. T. King, Private H. Lambourne, Private A. Lamborne, Private L. Rainbow, Able Seaman C. Claton, Private W. J. Walton, and Private G. H. Wise are engraved on the Kirtlington War Memorial.

The lord of the manor had also made his contribution to the war: on 3 May 1916 it was decided at a vestry meeting that 'a letter of thankfulness and congratulation should be sent to Lt. the Earl of Leven and Melville, on his sufficient recovery from wounds received at Mons, in August 1914, to be able to return to military home duties'.

During a parish council meeting in late 1918, Mr. Castleman proposed that a memorial card should be sent 'to every village soldier who served' as well as a special card to 'parents who had lost sons'.

The schoolchildren of Kirtlington were not forgotten when the Armistice was signed in November 1918. They were given a half-holiday, and the log book records that 'Mr. Ough, a visitor, gave each child a penny'.

If the children rejoiced at the end of the war which they were hardly old enough to understand, their parents and elder brothers who had returned safely to their families had even more reason for thankfulness. However, many of these young men found life very difficult, since it was hard to find a job. Harry King managed to get a little work digging allotments for five shillings a time, up at Crowcastle Lane, and

KIRTLINGTON.

"WHY WE ARE AT WAR,"

AND

"How we can help our brave Soldiers and Sailors."

. A .

PUBLIC MEETING

WILL BE HELD IN

THE SCHOOLROOM

ON

THURSDAY EVENING, OCTOBER 15,

WHEN

Addresses will be delivered by

THE RIGHT HON.

Viscount VALENTIA, C.B., M.P.

AND

J. A. R. MARRIOTT, Esq. (of Oxford)

Door open at 6.45; to commence at 7 o'clock.

Men of Bletchington and Kirtlington, attend the Meeting, and show your respect for our gallant sailors and soldiers

God Save the King.

OLIVER & SON, PRINTERS, 62 GEORGE STREET, OXFORD.

Fig. 15. A Patriotic Meeting, October 1914.

solved the problem of checking the time in a most ingenious way – by training his captured German binoculars on Tackley church clock! Later on, he was fortunate enough to get work on Kirtlington estate, when they were re-organising their tree-planting and felling. Harry married his Tackley sweetheart, Eva Clark, but never made a complete recovery from his war wounds, and died at the early age of 32 in 1928.

For a group of ex-soldiers who were unable to find jobs, time hung very heavily, and they resorted to card-playing. They also borrowed Ernie King's gramophone and a few records, as well as a drum – the last remnant of the village drum and fife band. Then, whilst three of them helped to wind the gramophone and change the records, the other three took turns banging the drum in time. They sat at the roadside doing this, hoping to get some money in the hat. Unfortunately the only donation they remember getting was sixpence from 'Fishy' Pitts of Woodstock, when he came to deliver fish and fruit one weekend!

One Kirtlington soldier only left his home to serve his country in 1919. This was Aubrey Giles from Flight's Mill. His battalion of the Oxford and Bucks Light Infantry was embarking on a 'clearing-up' operation in the war zone, although the Armistice had been signed on 11 November 1918. During the months Platoon Sergeant Giles spent overseas, he kept a diary, which is now in the possession of his son, Mr. Bill Giles, who has kindly permitted extracts from it to be quoted in this chapter.

The troops arrived in Antwerp on 27 March at 1 a.m., where a Scottish band was waiting to play them to camp. 'We needed something a bit cheerful, for it was raining like old boots, and has been all day' wrote Aubrey. 'This camp is called a "Discharge Embarkation Camp". A Scotch Battalion is building it – although there are about five or six hundred Belgian civvies supposed to be – but it's very little they do ...'. He thought the huts they were living in 'very peculiar', like the roofs of miniature 'Dutch barns laid on the ground'. Each hut housed between 16 and 20 men.

On 30 March they left Antwerp for Dunwald, travelling in cattle trucks – 'the delight of all British Tommies' – with three blankets each. Not far from Antwerp the railway line ran through a timber yard, and as the trucks passed along, the Belgian workers threw bags of wood into them. Each truck had a little stove in the centre, and they soon had a good fire to keep them warm. Suddenly, however, the top joint of their chimney came away and rolled off the truck, leaving the remainder just below the roof, which soon began to catch fire. 'It put the wind up me properly, but we managed to get out of the difficulty by putting the stove on a stack of timber, high enough to push the chimney outside'.

By eight the next morning they were marching through the town of Mulheim, and out into the countryside. After about five miles they came to a village school, which was to be their new quarters. They were surprised to find that travelling was free on any of the tramways running through German territory held by the British, and although the notices on board stipulated only six soldiers could ride in each car, they were usually so full of British troops that there was no room for German civilians.

Towards the end of April the troops were given their brigade distinction flashes, which were sewn on the arm, just above the elbow. Aubrey, by this time, was working hard in his capacity of Post Corporal and Sergeant. Sometimes he was inundated with food parcels from home, and sometimes these were delayed in the post and arrived in a most unappetising condition. In May letters and parcels were delayed by 'the strikes in England' – a situation which upset the soldiers, many of whom were used to getting a letter a day from home. On 15 April there was a flurry of excitement for the battalion when they were turned out about six in the evening to patrol 'as they heard the Bolshevists were doing a bit of scraping somewhere'. By Good Friday 1919, the company had been transferred to the 2/4 Hampshire Regiment. They were impressed by their new billets, with wooden bedsteads and straw mattresses. 'The fellows will take a bit of routing out now at Reveille!' Aubrey commented.

A few days later, when the company was returning from a cross-country run, the fire alarm was raised at camp. 'We reached our billet in record time and were immediately turned out and marched to the scene of the fire, which was in a German's house where some of 'A' Company were billeted. All the Battn. were turned out, bringing with them buckets, dixies, biscuit tins, and any old thing ...'. Practically all the villagers also rushed to help and a line of people with water containers quickly got to work – until 'the fellow at the end of the line said the first bucket had put it out!'.

Amongst the humour and humdrum incidents, there were moments of tragedy, when men lost their lives in accidents. A 'No.1' of a Lewis gun section was unloading his revolver when it went off and shot another soldier in the stomach, and during a demonstration of firing trench-mortars, a shell exploded in the barrel of one of them, killing three men, and wounding 16 others, some of whom subsequently died. Two of the dead men had been due for demobilisation the next day.

By 18 June there was 'a proper wind-up' owing to the continued uncertainty over the signing of the peace treaty. 'This morning we had orders to pack up and get ready to move, wearing fighting-order ... if they do not sign the Treaty, we shall advance on Ramscheid'. By 21 June it was learnt that the Germans had only two more days in which to sign. 'The troops are getting fed up with this messing about – I can see they will have trouble out here if they put it off much more'. At last, on 28 June, the peace treaty was signed by Germany. 'I suppose the War is quite at an end now' Aubrey wrote; and concluded his entry with a comment on the weather 'rotten this week – rain every day'. Perhaps there was something of a feeling of anti-climax for the soldiers, prepared for the 'trouble' that did not, in the end, materialise.

Gradually, the battalion was demobilised: the weather got worse, everyone was longing to go home, but strikes meant that leave and demobilisation were cancelled for a while. Aubrey was trying to be philosophical on 13 October – 'I suppose I shall be going home *any year* now', having watched 50 others leaving, with the band playing them to the station. In late October, his company was transferred to the 51st Hampshire Regiment ('the fellows all hate the idea') and news reached them that two other battalions had been posted to Poland, and that there was a prospect of their going to Russia! This unpleasant idea was made still worse by the awful weather; by 14 November six inches of snow had fallen. N.C.O.s were given a lecture about the journey to Russia and the life there, which was further cause for alarm; but at last things began to improve. On 18 November a thaw set in, and by the 20th all the snow had gone. It was a lovely day on 24 November, when at last Aubrey learnt that he was moving to Cologne, in preparation for demobilisation. On 5 December 1919, the diary ended – with Aubrey back home at Flights Mill, Kirtlington, in good time for a real Christmas celebration.

Part Three: 1939-1945

When Mr. and Mrs. Hugh Budgett purchased Kirtlington Park Estate in 1922, they had little idea that with the coming of world war, the historic mansion was to become the nerve centre of the village, as well as housing important Government officials, entertaining visiting American soldiers, and providing comfort for endless streams of tearful evacuees from London. The village institute hall, as we have seen, became an emergency schoolroom for the London children, and most cottage homes had their quota of children, like Martha Scarrott at North Lodge and Edith Blake at the Bushes. The East family at the Red House often had to work through the night to supply extra batches of bread and cakes and later in the war also did good business with the American forces billeted locally.

With her husband principally occupied in London, Hazel Budgett was responsible for keeping the estate going with a limited staff. The milking parlour (which was then opposite Dairy Cottage on South Green) was partly staffed with members of the Women's Land Army. More land had to be ploughed up for vegetables or turned over for arable use (including the polo field!), and as quickly as things were grown, they seemed to disappear to feed the ever-hungry evacuees, their parents and whoever else needed temporary sanctuary at Kirtlington Park.

As a little light relief, Hazel Budgett arranged social evenings for the American officers and the war staff from Blenheim who were living on the estate, and these events were enjoyed by all. The gratitude of the Americans manifested itself in the most useful way possible – just when the estate's food supplies were getting dangerously low, the door opened and there were boxes and bundles of food. Hazel Budgett still remembers this as a marvellous sight.

The R.A.F. were also nearby, stationed at Slade Farm, and at Heyford Camp, which was later taken over by the Americans. The Air Force had a splendid band which was willing to play for children's parties: its leader later became a well-known broadcaster.

When invasion seemed imminent, the Oxfordshire County Emergency Committee, like others throughout the kingdom, issued special instructions in the form of a confidential 'War Book', on 1 October 1942. The first part of the book concerned the Headquarters and the composition of the Invasion Committee, and gave the telephone numbers of local, military and civil authorities. Part Two dealt with the civil and military plans to be put into action if invasion took place. The officials and 'special departments' for Kirtlington were as follows:

Chairman of Civil Defence:	Colonel Cowie
W.V.S. Representative, Food Executive Officer:	Mrs. Budgett
Doctor:	Dr. Robertson, Islip
Headquarters:	The Estate Office
Deputy Chairman:	Rev. R. W. Bennett
Military Member:	Lt. Pearson, Manor Farm
Police:	A. Eeley, Bletchingdon
Town Clerk:	E. K. Truman, Bicester
Rest Centre Member:	G. Ward
Adopted Member:	Capt. Douglas

Home Guard Headquarters: ...   ...   Manor Farm, Kirtlington
Emergency Food centre,
   storage of reserves, etc.:   ...   ...   Kirtlington Park

The population of Kirtlington was then 530, plus evacuees. No public shelter was provided in the village, but each householder was expected to dig a slit trench in their garden. Should there be an invasion 'or other emergency' the church bells were to be rung, houses evacuated, and helpers to go on duty at the Rest Centre. The local inhabitants were instructed to 'carry on as usual'!

There were 32 wardens in the village, and the First Aid Post was sited appropriately at the War Memorial. There were also three labour squads, with ten people in each. The Home Guard had three vantage points – the roof of Kirtlington Park, the silo at Shipton Cement Works, and Truby's Cafe at Kidlington. A list of horse-drawn vehicles for emergency use was drawn up, the owners including Messrs. Bartlett, Smith, Pearson, Viner, Eeley and Lay. They each owned three '1-horse vehicles' which would be made available if drivers could be found.

Fortunately Kirtlington was not badly damaged by bombs; but some were dropped in Park Lake, and at nearby Tackley, close to the railway bridge.

In a recent copy of the *Village News*, Fred Cooper, who was a cattleman at Slade Farm for 35 years, remembers an incident towards the end of the war, when he was a member of the Kirtlington Home Guard. Their supply of rifles, shotguns and cartridges was very inadequate, and he doesn't know what they would have done, had the worst happened when they were guarding their positions. Apparently the throwing of hand-grenades was practised at Lazarus Bottom, and it was just a matter of outstandingly good luck that two of the grenade handlers were not blown up when the removal of the pin, and the actual throwing of the grenade, became rather confused on one occasion!

Fred Cooper also remembers German bombers flying low over the treetops, apparently trying to attack Heyford Aerodrome. Instead, they dropped their bombs on the outskirts of Northbrook Farm, towards Crowcastle Lane. Fortunately no-one was injured, but doors and windows shook and debris reached as far as the Heyford Road.

On 6 June 1944 the Reverend Reginald Ward Bennett recorded D-Day with some triumph in the Kirtlington Church Register of Services:

> On this day was announced the first great assault on the Nazi fortress of Europe, by our invasion of Normandy. During this first week of bitter fighting, there will be celebration of Holy Communion every day at 8-am, with occasional short services of intercession.

With the ending of the war in 1945, life gradually returned to normal – although it would never be the same for the families of four Kirtlington men whose names appear on the War Memorial – W. A. Cato, A. W. Jarvis, H. W. L. Johnson and J. C. Tatham Warter.

Ernie King recalls that 'It was the feeling of everyone pulling together, and the determination to win against sometimes overwhelming odds, that I remember most about the Second World War'. No doubt these sentiments were echoed throughout the towns and villages of England, and contributed to the feeling of triumph and joy when the sky was once more for the birds – and not for the machines of war.

CHAPTER TEN

The Struggle for Survival

During the 17th and 18th centuries, and even earlier, when many people were forced to leave their homes as the result of wars, epidemics or failed harvests, the roads and lanes around Kirtlington had many tales to tell. They were often sad ones, as the wandering poor made their way through the village, sometimes begging for food or a place to sleep, before being moved on by the constable or Overseer of the Poor, so they would not be a drain on the village's tightly-budgeted poor rates. For some it was too late for them to be either helped or moved on, as the parish registers tell us. During the winters of 1638 and 1642, two 'poor travellers' died whilst passing through Kirtlington parish, and their bodies buried in the churchyard. In 1624 a 'poore fellow' who had come from Middleton was apparently looked after by 'Goodie Woodward' before he died, although William Freebody, travelling from King's Sutton in 1645 was not so fortunate: he 'fell down dead as he was travelling by ye grove'.

In 1521 John Slatter, Thomas Fender, and their wives were declared to be vagabonds and ordered to be expelled from the parish, but 'a poor woman' who was travelling through in 1581 was no treated so harshly; her children Anthony and Joan were baptised before they died.

It was not unusual for children to born, baptised and buried within a short space of time – like Jesper, son of an unknown father, 'born of Smith's daughter' in 1609, and Alice, 'daughter of a woman travelling this way'. But at nearby Bletchingdon, the vagrant woman who gave birth to a son in the shelter of a capacious oak tree was fortunate enough to live to see him grow into a strong young man. Bletchingdon was the scene of another humble confinement when a beggar woman found shelter 'under a hovell in Christ[opher] East's backsyde abode' in 1609 and gave birth to her daughter, later christened Margaret Paradise (her father being one Anthony Paradise). Two kindly local women, Margaret Merry and Em Wells, acted as godmothers, and the godfather was 'a sheapheard of Christ. East'. As late as the early 19th century, Susannah Smith, a tall and handsome gipsy woman, gave birth to a daughter on a cock of hay in the hedgerow at Radris Bottom according to the diary of George Dew, the local Relieving Officer.

Some of the many travellers on the roads in the 17th century had genuine 'walking passes' granted by justices of the peace to 'persons not being either Soldiers, Marines or Soldiers'. One of these was Thomas Bonhem, but his pass could not save him from misfortune: Kirtlington was his final resting-place. A number of these wanderers were craftsmen, searching for work. They were known as 'journeymen', who had served their long apprenticeships – usually of seven years – and jealously guarded their hard-won skills against imposters. Kirtlington itself furnished lads for apprenticeship, like William Enser, who was engaged by the master wheelwright John Bunker on South Green, and William Woodley, who was apprenticed to master

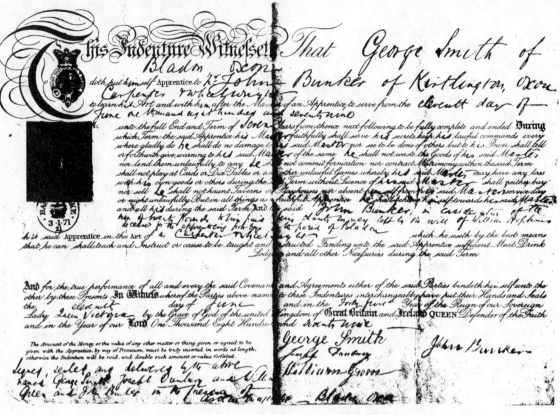

Fig. 16. Apprenticeship indenture for George Smith.

tailor John Hawkes at the age of eighteen. Journeymen who could not find the opportunity to set up a business of their own in the place where they had been apprenticed travelled round the country, looking for opportunities to take on temporary jobs or to settle permanently.

Some travellers were given the right to travel to a new home, and were granted settlement certificates to prove it. On 29 November 1769, for instance, John and Mary Spicer from Kirtlington, with their three-year-old daughter Mary, were granted a certificate to enable them to take up residence in St Aldate's, Oxford, ten miles away. Some fifty years previously, Thomas Kendal, probably a journeyman carpenter, arrived to settle in Kirtlington from Northamptonshire, with his certificate attested by two justices.

Kirtlington's own poor could look for help to several quarters. Their earliest benefactor, as we have seen, was Adrian Whicker, a former vicar of the village, who bequeathed £100 to be invested and used for the benefit of the 'very poorest sort'. A villager called Blatter contributed five pounds, which was distributed each year in the form of sixpences to poor widows. In 1911 Whicker's Charity still helped 25 widows by giving them sums of three and four shillings each, and the 'Fuel Charity' gave 95 householders 2s 9d apiece.

There was also 'The College', which had probably been first used as a brewhouse by the medieval lords of the manor, and later as a sanatorium by St John's College as patrons of the church. J. C. Blomfield, in his *Notes on Kirtlington*, describes it as a two-storey building, with a high thatched roof, and two very narrow doors and

Oxfordshire To wit. **W**E the ⸻

Churchwardens and Overseers of the Poor of the Parish of _Kirtlington_ ⸻ in the _County_ of _Oxford_ ⸻ aforesaid, do hereby own and acknowledge _John Spicer, Mary his wife and Mary their Daughter aged about three years_ ⸻ to be _our_ Inhabitant_s_ legally settled in the Parish of _Kirtlington_ aforesaid, In witness whereof, we have hereunto set our Hands and Seals, this _29th_ ⸻ Day of _November_ in the _Tenth_ ⸻ Year of the Reign of our Sovereign Lord _George the third_ ⸻ by the Grace of God, of _Great Britain, France, and Ireland_, King, Defender of the Faith, and in the Year of our Lord 17_69_.

Churchwardens ⎱ _John Hall_
⎰ _William King_

Attested by _us_

James Scot

George phillips _Overseers_ ⎱ _Thomas Young_
⎰ _Henry Drayton_

To the Churchwardens and Overseers of the Poor of the Parish of _Saint Aldates otherwise Saint Tolls_ ⸻ in the _City_ ⸻ of _Oxford_ ⸻ or to any, or either of them.

WE whose Names are hereunto subscribed, two of his Majesty's Justices of the Peace for the _County_ ⸻ of _Oxford_ ⸻ aforesaid, do allow of the above-written Certificate. And we do also certify, That _James Scot one of_ ⸻ the Witness_es_ who attested the Execution of the said Certificate ha_th_ ⸻ made Oath before us, That _he_ ⸻ did see the Churchwardens and Overseers, whose Names and Seals are to the said Certificate subscribed and set, severally sign_y_ and seal the said Certificate, and that the Names of the said _James Scot and George Phillips_ ⸻ whose Names are above subscribed as Witness_es_ to the Execution of the said Certificate, are of their own proper Hand-writing. Dated the _thirtieth_ ⸻ Day of _November_ ⸻ in the Year of our Lord 17_69_.

J. Dashwood

Thos Gregory

Fig. 17. Settlement certificate for the Spicer family.

windows. At one time it had a portico. It was used for a time as a 'dame school', but by the 19th century it was the local workhouse and was used to house up to 24 members of the 'labouring poor'. The vestry records show that it was in bad repair by this time. Eventually James Minn, Sir George Dashwood's steward, arranged for his master to buy the property in 1842, and it was subsequently pulled down.

Poverty continued to be a problem in 19th-century Kirtlington. In the year 1802-3, 75 people were given assistance totalling £476 17s 6d. In 1835, outdoor relief, which was given to people still living in their own homes rather than in a workhouse, amounted to £4 8s 11d in money and bread, and to £4 4s 11d in money only during September. Benefit was usually based on the price of bread, and fluctuated accordingly, and also on the size of the family to be fed. A man and wife with one child could qualify for 6s 6d a week when a widow could get only 2s 6d.

In 1835 plans were already well in hand for the erection of the Bicester Union or workhouse, which was to cater for the poor of the whole Bletchingdon district, including Kirtlington and Weston-on-the-Green. Each district was to have a Relieving Officer (at £60 a year), and the other staff members were a chaplain (at £50 a year), a schoolmaster, who had to be a tailor and shoemaker, and a porter who got £20 a year and ate the same food as the paupers. Tenders had already been submitted for a number of items including the inmates' uniform – hats at 11s 6d a dozen, stockings at between 8d and a shilling a pair, stays (corsets) at a shilling a pair, and jackets from 10s 6d each. The women were to have 'blue print for gowns'. Flock, not straw, was to be used for the mattresses, and iron bedsteads provided, whilst the working tools and equipment to keep the paupers usefully employed included spades, pickaxes, birch brooms and blacklead.

Different arrangements had been made for the handicapped poor: a Mr Tilsley 'had offered to take the Lunatics and Idiots at 9 shillings per week, when ten in number or upwards, with an entrance fee of 10s 6d for each': it is not hard to imagine the misery that was surely in store for this section of the population. For married couples, and perhaps for elderly people in particular, admission to the workhouse could be a dreadful experience when men and women were compulsorily separated, clothes and familiar possessions confiscated, and a rigid programme of hard work and scanty meals adhered to. No wonder that many elderly Kirtlington villagers chose to work and earn their keep until they were over eighty – like George Telley, Lydia Ashton and Richard Allen.

Workhouse children could hope to be apprenticed to a craftsman, or even perhaps decide finally on emigration. Those who did not live to have a choice were taken to the churchyard in tiny coffins costing 3s 6d apiece, usually made of unplaned elm boards, darkened with lampblack. The Reverend Chittenden, Kirtlington's vicar, was not only saddened by these pathetic burials, but horrified by the way in which the corpses of elderly paupers were sometimes left without clothes in their coffins. He felt so strongly in fact that he would apparently have liked to see the building pulled down altogether!

The lords of the manor also tried to ease the lot of the poorer villagers. Sir James Dashwood sold corn cheaply to them, and often gave them bread in bad winters, whilst Sir George Dashwood, himself the father of a large family, gave children mugs of hot soup or cocoa. At Christmas 1894, he gave one J. Pearman a scarlet 'comforter' or scarf, and scarves, serge petticoats, mitts and stockings were distributed to other needy folk.

The village also had its own self-help in the form of the Friendly Society or Box Club, founded in the early 1800s. The rules were numerous, detailed, and strictly kept. Amongst them it was stated that membership was not to exceed a fixed number, and that soldiers, bailiffs and 'bailiffs' followers' were to be excluded! The benefits paid ranged from seven to 12 shillings a week, and covered most forms of sickness. There was also a burial allowance payable, whilst payments made could vary from one halfpenny to 2s 6d a month, according to age. The village could also manage to put on special treats from time to time, like the Old People's Tea of January 1891. In spite of bad weather 35 out of 50 villagers came along to enjoy ham, beef and collared head, followed by tea and crackers. Later they were entertained by the schoolchildren's play *Beauty and the Beast*, and after community singing until nine o'clock, they all went home with a gift of a packet of tea apiece.

The best news for elderly people was contained in the *Oxford Times* of 2 January 1909, when it was announced that 'payment of Old Age Pensions begins on Saturday, between 8 a.m. and 9 p.m.' This was truly a momentous day when your income was only 10 shillings a week, or less. A single elderly person could claim five shillings and a married couple 7s 6d, without having to work for it!

With membership of the lively 'Welcome Club' open to them, with coach trips to places of interest, shopping expeditions and birthday treats, Kirtlington's senior citizens nowadays have a lot to enjoy. The 17th- and 18th-century poor, often with nowhere to turn to for help, would have thought themselves already in paradise.

Deer.

CHAPTER ELEVEN

The Ways of Village Government

On 18 October 1760 'in the thirty-fourth year of the reign of George II' an important notice, signed by Thomas Walker the steward, was submitted to the bailiff of the manor of Kirtlington, who would either have fixed it to the church door or handed it to the parish clerk to read during the service. This document was one of the regular summonses to the Court Baron and View of Frankpledge of Sir James Dashwood, held 'at the usual place within the Manor'. On Thursday, 30 October, it would be the duty of 'four and twenty honest and lawful men of the same Manor' to attend and perform the 'Suits and Services' they owed the court.

The manor courts were a very important part of the tight-knit community life of the village, and were in fact a continuation of the early tradition of the folk moots of the Saxon chieftain Cyrtla, who would have called his people together at regular intervals to discuss matters of importance and to order any punishments necessary.

The court rolls provide an essential record of Kirtlington's administrative history from medieval times. They could also be used to provide proof of tenancy for 'copyholders' who wanted to obtain land from their lord in return for services or a money rent. The Court Baron was the lord's private court, and fines or a forfeit could be imposed for non-attendance without a suitable excuse. Village officials were appointed, including the bailiff and the beadle, who collected fines. In the 17th century, for instance, one Kirtlington steward was called John Ellys, and the bailiff was John Reeve. The 'hayward' or guardian of the hedge, who was in charge of the common or waste ground, ensured that fencing was stock-proof and impounded stray cattle which would be taken into custody by the 'pinder' and held in the village pound. This was usually a sturdily walled or fenced enclosure about five feet high, with a water trough and perhaps a manger. The Kirtlington pound was situated close to the old forge at the junction of Mill and Crowcastle Lanes. In 1897, some years after the pound had been demolished, a tree was planted on the site to commemorate Queen Victoria's Diamond Jubilee. Although the *tree* was parish property, the length of tenure of the site resulted in it becoming council property!

It was the responsibility of the 'woodward' to care for the forest land and the timber, whilst the fieldsmen or herdsmen like the 16th-century villagers Thomas Shadd, Thomas Hogges and Thomas Myles, allocated the common meadowland, which was done by lot until about 1748. In the mid-17th century these men would have received 4d and 'a peck of maslin' for every yardland they dealt with. They also had to ensure that no more than the statutory number of animals were grazed by Kirtlington farmers, and that the fields were used at the correct times of the day.

The village constable was another important member of the community, whose duties included the removal of vagrants and the supervision of sheep-dipping. The apprehending of criminals was a community affair and, after the hue and cry had

Manor of Kirtlington with its Members in ye County of Oxford

These are to will and require you to Summon and give Publick Notice within the said Manor of Kirtlington That the View of Frankpledge of our Sovereign Lord the King for the same Manor with the Court Baron of Sir James Dashwood Bart. Lord of the said Manor will be holden at the Usual place within the Manor aforesaid on Thursday the Thirtieth day of October Instant by ten of the clock in the fore noon of the same day And that you Summon and give Notice to all ye Tenants of the said Manor and Resiants within the same that do owe Suit & Service at the said Court That they and every of them personally be and Appear at the time and place aforesaid then and there to do and perform the same Suits & Services **And Likewise** that you Summon four and Twenty Honest & Lawful Men of the same Manor to be and Appear at the Time & place aforesaid to Enquire for our Lord the King of all such matters as to the said Court do belong **And** that you yourself be then and there personally present and have you there the Names of such Persons as you shall so Summon and this Precept Given under my Hand and Seal this Eighteenth day of October in the Thirty fourth Year of the Reign of our Sovereign Lord George the Second King of Great Britain &c. And in the Year of our Lord Christ One thousand seven Hundred and Sixty.

To the Bailiff of the Manor of Kirtlington aforesaid

These

Tho Walker

Steward.

Fig. 18. Summons to the Court Baron, 1760.

been raised, it was often a joint effort which brought a wrongdoer to justice, with everyone acting to preserve the good name of the village. Serious lawbreakers, like the man who attacked Gilbert Fowler the village priest in 1515, would no doubt have then been dealt with in the courts at Oxford. John Andrews was the constable for 14 years continuously in the 17th century, and he was followed in the post by well-known villagers such as Rowland Bennett, the Northbrook farmer, Sam Garnett the Kirtlington tobacconist, and Ralph Pearman, whose descendants were talented Morris dancers. These hard-working men were given no salary until the 19th century, but were no doubt allowed 'disbursements' when criminals had to be found and taken to court.

Other officials ensured that the weights, measures, and quality of ale, bread, fish and tanned leather was correct, or acted as 'hog-ringers', 'dog-muzzlers', or maintained the boundaries.

The lesser court leet, held twice a year, was presided over by the steward, and had to be attended by all village males over the age of 12, and by widows of farmers who had taken over their husband's lands, or who were owners in their own right.

In 16th-century courts we find fines imposed for illegal wood-picking. This was only allowed on Sundays, and then only by one member of each household. In 1592 there was a choice of a two-shilling fine or 24 hours in the stocks, but by 1593 this penalty had been reduced to a 12 pence fine, or six hours in the stocks. Gutters that had not been cleaned, untethered dogs – like the mastiff belonging to William Barre – and the troublesome people who 'did most wickedly and maliciously' break down either fences, doors or windows; those who neglected archery practice; and those who indulged in card and dice games were all subject to fines at various times in Kirtlington's history.

Towards the end of the 18th century the form of village government began to change. The first step was the creation of the parish vestry, where not only was the church rate levied, but the relief of the poor and the management of the highways was dealt with. The vestry, a committee of responsible villagers, appointed parish officials like the clerk, the sexton and the churchwardens, and they would also recommend suitable villagers to be appointed as constables, overseers and highway surveyors to the justices of the peace. Thus in 1839 we find the parish clerk paid an extra five shillings (making a total of a pound per year) for 'keeping the clock' and sweeping and cleaning the church. In 1841 the overseers of the poor were John Walker and John Trafford, and the surveyor was Samuel Street, who became 'guardian of the poor' in 1842.

The upkeep of the highways which passed through the village entailed the creation of a series of posts after 1555. The 'waywarden' or surveyor of the highways was at first appointed by the parishioners, but later he was chosen from a list of landholders by the justices of the peace. The highway had to be surveyed three times a year, and he had to organise the necessary labour for repair work, or else collect the 'commutations' or fines payable in lieu of the labour, which were used to pay other villagers to do the work instead. A waywarden had many other responsibilities connected with the roads – that no hay, manure or timber was stacked on them, and that they obeyed the regulations concerning the number of horses required to pull a wagon, and the size of the wheels.

When John Hall and George Weston were in charge in 1779, the accounts show that Walter Prior earned £1 12s 0d for 'spreading and breaking stones and other works', whilst Mr. Cox measured stones three times. Thirty-four villagers each paid their two shillings commutation, which brought in £3 8s 0d, but Thomas McGregor paid for two days only at 1s 4d and worked one day himself. Sir Henry Watkin Dashwood, the lord of the manor, naturally did not work on the roads himself, and was liable to pay £1 19s 6d in lieu (a sum calculated on the size of his landholding). This sum paid for the digging of 400 loads of stone. In 1786 his liability was £2 11s 6d, covering the cost of 580 loads of stone. With all this hard work, it was natural that the men developed quite a thirst, a problem fortunately taken care of by the surveyors, who noted such needs as 'Expenses at the Bells at the time of measuring 1s 3d'. The public houses most in use were the *Six Bells*, situated close to the gravel pit in Mill Lane, and the *Dashwood Arms* on South Green, previously known as the *Greyhound*.

From the late 18th century onwards, private groups of investors bought the right to build and maintain better roads in their locality, and covered the costs of so doing by charging tolls to those who subsequently travelled along them. These roads were known as turnpikes. A turnpike ran through Kirtlington parish, and we find records of those who sought to evade the tolls like John King, who took the horses off a carriage before passing through the gate in December 1850. At Bicester Magistrates' Court King was fined eight shillings, and 12 shillings costs. In 1841 the census shows that James Busby (aged 15) and nine-year-old Edmund Cato were acting as toll-gate keepers, but this may have been only a temporary arrangement. The exact amount of the tolls charged is not known, but the average cost of taking a horse and cart through a tollgate was four or fivepence, and for a score of cattle about tenpence or a shilling. Smaller animals (calves, sheep, or pigs) cost only sixpence a score. All prices were doubled on a Sunday, but churchgoers were exempt, as was the vagrant's cart, carrying unwanted visitors out of the parish.

Not everyone in Kirtlington went through the gate, however: with just a few cattle to drive it was quite easy to slip down Tinker's Ditch to South End, and so evade the gatekeeper.

At noon on 1 November 1877, all tolls ceased, the gates were removed, and the auctioneers Messrs. Jonas Paxton held a large sale of equipment and of the local toll-houses themselves.

In 1894 the parish councils as we know them today were formed, and their legislation altered the village's organisation. On 4 December 1894 the first Kirtlington parish council meeting took place in the school, and voting commenced on the election of various officers. The first seven councillors – Mr. Austin the schoolmaster, William Collett, a labourer, Godfrey Blount, an artist, A. George the bootmaker, James Castleman, a local farmer, Urban Simmons, a groom, and W. Gillman – were sworn in. Sir George Dashwood was elected chairman.

One of the council's new responsibilities was street lighting, and an estimate for keeping four oil lamps lit in 1901 amounted to £3 10s 0d a year. In 1915 the lamplighter was Mr. Brackley the shopkeeper. The lamps were positioned at convenient spots, such as outside the *Dashwood Arms* (handy for lads playing football on the Green), by Toll Gate Cottages, at South End and in the Heyford Road. Several attempts were made after the Second World War (when the lamps had of course been removed) to reinstate the lighting in Kirtlington, but without success.

One of the matters currently under discussion at parish council meetings is the erection of a new village hall. Opinions are naturally divided – some fear that it will be too expensive to construct and maintain, but local fund-raising has been fruitful, and some building-stone has been donated.

The pattern of village government shows that a sense of tradition and a love of the past have not been lost. In 1977 a special tree-planting ceremony was held to install new oaks and lime trees on North and South Greens, to replace the trees killed by Dutch Elm disease. In the same way, perhaps, villagers may have gathered over 500 years ago, when the great oak forest was planted by royal command.

Rustic figures.

CHAPTER TWELVE

Farm and Field

At his beds feete
feeden his stalled teme
His swine beneath,
his pullen o'er the beame ...

Hall's Satires, 1599

The Black Death of 1348-9 must have been a terrible blow to the economy, although it only temporarily halted the development of sheepfarming. It appears that by 1422 there were definite roads leading to the sheepwash in Kirtlington, known as 'Overwasyng' and 'Netherwasyng'. One of the present-day fields leading down to the old mill and canal was the probable route along which flocks were driven from the village centre in medieval times. It still bears the name 'Sheepwalk' although it is now used by Marion and Arthur Kirtland to graze their beef cattle. Other lost place-names from the Middle Ages also point to the important role which sheep-rearing played in village life: manorial records refer to 'Wamper's Way' and 'Plumper's Way', which are both terms used in preparing wool, whilst in 1593 'Wolwell Way' was recorded as part of the East Field where sheep were allowed to graze the stubble after harvest.

The original two-field system of agriculture had been gradually changing. In 1522 the meadowland was still allocated by lot; each tenant was responsible for planting thorn hedges with a ditch on either side in their part of the common field, which lay between Mill Mead and Pyngey meadows. During 1585 'living' hedge boundaries and ditches were made around Northam meadow, in the hamlet of Northbrook. Grazing on the common land was still strictly controlled by the manor court. For every yardland a free- or copyholder held, he could graze seven ploughbeasts, five other cattle, and 50 sheep in the East Field or 40 sheep and the same number of cattle in the West Field when either of them was fallow. Good harvests, which were fairly general between 1599 and 1605, encouraged farmers to increase their flocks and herds. There was also an increase in the number of 'hitches' allowed. By 1650 there were seven quarters in the East Field and five in the West. This system remained practically unchanged until the passing of the Kirtlington Enclosure Act in 1811.

The 16th and early 17th centuries were probably the most prosperous time for Kirtlington sheep farmers, in spite of the many restrictions laid down by the lord of the manor and his court. The average flock owned by a villager numbered about 30 animals, and they were looked after all together by one shepherd on the common land. In 1538 Robert Barrett was one of the more prosperous farmers, owning 200 sheep. With such a large flock, he might have even employed his own shepherd. Hungry men were sometimes tempted to steal, like the Kirtlington labourer who in 1518 killed and skinned a wether lamb, or his fellow thief who attempted to steal 20

ANNO QUINQUAGESIMO PRIMO

GEORGII III. REGIS.

●●

Cap. 160.

An Act for inclosing Lands in the Manor and Parish of *Kirtlington*, in the County of *Oxford*.

[10th *June* 1811.]

WHEREAS there are within the Manor and Parish of *Kirtlington*, in the County of *Oxford*, several Open and Common Fields, Common Meadows, Common Pastures, Commons, Waste and other Commonable Lands and Grounds: And whereas Sir *Henry Watkin Dashwood* Baronet, is Lord of the Manor of *Kirtlington* aforesaid, and Proprietor and Owner of very great Part of the Lands or Grounds by this Act intended to be divided and inclosed: And whereas the President and Fellows of *Saint John Baptist College*, in the University of *Oxford*, and the said Sir *Henry Watkin Dashwood* their Lessee, are seised of the Rectory Impropriate of *Kirtlington* aforesaid, and in Right of the said Rectory entitled to certain Glebe Lands, Part of the Lands and Grounds intended by this Act to be divided and inclosed; and also to all the Great Tythes whatsoever arising, renewing, or payable, for or in respect of the said Open and Common Fields, Common Meadows, Common Pastures, Commons, Waste and other Commonable Lands and Grounds, and of all the old Inclosures within the said Parish of *Kirtlington*: And whereas the said President and Fellows of *Saint John Baptist College*, are also seised of the Perpetual Advowson, Right of Patronage, and Presentation of, in, and to the Vicarage of the Parish Church of *Kirtlington* aforesaid; and the Reverend

Fig. 19. The Kirtlington Enclosure Act, 1811.

In the Name of God Amen the Seventh Day of Novem: Anno Dom: 1730 I Richard Bryon of Kirtlington in the County of Oxon being sick and weak in Body but of good and perfect Memory thanks be to Allmighty God and calling to Remembrance the uncertain Estate of this Transitory Life and that all flesh must yield unto Death when it shall please God to call I Do make and Declare this my Last Will and Testament in Manner and form following: First being penitent and Sorry for all my Sins most humbly Desireing forgiveness of the same I Commend my Soul unto Allmighty God my Saviour and Redeemer in whom and by whose Merrits I trust and believe to be saved and to have full Remission and forgiveness of all my Sins and to Inherit the Kingdom of heaven and my Body I commit to the Earth to be Decently buryed in a Christian like manner at the Discretion of my Executor hereafter Named: and for the Settling of Worldly Goods and Chattles as it hath pleased Allmighty God to bestow upon me I do order give and Dispose of the same in Manner and form following that is to say

Imprimis I give and bequeath unto my Son Robert Bryon one Shilling and my best Shute of Cloths I give unto my Daughter Mary Bath all that [debt] which was Due to me from William Bath I give unto my Son Richard Bryon all my houseall Good and all my Linnen and two horses which he shall chuse and two Cows which he shall chuse and forty Sheep I Likewise appoint my Son Richard and my Son Edward [Bryon] full and Sole Executors of this my Last will and Testament but if my Son Richard Bryon Shall think fit to pay unto my Son Edward Bryon fourty Pounds of Good and Lawfull Money of Great Britain within four Years after My Decease to pay [him] ten pound a Year then My Son Richard shall be Full and Sole Executor of this my Last Will and Testament and my Will is my Executor shall pay all my Debts and funeral charges whereby Revoaking Disannulling and Making void all former Wills and Bequests by me Made and Declare this only to be my Last Will and Testament whereunto I have Sett my hand and Seal the Day and Year above Written

Seald: Signd: and Delivered in the Presents of

John Sanford

Thomas Tolley

Aled [mark] Condys mark

Richard Bryons R mark

Probat et 24 Maij 1732 Coram Venli Viro Hen Brooke ... Dni Archus Oxon Offli ... Testo Ricardi filij et Extoris ... cui comissa fuit ... Admio ... Dei Evangel in forma juris jurati et Salvo ...

Geo: Cooper Regr

Fig. 20. Will of Richard Bryon, farmer.

pounds of wool from John Cockes, 'yoman' or 'wolman' of the village, that is, the local sheep-dealer. He himself was not always virtuous, however, for the manor court repeatedly found him guilty of allowing his 500 sheep to go on the common fields at the wrong time, and Henry VII twice pardoned him for unlawful wool dealings.

In the late 17th century, however, the English wool industry fell on hard times. Parliament passed an act making it compulsory for all corpses to be buried in a woollen shroud, but this and other acts intended to boost the industry's fortunes had only a limited and short-lived effect. In addition to being buried in a woollen shroud, and having his coffin borne to church on a sheep hurdle for a bier, a shepherd was usually buried holding a tuft of wool in his hands, to ensure that St Peter would be aware of his profession and make allowances for his non-attendance at church!

From wills and inventories of 17th-century farmers, it appears that some of them certainly prospered. Thomas Woodward, for example, had 17 hogs worth £11, five cows, four calves, and six yearlings worth £16; five horses and harness valued at £22; sheep and lambs to the value of £24; a waggon, cart, plough and other instruments of husbandry, amounting to £12 in value; and corn in his barn and rickyard valued at £65, as well as hay in the field and yard worth six pounds.

After 1650 the pattern of ownership changed, when many farmers sold out to Sir Robert Dashwood, the new lord of the manor, and former copyhold, leasehold and freehold farmers became his tenant farmers. In 1746 his heir Sir James Dashwood became the first resident lord of the manor. Although some of the common land was enclosed to form the park of his new mansion house, there was still over 700 acres left, as well as waste land for gathering furze behind Northbrook Manor. By 1750 there were 17 Kirtlington farms with over 30 acres each, and most of these were Dashwood tenants. Nine others held more than 100 acres, and three farmed 200 acres. There were also a number of smallholdings, each with a cottage, and others, less fortunate, with no land in the open fields.

The style of life enjoyed by the wealthier farmers was changing, and the old days when the farmer and his workpeople sat down together to eat were fast disappearing. With the example of the fashionable and wealthy Dashwoods before them, farmers' wives and daughters wanted new luxuries – a piano perhaps, new dresses, and visits to balls and assemblies at Woodstock and Oxford. Their husbands and fathers were also influenced by new trends in the outside world – not only to travel to race-meetings and cockfights, but more significantly, to take a new interest in livestock breeding, adopt a wide range of new farm implements, and plant different crops which could improve the fertility of the soil, or provide fodder to keep cattle alive through the winter. Previously farmers had had to slaughter the majority of their animals and salt the meat down, since they could not provide them with food.

Sir James Dashwood, who was a keen and progressive farmer, started to plant a turnip crop in 1751, several years ahead of his neighbours. By 1813, when Arthur Young, a farming expert from the newly-formed Board of Agriculture, toured Oxfordshire, he noted that several farmers in the area were feeding the new fodder crops of vetches and ryegrass to their sheep. In other cases, when grass was short, they were fed straw, beans or peas.

Although the 1811 Enclosure Act was resented by many farming families who disliked such a sweeping change which deprived them of their traditional access to the common land, it did present a new challenge to forward-thinking farmers. Once the initial cost of fencing, legal fees and labour had been met, there were less quarrels

KIRTLINGTON PARISH ALLOTMENTS

I .... do hereby acknowledge that I have taken from the Parish Council of the Parish of Kirtlington (hereinafter called the Lessors), for the time being in trust of the hereinafter demised Premises, an Allotment or Piece of Land, situate in the said Parish of Kirtlington, containing about One Chain and a Quarter, and known as part of the Parish Land, and I do hereby acknowledge and agree that I hold the said Allotment on the following conditions :—

1.   On a yearly tenancy from the 29th day of September,   determinable at the end of any current year by six months previous notice in writing, to be given by either party, such notice when given by the undersigned to be delivered to the Clerk of the Parish Council for the time being of the said Parish.

2.   The Rent for each Allotment to be   per annum, payable on the 29th day of September of each year to the said Clerk of the Parish Council, the first year's rent being due September 29th,   .   The Lessors to pay all rates.

3.   May erect a Pigsty, Meal, or Tool House ; but must see that his gates are properly locked, and so prevent his pigs from straying over and damaging the Allotments; or if such should get out he must be answerable for any damage done, the amount of such to be decided by the Lessors, or should he wish to give up his Allotment he must remove either of the above if he cannot sell same to the incoming tenant.

4.   Not to throw cabbage stems or rubbish over the hedge into the roadway. The land to be cultivated as Garden Allotment, and at all times to be kept clean and well cultivated, and left in like manner at the termination of the tenancy.

5.   The Lessors to keep the fences trimmed yearly, also to keep the gates in repair.

6.   That if the said rent shall be in arrear fourteen days next after the day hereby appointed for payment thereof, or if the undersigned shall make default in the observance or performance of any of the conditions and agreements on his part to be observed and performed, then in either of such cases the Lessors may re-enter on the premises occupied by such defaulter as in their former estate, and upon such entry the said tenancy shall absolutely determine.

7.   No cart to draw on any Allotment after the first day of April of any year.

As witness my hand,

....

Fig. 21.   The Parish allotment agreement.

about human and animal trespassers; the vicar no longer demanded tithes, as land had been allocated to the church in lieu of further payments; and good cattle and livestock could be separated from the rest and bred to improve the quality of the herd. The fields were also provided with better drainage systems. The poorer villagers were worst off, as they lost the perquisites of free fuel, free grazing for their animals and so on, but even they were given allotments to compensate them to some extent.

Well into the 1900s the tradition of gleaning wheat – going round after the harvest had been gathered to collect what had been overlooked or dropped on the ground – continued to flourish in Kirtlington. When the price of corn or bread was high, such gleanings could be of great value, as they could be exchanged for a bag of flour which might last a small family through the winter. Four Kirtlington villagers were a little over-eager to take their gleanings in 1809 and found themselves before the Oxford County Court: although the point was conceded that they must not start until the farmer had cleared the field to his own satisfaction, their right to glean as an ancient right was granted and they were acquitted of any offence.

Another part of the cottage economy which continued to be a vital factor for many people until this century was the family pig, fed on household scraps. It was common knowledge that shunters at Bletchingdon railway station moving a waggon-load of turnips could easily 'lose' a few on the line! Oxfordshire pig farmers had seen their local animal evolve into the prize-winning Berkshire and Middle White pigs, and good-quality animals lived on the best their owners could find for them. When they were brought to the show ring, they often had great difficulty in walking, and the judges had to inspect them in their pens, where their heads had to be supported by wooden frames.

Before the advent of the motor car, practically everything needed by farming people could be bought or made in the village. A glance at *Kelly's Directory*, or any other similar publication produced between 1841 and 1900 will show how many small businesses there were in Kirtlington, including the following:

> *Blacksmiths and farriers:* Joseph Walker and later the Kirtland family.
> *Wheelwrights:* Anthony Hawting, Matthew Lee, Thomas Townsend, William Nobley, John Bunker, William Giles.
> *Cattle dealers:* James Enser, Thomas Horwood.
> *Pig dealer:* Thomas Rogers.
> *Corn merchants:* William Sandeland, Richard Curtis Enser.
> *Saddlers:* The Scarsbrook family (who were also involved with the running of the *Six Bells* and the Coffee Tavern).
> *Tailors:* John George, Thomas Powell, John Hawkes, Edwin Hoole.
> *Shoemakers:* Phillip Wakefield, John Jessett, Thomas George.
> *Cooper:* Joseph Hawkes.
> *Hurdlemaker:* William Walton.
> *Miller:* Richard Enser.
> *Dressmakers:* Martha Eaglestone, Eileen Griffin, Ann Davis, Sarah Busby.
> *Gloveresses:* Leah Coxhill, Sarah Coxhill.
> *Straw bonnetmakers:* Elizabeth Davis, Elizabeth Dean.
> *Straw hatmaker:* Emma Evans.
> *Lace maker:* Sarah Stanley. In 1871 she had to become an agricultural labourer, perhaps because of the increasingly widespread use of factory-made lace.

The shepherd was one of the most important members of the traditional village community, and his responsibilities changed little over the centuries until very

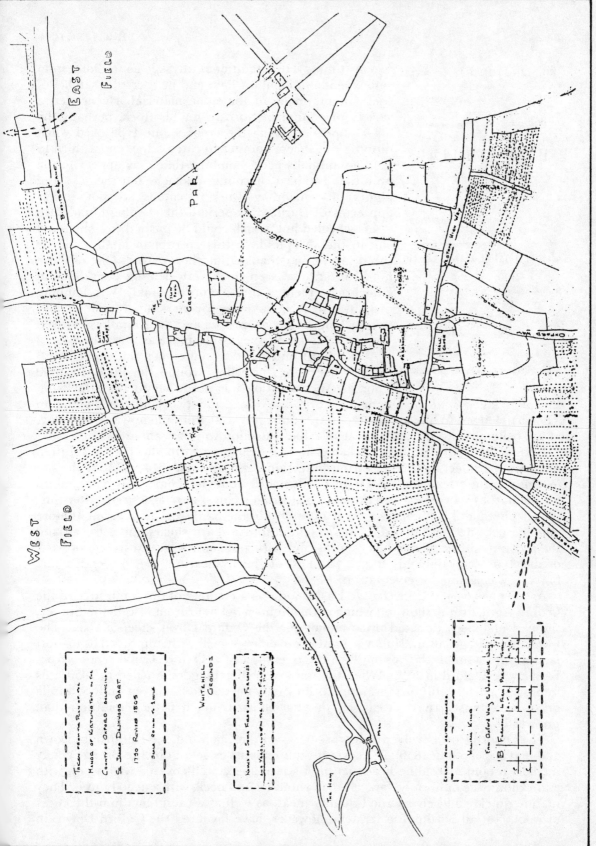

Fig. 22. The pattern of the plough – Kirtlington farmlands c.1805.

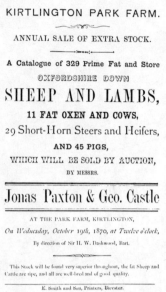

KIRTLINGTON PARK FARM.

ANNUAL SALE OF EXTRA STOCK.

A Catalogue of 329 Prime Fat and Store

OXFORDSHIRE DOWN

SHEEP AND LAMBS,

11 FAT OXEN AND COWS,

29 Short-Horn Steers and Heifers,

AND 45 PIGS,

WHICH WILL BE SOLD BY AUCTION,

BY MESSRS.

Jonas Paxton & Geo. Castle

AT THE PARK FARM, KIRTLINGTON,

On Wednesday, October 19th, 1870, at Twelve o'clock,

By direction of Sir H. W. Dashwood, Bart.

This Stock will be found very superior throughout, the fat Sheep and
Cattle are ripe, and all are well-bred and of good quality.

E. Smith and Son, Printers, Bicester.

Fig. 23. Stock sale at Park
Fark, 1870.

recent times. His traditional dress was a homespun smock made of hemp or flax, and he carried a satchel of useful items made of the same material. He needed a variety of equipment to care for his flock, perhaps the most important being the crook – one type used when dipping the sheep, another to catch a leg, and a third to hold an animal's neck. Lambing-time may appear to the uninitiated to be a charming spectacle, but the days and nights of demanding work it entails are not always appreciated. During this period, the shepherd made use of his wheeled hut, which could be pushed to a sheltered site in the sheepfold. In this an orphan lamb could be cared for, or an exhausted mother revived. One of these huts can still be seen, in a very derelict condition, in Drawbridge Field at the side of the canal. With lambing over, the next tasks were ear-marking, branding, and tail-docking. Many shepherds and their families enjoyed the lamb's tail stew they could make as a result.

A shepherd and his dog sometimes had to fight off rogue village dogs prowling around the flock. In 1550 Thomas Andrews' dog was notorious for its attacks on sheep: it killed nine belonging to Anthony Arden, and two lambs belonging to Thomas Hedges. While such attacks are, unhappily, far from unknown even today, at least there is not the added fear of rabies infection to worry about.

During the 19th century it became normal practice to dip sheep in a solution intended to protect them from various infections, and between 1914 and 1920 the site for this was the stream leaving Flight's Mill, which would be temporarily dammed-up for the purpose. In later years the waters at Brian's Hovel were also used. After this, the shepherd and his helpers were ready to begin the hard work of shearing. Before clipping became mechanised, it was essential to use sharp shears and scissors, and the accounts of the village blacksmith John Kirkland show a steady stream of work of this type came into his forge. The end of sheep shearing, like the end of the harvest, was a time for celebration.

As long ago as 1903, Sir George Dashwood was a member of the committee of the Oxford Agricultural Show, on which occasion his neighbour from Middleton Stoney, the earl of Jersey, donated prize money for the Oxford Down sheep classes. The formation of agricultural shows in the area developed with improved transport facilities for animals, beginning with the opening of the Oxford Canal section from Banbury to Oxford in 1790. When the railway at Bletchingdon opened in 1850, this improved matters still further: animals now only needed to be driven on foot a mile or so, and thus arrived at market or at a show in much better condition than previously.

The Oxford Down evolved as a cross between the Cotswold and Hampshire Down and first appeared in 1830. The current requirements as set out by the Breed Society include 'a bold masculine head, set on a strong neck, well covered with wool, with a top knot. Face uniformly dark, a broad shoulder and neck, with a deep barrel'. They mature quickly and give a good-quality meat, as well as a useful medium-thickness of wool. Not all Kirtlington farmers, however, have favoured the Oxford Down. In

1920 Joseph Eeley of Northbrook farmed Border Leicester/Cheviot cross sheep sent down from Scotland, and also had Hampshire Down sheep at a later date, and Arthur Budgett exhibited pens of his Hampshire Down ram lambs and ewes at the Oxford Royal Agricultural Show in 1950.

Mr. Sam Miller, a long-established livestock auctioneer at Bicester Market, reports that today young ewes can fetch between £75 to £80, whilst 'full-mouth' ewes nearing the end of their breeding lives go at about £45 to £55. A good breeding ram, however, could fetch 120 to 200 guineas. In the pens at the market today, it is rare to see the old Oxford Down: Mr. Miller considers that the Border Leicester sheep make up about 50 per cent of local flocks, followed by the Suffolk Cross and other cross-breeds.

In the 18th and 19th centuries, it was commonplace for those seeking work or employees to attend one of the hiring fairs which were held all over England. The nearest one to Kirtlington was at Bicester, as we see from this notice which appeared in *Jackson's Oxford Journal* in 1792:

FRIDAY 18th June, 1762
Notice is hereby given that a Statute will be held for the hiring of servants, and will be continued to be held on the Friday next, before the 20th June yearly. There will be at the said Statute Fair, a large show of fine cows, horses, sheep, hogs, etc.

According to the records of George Dew, the local relieving officer at the time, servants could still be hired at Bicester in 1876.

Many gentlemen interested in farming formed companies in the late 19th century which negotiated loans to enable farming communities to make important improvements to their land – update decaying farm buildings, improve drainage, roads, build bridges, clear waste ground – in fact, anything that would improve the efficiency of the farm and its land. Frederick Loftus Dashwood, J.P., was the son of Sir George Dashwood, the fourth baronet. Frederick served as a major in the 16th Lancers, and was an adjutant of the Oxfordshire Yeomanry for several years. He also farmed Northbrook Manor for a while, and took an interest in anything which might improve the Kirtlington estate, for which he acted as land agent. In 1898 he was involved in the formation of the 'Lands Improvement Company', which charged each client five per cent of the costs incurred, but for that sum undertook to obtain the permission of the Board of Agriculture and oversee the implementation of the improvement.

There were other members of the community, however, who did not share in the farmer's prosperity. The need to feed a large family, or for old people left on their own to keep bread in their mouths, meant that often the very young or the very old had a hard time of it. Harriet Hounslow and James Walton, both aged ten, were classed as 'agricultural labourers' in the census returns. The oldest labourer listed seems to have been Richard Allen, aged 82: Thomas Welch, Lydia Ashton and Rachel Smith were all eighty.

It was accepted, however, that the harvest did demand 'all hands', and the school authorities planned the summer holiday to coincide with it. Children could earn between three- and ninepence a day at this busy time. Very often families worked together in the harvest field – father cut and mother gathered sheaves, while children helped to twist the straw bands to bind them. When the hard work of threshing wheat

THE
LANDS IMPROVEMENT COMPANY

Amalgamated with the LAND LOAN AND ENFRANCHISEMENT COMPANY.

INCORPORATED AND EMPOWERED BY SPECIAL ACTS OF PARLIAMENT
1853, 1855, 1859, 1860, 1863.

Board of Directors.

FREDERICK L. DASHWOOD, Esq.,
            Kirtlington, Oxford.
HENRY FARQUHAR, Esq.,
      Gilmilnscroft, Mauchline, Ayrshire, N.B.
THE EARL OF GALLOWAY,
      Galloway House, Wigtonshire, N.B.
EDWIN GARROD, Esq.,
      Park Hill, Richmond, Surrey.
The Right Hon. ALEXANDER STAVELEY
  HILL, Q.C., M.P., 4, Queen's Gate, S.W.

PERCY MORRIS Esq.,
      77, Cambridge Terrace, Hyde Park.
GRANVILLE R. RYDER, Esq., *Managing
Director*, 60, Ennismore Gardens, S.W.
G. H. SANDAY, Esq.,
      Blackwell Hall, Chesham.
A. W. WILLIAMS WYNN, Esq.,
      Coed-y-Maen, Welshpool.
E. PARKER YOUNG, Esq.,
      30, Westbourne Square, W.

Bankers—LLOYD'S BANK, LIMITED, 16, St. James Street, S.W.

Solicitors—Messrs. WEST, KING, ADAMS & CO., 66, Cannon Street, E.C.

Agents in Scotland—Messrs. HOPE, TODD & KIRK, W.S., Edinburgh.

Secretary —GEORGE HAMLIN, Esq.

Offices of the Company—1, GREAT GEORGE STREET, WESTMINSTER, S.W.

IMPROVEMENTS FOR WHICH LOANS CAN BE GRANTED.

1. **Drainage of Land**, and Improvement of Drains, Streams and Watercourses.
2. **Irrigation** and Warping.
3. **Embanking** from the sea, or Tidal Waters, or from Lakes, Rivers, or Streams.
4. **Inclosing**.
5. **Reclamation**.
6. **Making permanent Farm Roads** and permanent Tramways and Railways for Agricultural purposes, Private Roads, Roads or Streets in Villages or Towns.
7. **Clearing**.
8. **The Erection of and additions to** Farm Houses, Farm Buildings, Farm Labourers', Artizans' and Miners' Cottages, and Cottages for Labourers employed on the Estate or not, also for making any additions to or alterations in buildings necessary or proper to enable the same to be let.
9. **Planting** for shelter, or for any beneficial purpose which will increase the permanent value of Land.
10. **Bridges**.
11. **For the Construction and Erection** of Reservoirs, Tanks, Conduits, Watercourses, Pipes, Wells, Ponds, Shafts, Dams, Weirs, Sluices and other Works, and for Machinery for the Supply and Distribution of Water, for Agricultural, Manufacturing and other purposes, or for Domestic or other consumption; also for the Subscription towards the construction of Waterworks by any Water Company.
12. **The Constructing and Erecting of** any Engine House, Waterwheels, Saw and other Mills, Kilns and Bridges, which will increase the value of the Land for Agricultural purposes, or as Woodland or otherwise.
13. **The Construction of Railways**, Canals, Tramways, Docks; including, in the cases of Railways and Canals, the subscription for Shares in Railway or Canal Companies, and Light Railways under the Light Railways Act.
14. **Construction or Improvement of Jetties or Landing Places** on the sea coast, or on the banks of navigable Rivers or Lakes, for the transport of Persons, and of Agricultural Stock and Produce, and of Lime, Manure, and other articles and things for Agricultural purposes, and of minerals and things required for mining purposes.
15. **Markets and Market Places**; Streets, Roads, Paths, Sewers, Drains, and other Works necessary or proper in connection with the development of Land (being part of Settled and other Estates), for Building purposes, including Pipe, Brick and Tile making, in connection with any of the objects aforesaid.
16. **Trial Pits for Mines** and other Preliminary Works necessary or proper in connection with the development of mines.
17. **For the Contribution** due from any Landowner towards any Public or General Works of Drainage or other Improvements, the Cost whereof shall, by Act of Parliament or Royal Charter or Commission, be directed or authorised to be assessed or charged upon the inheritance of the Lands improved.
18. **To the Owners** of settled estates in England and Wales for the erection and completion of, or additions to Mansions, Stables and Out-buildings, Coachmen's and Gardeners' Cottages, Entrance Lodges &c., for supplying Water thereto, for their general Sanitary Improvement, and Electric Lighting.
19. **The Reconstruction**, Enlargement or Improvement of any of the above works.

[OVER.]

Fig. 24. An opportunity for Kirtlington farmers.

in a barn or granary began, children helped to rid the workplace of rats and mice. Mary Viner and her terrier dog thought nothing of this job in the early 1900s. After all the hard work, there was the harvest supper – good food and ale provided by the farmers and the lord of the manor, and some hearty singing.

Nevertheless, it was a hard life, and at the end of the last century some young people decided to try their luck elsewhere. In some cases they were encouraged in this decision by the newly-formed Agricultural Labourers' Union, which in some cases was able to give them some financial help. There were many advertisements like that which appeared in the *Oxford Times* in 1911 – 'Farm workers wanted in Canada and Australia ...'

The Kirtlington Union Secretary at this time was John Jessett the shoemaker, who collected the dues of tuppence-halfpenny a week. There were also active groups in Bletchingdon, Tackley and Weston-on-the-Green. Union membership sometimes inspired a man to show his opposition to those he regarded as his oppressors, perhaps by refusing to attend the parish church, which he saw as the creation of the 'bosses'. The vicar, the Reverend Thomas Chittenden reported to the bishop in 1881 that 'the parish has never recovered the effects of the Labourers' Union', and a similar opinion was expressed by the Reverend William Dry of Weston-on-the-Green.

In 1891 the Reverend Deane recorded in his diary that 40 men had joined the Dockers' Union. At harvest-time that year, 10 men at Park Farm struck for an additional rate of a shilling per acre. The older men felt it was unfair to strike when Sir George was away and the agent Mr. Scott was ill, so the strike call was overruled. One farmer, Mr. Castleman, voluntarily gave his workers sixpence more per acre. A delegate from the Dockers' Union met Mr. Scott and eventually the rate of 5s 6d per acre was agreed upon. In response to the unionisation of the workforce, the farmers also sought to 'protect the interests of the employers of agricultural labour' as *Jackson's Oxford Journal* put it in July 1872. The Oxfordshire and Adjacent Counties Association of Agriculturalists invited subscriptions at ten shillings per annum.

Fortunately in Kirtlington today strikes are unknown, although there is still a local representative of the Agricultural Workers' Union. The farming pattern is also a little different, as I learnt from Mr. Philip Thorman, manager for the Kirtlington Park Estate, covering about 1,800 acres, which is owned by the Budgett family. Although woods are uneconomic today, and there are no longer three forestry staff employed as formerly, planting and maintenance work is still necessary. Tree plants only cost 50p each, but the wooden guards to protect them from cattle and deer cost thirty pounds! Many of Kirtlington's beautiful trees fell victim to Dutch elm disease, and ended up at Ercol's furniture workshop in High Wycombe. At the present time, oak, ash and walnut are doing well. The estate's most important crops are wheat and barley. Oil seed rape is doing well too, although it has taken about six years to become established. The soil here is considered good, although ideally it needs rain at least once a week as it is thin and 'brashy'. As far as livestock is concerned, Kirtlington has been fortunate enough never to suffer an outbreak of foot-and-mouth disease, although it was a restricted area in 1945. The animals are also free of brucellosis and T.B. The Jersey herd, originally formed by Mrs. Budgett, and which still usually numbers between 60 and 65 animals, are milked at Home Farm, which used to be the old timber yard. Slade Farm has about 120 head of milking Friesians at present. Until about six years ago, cattle to be slaughtered were sent down to

North Green, but the old building has now been converted to a private house. Apart from Mr. Thorman himself, the other employees are a gamekeeper, groom, three herdsmen, three tractor drivers, two maintenance men who also help out with field work, an office clerk and a temporary student to help at harvest time.

The modern Kirtlington farmer no longer sleeps with his 'stalled teme', but he still relies on the natural resources of the soil, the water and the woodland, just as his predecessors have for centuries.

Rustic figures.

CHAPTER THIRTEEN

The Horse in the Village

Hunting

> Oft listening how the hounds and horn
> Clearly rousse the slumbering morn,
> From the side of some hoar hill
> Through the high wood echoing shrill.
>
> *Milton, 1645*

Hunting

The open countryside of the royal manor of Kirtlington was often hunted by the reigning monarch, with his retinue of servants, horses, hawks and hounds, and they would expect to be accommodated and entertained by the lord of the manor and the villagers, as part of their duty to the king.

The preparations for a day's hunting were quite lengthy. The

Fig. 25.   The mad mysterious hare.

feuterers who led the greyhounds had to make a lodge of green boughs to keep the king, queen, gentlemen and greyhounds 'from the sun and evil weather'. When all this was in readiness, the Keeper of the Forest mounted his horse and rode to meet the king and queen. In 1422 this post was held by Thomas Brokenton, who had been appointed in the customary manner by the manor court of Kirtlington.

Early hunting was primarily intended to supplement the larder, but with improved farming methods livestock could be fed throughout the winter, and hunting became more and more a matter of sport, of pitting oneself and one's horse against the speed and ingenuity of the prey. Sir Robert Dashwood, who became lord of the manor of Northbrook in 1682, soon acquired his own pack of hounds, and appointed his own huntsman, Ralph Rawlins. In 1686 Richard Blome considered Sir Robert to be an expert on hunting the elusive quarry of the hare, and dedicated a print to him in his book *The Gentleman's Recreation*, showing the 'field' and a variety of hounds surrounding a captured animal.

Ralph Rawlins clearly became a prosperous man: when he died in 1751 aged 83, he not only left considerably property, but also cash and gold coins to his family and money to the poor of the neighbourhood.

Fig. 26.   The 'new entry' (print of 1842).

Towards the end of the 18th century, John Warde, who has been described as 'one of the fathers of fox-hunting', set up his kennels at Weston-on-the-Green in Kirtlington parish, and the long and successful history of what was to be the 'Bicester and Warden Hill Hunt' began. Mr. Warde was a cheerful, down-to-earth man, weighing at least 18 stone who favoured large, bony hounds, known at one time as 'John Warde's Jackasses'. Hunting was now essentially a sport, and gentry and well-to-do farmers invested in better quality horses, especially when enclosures and hedges meant that jumping could be included in a day's sport. There was also some construction of artificial coverts to increase the game available.

The hunting squire of the 1790s often breakfasted at four a.m. on 'underdone beef, washed done with eggs beaten up in brandy. Thus fortified, he was ready for a 50-mile ride if need be'. At the end of the day, these hearty men adjourned to the nearest tavern where, with hounds at their feet, they sat in front of the fire drying out their wet clothes. As the beer tankards were drained, succulent beef was roasted and piled high on to plates; to follow there would probably be thick wedges of rich fruit pie and cream.

After John Warde, the hunt's new master was Sir Thomas Mostyn, and the kennels were moved from Weston-on-the-Green to Bicester, about eight miles away. Those who hunted during Sir Thomas's 30 years in office were very fortunate, as he never asked for a subscription.

In 1809 Northbrook achieved some fame, when the first hunt racing in Oxfordshire was held there. This new sport, however, had its critics, like William Youatt of *The Horse* who wrote of the steeplechase as 'an abuse of hunting ... an outrage to humanity'. The first event was a ten-guinea sweepstake for 'horses the property of Sir Thomas Mostyn's hunt, 3 miles to be rode by members of the Hunt, 13 stone each'. There was also a farmers' race. In 1811 a splendid gold cup was offered as a prize, valued at £100, and there was another ten-guinea sweepstake. Unfortunately, 1811 was the year of the enclosure award for Kirtlington and Northbrook, which put a stop to the race meetings there. They had transferred to Bicester by 1819.

Despite the long association of the Dashwood family with Kirtlington, not a great deal is known about their hunting activities. They were certainly not prominent in racing circles like their neighbours the earl of Jersey at Middleton Stoney, or the hunting and racing Valentia family of Bletchingdon Park – Viscount Valentia was master of the Bicester between 1872 and 1885. The earl of Leven and Melville, who bought the estate from the Dashwoods, was, as we have seen, killed in a hunting accident, and his brother, the Honourable Archibald Alexander Leslie Melville, seems to have been equally keen on the sport, as he was a subscriber to the Bicester in 1919.

During the 1900s, in the years before the First World War, hunt-racing was in full swing at Bletchingdon, and drew quite a crowd, helping the Bicester's finances

1. Sir Robert Dashwood, M.P., J.P., by an unknown artist.

2. Miss Muriel Dashwood, 1982.

3. Kirtlington Park, 1983.

4. Christopher Buxton, O.B.E., M.A., M.B.A., Lord of the Manor : a painting by Carlos Sancha.

5. Mrs. Hazel Budgett with 'Pepper', 1983.

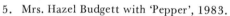

6. A shooting party, c.1900 : Sir George Egerton Dashwood, his six sons and the gamekeeper.

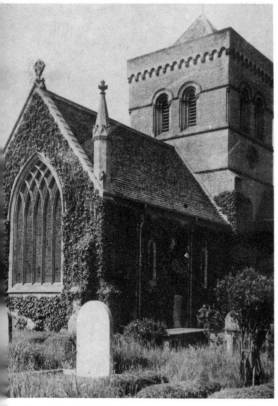

. The Church of St Mary the Virgin, about 1920.

8. The Reverend T.K. Chittenden, 1858.

9. The Reverend Reginald Ward Bennett, 1929.

10. The Reverend Reginald George Bennett, 1961.

11. Mary and Bob Viner, about 1900

12. Sophia and Jeremiah Keys, with Lilian,
Arthur and Bertha, about 1900.

13. Mrs Lilian Wickson, with Wilfred and Nora
about 1920.

14. Edwell Walter Talbot, with his sons Jack and 'Turp'.

15. The forge, about 1890.

16. Bill Johnson with 'Jolly' at a ploughing match.

17. Frederick Blake, gamekeeper.

18. Workers at Park Farm, c.1930 : from top left to bottom right, Bill Scarrott, Ron Hayes, Ted Waters, Joseph Reeves, Bill Johnson, Ken Hayes, John Reeves.

19. Percy East, 1914.

20. Albert East, sitting cross-legged in the foreground, 1914.

21. 'Prince' and the Kirtland's water cart.

22. A concert party, 19

23. Village children at the turn of the century.

24. Kirtlington Football Team wins the coveted Jersey Cup, (1908-9 season).

25. Jack Talbot, band leader.

26. 'A remarkable grandmother'. Martha Scarrott with Kathryn Faulkner, 1952.

7. Ernie, Winnie and Ivor King in the early 1940s.

28. Marion Kirtland and the Easter lambs, about 1940.

29. (*left*) Victor Tugwood, aged 10, with 'Nell'.

30. (*above*) Aubrey and Edith Giles with Monty, Stella, Laurie, Bill, Victor, and Godfrey.

31. (*below*) Albert and Jessie East with their nephew and the new bread van, about 1920.

32. A 'Number One' boatman on the Oxford Canal.

33. Unloading coal, Washford Pits landing stage, c.1920.

34. Cement packers at Washford Pits, about 1920.

35. The workforce of the Oxford and Shipton Cement Company Ltd, about 1930.

37. One of the prehistoric mammal teeth found at Washford Pits (greatly enlarged).

Remains of the Kirtlington dinosaur.

Erection of the kilns at Washford Pits, 1906-7.

40. A stirrup cup for the Bicester Hunt at Kirtlingt
Park, about 1913.

39. 'Morston', winner of the 1973 Derby, is toasted by
his owner and stable lad.

42. H.R.H. Prince Charles at the 1983 Varsity
Polo Match at Kirtlington Park.

41. Ready for the next chukka.

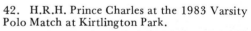

3. (*above*) The choir outing, about 1920.

4. (*right*) Colonel Henry Shellard, present editor of *The Village News*.

5. (*below*) The Kirtlington Morris Men, 1980, with Squire
en Berry (back row centre), Barbara Berry, 'Elmo', the Mace
id the Forest Feathers.

46. School group, 1908. Mr. A. M. Austin, headmaster, is on the left of the group, and Mrs. Nellie Bunker, née Fruin, schoolmistress, is on the right.

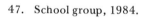

47. School group, 1984.

considerably. According to *Jackson's Oxford Journal*, the hunt was well subscribed between 1911 and 1913, with a field of as many as 400 on some occasions. The war saw the deaths not only of many young men, but of many thousands of good horses on the battlefields. The 1920s brought further problems, when the motor car began to replace the horse as the principal means of transport, which meant hard times for the corn-merchant, horse-dealer, saddler and farrier.

Nevertheless, the Bicester country continued to have its hunt. When Mr. and Mrs. Hubert Budgett came to Kirtlington in 1922 as owners of the manor, they joined the hunt. Mrs. Budgett was also regarded as a notable 'whip' – she once raced a steam bus with her cob and rally cart, and won! Mr. Budgett became joint-master and then master of the Bicester in 1925. Hunting took place four days a week, and an ample supply of horses was needed to mount the Budgetts and the hunt servants. Perhaps the most memorable season under Mr. Budgett's mastership was that of 1930, when 100 brace of fox were taken. The following year, however, was his last in office. He had suffered a bad fall in 1929, and decided that he must now give up.

Apart from his valuable contributions to the Bicester as master and hound breeder, Hugh Budgett's expertise resulted in a most interesting and original book, entitled *Hunting by Scent*, which was published in 1933. In this he went far beyond the discussion of the modern problem of motor-car fumes to the very basis of scent – the how and the why, and the workings of a hound's nose. In addition, he invented and marketed a 'Scent Indicator' and a 'Thermometer Stick', which were put to excellent use during his mastership, when readings were taken at set times during the day. The book was dedicated to Lionel Edwards, the well-known sporting artist, whose 'sympathetic encouragement and valuable suggestions' had originally inspired the work.

Not only did hunting give the mounted followers a wonderful chance to appreciate and understand the countryside – children, like young Ernie King, were also aware of the advantages. 'One hour out with hounds taught me more about the Parish than years at school' he said in later life. He and his friends learnt the names of the coverts, 'Cockshot', 'The Bushes', 'Plantations', and places like the trees behind 'the Big House', which were favoured by 'roosting' foxes! The fields most commonly ridden across included 'Rye Furlong', 'Sandy Briton' and 'Pope's Close'.

A successful hunt has never been cheap to run. In the 1930s, when hay was 50 shillings a ton, oats eight pounds and hound meal up to £19 a ton, costs were in the region of £9,000 a year – but in the 1980s the total is nearer £70,000. The account books of Mr. Leslie Kirtland at the forge, who specialised in shoes for hunters, show that a set of four shoes cost ten shillings in 1927, and the average monthly bill for the Budgetts was about eight pounds.

But perhaps these problems, as well as aching, bruised limbs, and your best hunter 'gone lame', were all forgotten during the gaiety of a Hunt Ball. On Friday, 20 December 1929, there was a brilliant gathering at Kirtlington Park, when 'the Clifford Essex band played, Viscount Valentia was a steward, and his daughter, the Hon. Hilda Annesley, was also present with a party'.

Many people today ask those who follow hounds 'why do you do it?'. Where else but out hunting would you find so many different people united by a common interest? The lord of the manor on a mane-plaited thoroughbred – the local farmer on a hog-maned cob; visitors from the city, or university students, on horses hired for the day; and the children's ponies, with their unruly manes and forelocks brushed tidily for the occasion.

The quarry, the fox, is swift and cunning, and has many tricks to elude capture; but he is a handsome creature, grudgingly admired even by the keeper or farmer whose gamebirds or poultry he has killed. Excitement and the element of danger is another factor – when you've had the sort of run that sets even a quiet cob alight – racing through woodland whilst brambles and thorns graze your face and tear at your clothes – you don't have to be a little mad to hunt, but it helps! There is one thing which makes it all worthwhile, and that is the special bond with your horse, who has shared the day and your excitement.

Today hounds still meet at Portway House in Kirtlington: it would seem that like the Olympic torch, the flame passes on eternally to a new generation of enthusiasts.

Racing

With their heavy involvement in the political life of Oxfordshire, it doubtful if the earlier Dashwoods had the time or money to devote much attention to the racing scene, but nevertheless, in September 1752, Sir James recorded in his account book:

> Josiah Marshal for a Burford plate, by note on Mr. Hoare ... £50.0.0

Racing at Burford had begun as early as 1621. In a 50-guinea sweepstake in 1772, the runners included Lord Abingdon's filly by Julius Caesar – out of Sir James Dashwood's mare. In 1759 he had been elected High Steward of Oxford, and in this capacity he no doubt visited the Port Meadow track, where racing had begun in 1630. Visitors arrived by boat, coach, or on horseback to watch the contestants. At the Oxford races of 1810, Sir James's grandson George Dashwood was one of the subscribers to the 100 guineas cup.

Fig. 27.   The country mare.

One of the Dashwoods' neighbours, Lord Jersey of Middleton Park, had a great deal of success with his horses in the early 19th century. In 1825 and 1827, he won the Derby with Middleton and Mameluke, and again in 1843 with Cotherstone. Bay Middleton, who won it for him in 1836, was described as 'the best horse ever foaled in Oxford'. Lord Jersey's stallions were available at stud, like Hyperion, 'got by Highflyer, his dam Coheiress by Pot-bo, who was got by Eclipse, his grand-dam Manilia by Goldfinders. G.G. dam Mr. Goodrick's Old English mare. He is a good bay with black legs, 16 h. high, with great prowess and excellent temper'. This fine horse 'stood' only a few miles from Kirtlington: it would be interesting to know how many local horse-owners took advantage of his availability.

There was no excuse not to have good young stock by this time, as the introduction of enclosures had cut down indiscriminate breeding, and well-to-do country folk could provide excellent accommodation for their horses, and good food and grazing for the brood-mares and young stock.

These early days of selective horse-breeding, when the 'thoroughbred' gradually evolved from the famous Arabian bloodlines of Godolphin, Darley, and the Byerley Turk, seem a long way from the achievements of Arthur and Alan Budgett, who were born and grew up in Kirtlington, and who have made their own contribution to racing history. Arthur began his long and successful career shortly after the Second World War, when he took out his trainer's licence, and later acquired the splendid establishment at Whatcombe. In 1969 he was top of the Trainers' Table for the Flat Season, and third in the Owners' Table. It was a wonderful day for the Budgett family and for all the staff at Whatcombe when young Ernie Johnson brought Blakeney to the front to win the 1969 Derby by more than a length. Arthur Budgett thus became the first owner since 1908 to have bred and trained a Derby winner. Harry Deakin of Kirtlington, who helped to rear the champion, shared the triumph of this special day.

Another great day came in 1973, when Morston (with the bloodline of the Darley Arabian) galloped home to win the prize-money of over £66,000 by half a length. 'Budgett's patient handling of Morston has been typical of a man whose quiet modest attitude to life conceals, but cannot totally hide, his very real skill' said 'Audax'. Arthur Budgett ascribes his success to a policy of early feeding to let his horses have plenty of time to digest their food before exercise; and to a keen eye for 'racing readiness'. Another important principle, sometimes overlooked by other racing establishments, was his refusal to tolerate bullying of horses or humans. A loud-mouthed groom had a very short stay in his yard.

Kirtlington could remember an earlier Budgett triumph, when Commissar won the Lincoln, beating a field of 58 horses, the largest in the history of flat racing. His lad at Kirtlington was Chick Hayes, who came to the village as an evacuee in the Second World War.

Alan Budgett, who still lives in Kirtlington with his family, has somehow or other managed to be a businessman, polo-player, joint M.F.H., racehorse owner and breeder. He has also had to fight ill-health in recent years, but this is in no way apparent. Over the years his horses have appeared at most of the flat race meetings in England, ridden by, amongst others, such famous names as Lester Piggott, Willie Carson and Pat Eddery, whilst two of his race stallions are at stud in South Africa and the Argentine. Between them, Arthur and Alan Budgett have made a great contribution to racing history.

Fig. 28.   The new thoroughbred.

Kirtlington Park and Oxford University Polo Club

Polo may well be one of the world's oldest sports, first recorded in 525 B.C. It appears to have originated in Persia, where at Isfahan what appears to be a ruined polo-ground with stone goal posts has been found, of similar dimensions to those of the present day. The game's popularity gradually spread throughout the Eastern world, until it caught the attention of British officers serving in India. In 1859 the first British club was formed in that country, consisting of officers and tea-planters from the neighbourhood of Cachar. When enthusiasts returned home from India, they continued to play, the first match in this country taking place in 1871, and four years later the Hurlingham Polo Association formulated rules for the game which are still adhered to today. Visiting teams from India were soon joined by others from America, and the latter country took the famous West Chester cup for the first time from British hands in 1909.

During this time, the animals used were truly 'ponies', limited to a height of 14-2 hands. After the First World War, however, to help the revival of the game, the height limit was abolished, and a 'polo pony' was usually a horse of well over 15 hands. It was about this date that teams first arrived from the Argentine. Although England is well endowed with a great variety of excellent native ponies, ours cannot match the Argentinians.

It was a former inhabitant of the Argentine who first brought polo to Kirtlington. Major Deed – known to his friends as 'Deedo' had served with the Indian army and then gone to South America. 'He was a very canny and persuasive horse-dealer' Mrs. Hazel Budgett recalls, 'but everyone liked him. For a while he kept only grey horses to sell, as he thought this was the fashionable colour at the time!' 'Deedo' had brought over a small string of polo ponies with him, which he used to school regularly in the grounds of Kirtlington Park. With the Budgett family's keen interest in all aspects of sport, it was not long before Hugh Budgett was being told 'you're a natural polo player!' He did not need much persuading to lay out part of the estate parkland as a polo ground. There was good local support for the venture, and in 1926 the Club was formally established.

Fig. 29. Polo, 1983.

The venue is attractively sited, and conveniently reached from major roads. The horse lines are well-positioned under shady trees, and even 'treading in' the pitch between chukkas is a pleasant chore in these surroundings!

Not surprisingly, Alan and Arthur Budgett were given polo instruction by their father. In 1936 the 19-year-old Alan was a member of the Kirtlington team when they retained their cup, and both brothers have captained the team.

The Second World War meant that the Club went into abeyance for the duration, and the ground was dug over as part of the 'Dig for Victory' campaign. In 1954 it was reopened by its President, Alan Budgett, and has flourished ever since, as one of the 17 English clubs. The present captain is John Tylor, husband of the former Miss

Heather Budgett. The Budgett polo tradition is also continued at Kirtlington by her cousin James, son of Arthur Budgett.

A polo-player now has to dig deep into his pocket if he wishes to buy a 'made' pony. A match played at Kirtlington is divided into four separate chukkas, with short intervals, and the four animals needed can each cost over £5,000. In spite of the Falklands War, which means that Argentinian teams are no longer invited over here, private individuals are allowed to import an Argentinian pony for their own use. The equipment needed for horse and rider is also expensive. The horse is protected against injury by bandages and boots, whilst the rider wears a helmet. One of Kirtlington's more recent members, who can afford to indulge his keen interest in the game, is Stewart Copeland, drummer with the rock group Police. He now owns three polo ponies, and is currently working on the background music for a documentary about the sport.

During the season, there are several weekends when a marquee has to provide extra space for an influx of visitors, and champagne replaces homely beer in the refreshment tent. These are the times when a tournament or university match is being played, or when the famous team 'Les Diables' is competing. Kirtlington has had some notable visitors. Her Majesty the Queen presented the winners' trophy in 1970, and Prince Philip has come to the club on two occasions; but the most frequent royal visitor is Prince Charles, playing for his team, the 'Cambridge Old Blues'.

SUNDAY IN KIRTLINGTON

Lush parkland dotted with oaks and sheep,
A line of chestnuts forms the background
To our Polo field,
One Sunday in summer, an ancient Rolls
With open dicky, lords it over the TR7
Though the latter has bottles on the roof,
Pimms No. 1, and a Teachers, two glasses,
Side by side, half empty.
Further down the line, a cream Mercedes
Squats, with an arranged bowl of fruit
On the back window ledge.
Horse boxes tower, veritable juggernauts,
Disgorge ponies, which stand, proud of hoof,
And champ bits, whilst tails are plaited.
Slim aristocratic youths, heavily paunched
Elders, darkly handsome South Americans
And Asiatics,
Play.
The watchers gossip, a few follow
The game, count the goals,
Enjoy the tea with home-made cakes,
Whilst in the distance parachutists,
Held up by brightly coloured balloons,
Fall in streams out of the sky.

Barbara Dunkerley

CHAPTER FOURTEEN

Money and Muscle: the Oxford Canal

The cheering of spectators, and the bells of St Thomas's church, greet the large fleet of boats slowly entering the canal basin. The band of the Oxford Militia are playing enthusiastically in the leading craft, under the shade of a Union Jack: but it is perhaps the sight of the long-awaited cargo of 'black diamonds' – coal to be sold at only sixpence-halfpenny a hundredweight – which arouses most enthusiasm on this January day in 1790. At last the Oxford Canal has reached its terminus at Hythe Bridge, fulfilling the dreams of a handful of dedicated men, the canal builders who planned for a national network of canals.

The cost of constructing the 63¾ miles of waterway amounted to a little over £205,000, the smallest item of expenditure appearing to be £150 for the purchase of horses, and the largest, for cutting canal culverts and 'puddling', amounting to over £43,000. Almost 20 years had elapsed since James Brindley, the brilliant and innovative canal engineer, had first demonstrated the art of 'puddling' to an astonished examining committee, before the necessary Act to permit the building of the canal had been obtained. Brindley had been equally persuasive when addressing the inaugural meeting of the Oxford Canal Company in October 1768, held in the bar of the *Three Tuns* inn at Banbury. The titled and important company present approved his design for a contour canal which would avoid too much expensive excavation and were quickly able to raise the sum of £50,000 in subscriptions, so that work could begin.

Canals were proving to be of vital economic use in the industrial revolution which was taking place in England. Not all manufacturers were within easy reach of river barges to move their goods, and the turnpike trusts which transformed the major roads had barely begun their work, but these new inland waterways could replace the packhorse or wagon system, when teams of heavily-laden beasts struggled along deeply rutted and muddy roads. Those of Oxfordshire were reputed to be amongst the worst in the kingdom.

Sadly, James Brindley did not live to finish the task he had undertaken, and it was completed by his assistants, Robert Whitworth and Samuel Simcock. James Barnes of Banbury later became the canal's engineer until 1794, at a yearly salary of £200. Time was money, and the shareholders were anxious to see a return on their investment: but delays were caused by disagreements with other canal companies over matters like the positioning of junctions and locks, and negotiations with landlords over the purchase of key sites. However, in 1791 the Canal Company paid its shareholders their first dividend, and by 1793 the £50 shares had risen to £200 in value. The investment was to prove worth while. By 1827 the Canal Company held its meetings in its own magnificent premises – 'Canal House' in Oxford, designed in the Greek Doric style by Richard Tawney.

The Dashwoods of Kirtlington were naturally most interested in the process of development. Sir Henry Watkin Dashwood was in fact one of the original investors, but the costs he incurred when introducing enclosures on his estates forced him to sell half his holding in canal stock. In 1787, Lady Newhaven wrote to her friend Lady Dashwood to congratulate her on the canal reaching Northbrook on 30 August, although 'if the Wharf is to be at Enslow Bridge as they say' she believed 'this would be equally convenient'.

No doubt Sir Robert Dashwood of Northbrook Manor would have been glad of a local wharf in 1730, when he had to pay 10 shillings to have coals brought from Abingdon, 17 miles away. However, even after the canal was built it could be rendered inoperable when it froze, as in the winter of 1793-4: coal had to be brought from Birmingham at 4s 8d per hundreweight. A frozen canal meant hard work for the ice-breaker boats, often pulled by as many as 12 horses. Several men stood in the centre of the craft, where there was an iron chain or bar, and this was used to rock the boat to and fro and break up the ice. Icy conditions also meant that the boatmen could earn no money, and this could lead to such severe economic measures as 'wife selling'. In the winter of 1788-9, the wife of an Oxford Fisher Row boatman was sold at a public auction for three shillings.

As the canal was gradually extended, more facilities were required, such as houses for the company's wharfinger, who was paid a pound a week and lived rent-free. Lock-keepers also needed housing, and sometimes a public house and stabling had to be built, if there was none close by. The materials used for these buildings, and for canal bridges and tunnels, were generally whatever was available locally – if there was no stone, brick was used. In Kirtlington it is likely that clay for 'puddling' was obtained from a field in Mill Lane, near the quarry entrance. In later years the village boys certainly found this spot useful for making clay marbles! On the canal bank, adjoining Mill Lane, there are the remains of a building which could have been a keeper or lengthsman's hut. These men would have taken care of Pigeon's Lock, and attended to the maintenance of the canal banks, removing water weed, and getting rid of moles.

The original *Three Pigeons* alehouse, on the opposite side of the canal, was sited further back than its successor, and its earliest recorded landlord was James Good, in 1869. It had eight stables for barge horses and they were bedded down for 3d a night in the early 1900s. A short distance away is Flights Mill with its rush of river water from the Cherwell, which used to have profitable eel-traps. The Domesday Survey mentioned two mills on this site in 1086. It is now the home of a well-known rock group.

The proprietors of the Oxford Canal Navigation could make money from sources apart from the canal itself. In 1811 the Kirtlington Enclosure Act recorded that they owned 'an osier bed at the Mill'. No doubt the osiers sprang up as a result of 'spoil' being thrown on the canal banks during construction, and they would have been a useful source of income when sold for making basketware. The osiers were first boiled in coppers, then taken out, red-hot, and pulled through a special machine to strip them in readiness for weaving. A lot of this hard and sometimes painful work was done by women and girls in the 1890s and 1900s on the premises of Oxford boatmen, like the Beesleys. In Kirtlington in the 1920s there was additional revenue from 'bicycle tolls', charged to regular users of the towpath. Ernie King and other workers at the Washford Pits Quarry tried to dodge paying their half-a-crown a year, but they always had to settle up in the end, in spite of racing to get to and from work before they were stopped.

Fig. 30. Osier cutting.

Fig. 31. Osier peeling.

Fig. 32.   Canal boy on the tow path.

Fig. 33.   A 'fly' boat and passengers, c.1810.

In the mid-19th century, attempts were made to introduce faster methods of travel on the canal. Something better was required than the leisurely old market boats which had plied between Oxford and Banbury, owned by firms like J. Couling and Thomas Sherratt. Charges were about a halfpenny for two miles' travel, and the passengers could sit comfortably by a fireplace, enjoying a good gossip, with their livestock tethered close by. When the canal froze, the journey was made by wagon. After 1830, however, Pickfords the carriers introduced a new 'fly-boat' service on the Oxford canal. Carrying only light freight and passengers, who paid '6d in the cabin' and '4d in the steerage', these boats operated six days a week, night and day, and a crew of four worked in shifts. They were drawn by galloping horses, ridden by uniformed postilions, sometimes known as 'horse marines'. As they raced along, slower craft were supposed to give them priority and drop their tow lines in the water to prevent them being cut.

This speedy travel was exciting for the passengers, but not economical for the company as only light goods could be carried. It was also damaging to the canal banks, which were being eaten away by the wash from the boats, and eventually they were taken out of service.

However, it was not the competition of the fly-boats which caused John Weaving to discontinue his market boat service in 1852, as much as that of the railway, which was to prove the death-knell of the canal system. Investors who had previously put their money into canal company shares now turned to the 'Iron Horse' which offered more speed, and more scope.

Kirtlington's nearest station was just over a mile away at Enslow hamlet, near Bletchingdon. It was close to the canal and the *Rock of Gibraltar* inn, and was well-used by the villagers who sought town employment, or town amusements. Farmers also found the railway a much quicker way of sending their stock to market, or to be exhibited at the increasingly popular agricultural shows. Although the station was closed in the 1960s, the railway line is still in use, and while goods trains rattle along it overhead, holiday narrowboats glide gently under the bridge, making for Oxford or Banbury.

In a desperate effort to compete with the railway, which was taking the bulk of the freight trade, the canal company reduced tolls from 5s 11d a ton to 2s 7d a ton. Boatmen adapted themselves as best they could to changing times. The 'Number Ones' who owned their own craft gave up their homes on the land and took their wives and families on the boat with them, which saved paying out for a crew, whilst others sold up and went to work elsewhere, or tried to let their boats for holiday use.

The names of two Kirtlington boat families appear in the 1861 census lists. They were George and Esther Coles, both aged 27, who had two young children, and a couple with a teenage son. In 1851 '2 males' were recorded, and in 1841 '3 males', as living in boats. By 1877 all boats had to be registered, and the number of people living on board recorded, with their ages and sexes, to ensure that sleeping accommodation was suitable, and that there was no overcrowding. They were regularly inspected, and the inspector would be particularly displeased if he discovered that the children were not attending school. The condition of the boat was also examined, and matters like dirty water carriers or faulty pumps incurred fines.

The problem of educating boat children led to an Act of 1884 which stipulated that they must have at least 200 days of schooling a year. The Rice family sent their children to the Kirtlington school in the early 1900s, but they sometimes had a tough time. Perhaps because they dressed or acted a little differently from them, the Kirtlington youngsters would chase them down Mill Lane, with shouts of 'Boatie, boatie!'.

As the children grew up and thoughts turned to courting, it was usually a member of another boating family who caught their fancy. One young man from Bletchingdon used to hitch a lift to Tackley on his sweetheart's family boat, and then walk home afterwards, repeating the process whenever the boat returned to Bletchingdon. Composing a love letter was a complicated matter, and often a lock-keeper would be pressed into service: but in Kirtlington young courting couples could call on the help of the Wickson family of the *Three Pigeons* alehouse. One unusual love story they heard was that of Tom Pikely who went into Banbury on market day, where a smart pair of green trousers caught his eye. Dressed up in them that evening in the village street, he knew he was attracting a good deal of attention. He hadn't been long in the pub when he was told 'Mrs Tupple wants to see you': sitting with the good lady was her daughter, who had an important question to ask him. 'Will you walk out with me?' she said. 'I sin you go by, and they trousers took me fancy.' Six months later, they were married!

A boatwoman's life could be very hard, with scant time to recover from having babies, particularly if they had to help load or unload cargo, or take their turn 'legging' the boat through a tunnel. The day often started about four a.m. Any delay or bad weather could send the boatmen to the nearest alehouse. On their return their unfortunate wives might get a beating, or they might take it out on their horse. Not for some of these horses a nose bowl filled with oats and bran, and a sheltered stable in rough weather: they were lucky if the sweat-stains were brushed off their backs when their dirty and ill-fitting harness was removed, and they were turned out on

Fig. 34.   Canal scene, *c.*1870.

whatever rough grazing was nearest. On the Kirtlington stretch of the canal, however, most of the Number One boatmen treated their animals well, and took a pride in having them well turned out.

In some cases donkeys and mules were used instead of horses. One famous mule was Dolly, owned by Joe Abel and Rose Skinner, who was well-known along the canal, and hauled coal and cement loads. Some years ago holidaymakers passing a meadow near Flights Mill would see the donkeys belonging to 'Mr. and Mrs. Clark', who lived in a beautifully-fitted out narrowboat and also had a gipsy caravan, both pulled by their animals. Their happiness was disturbed when a journalist discovered that they were in reality Lord Justice Eve and his wife. Some days later the meadow was empty. 'Mr. and Mrs. Clark' had moved on to find solitude elsewhere.

Apart from horses, donkeys and mules, a number of boatmen owned dogs – sometimes ferocious guardians, or favoured lurchers. These latter were ideal for getting a free supper, provided the gamekeeper didn't spot you making off with the hare, pheasant or rabbit! Other boatmen resorted to stealing vegetables from the fields adjoining the canal, and several were fined for this by Bicester magistrates in the 1850s.

Shopping could be a problem, but again the Wicksons of the *Three Pigeons* helped out by stocking basic items like bread and a few groceries. If the boat people couldn't pay at the time, the right money would be slipped under the door at their next visit to the Oxford Canal.

There have been tragic occurrences on the canal. Dead animals and other refuse were sometimes thrown into it, and this practice, although officially forbidden, may have contributed to several serious outbreaks of cholera in Oxford between 1832 and 1854, when many boat families from Fisher Row were amongst those who suffered. Typhus was also an ever-present hazard. Perhaps the most common misfortune was that of falling in. Ernie King once went to the rescue of a man who had fallen through the ice of the frozen canal with his bicycle. Ernie's most vivid recollection was of the bicycle lamp, shining up through the ice. By far the saddest accident occurred on Christmas Eve 1874, when the bridge at Hampton Gay collapsed as a train was passing over it. Thirty-four people were killed in this dreadful accident.

At a meeting of the canal company in April 1900, trade was described as poor, owing to a shortage of water after a hot summer, followed by a hard winter. One major problem for boat-owners was that they could not take a lot of different one-ton loads to make up a total consignment, as the railways could. By May 1909, however, conditions had improved sufficiently for the company to consider purchasing a heavy dredger costing £150.

The early 20th century saw, in fact, an increase in canal traffic. The ancient quarry at Washford Pits, only a short distance from Pigeon Lock, was leased to the Oxford Portland Cement Company by Sir George Dashwood, and it was not long before their immaculate blue and white boats became a regular feature, in sharp contrast with the grimy coal boats from Staffordshire and the northern collieries who unloaded their cargoes at the company's landing stage. Another regular visitor was the Cadbury Company's boat from Bournville in Birmingham, taking their staff on outings; the quarry featured on their itinerary as a place of interest. The cement company used both the canal and the railway to despatch their products.

Today the canal is principally used by holidaymakers, but its maintenance and supervision still requires constant behind-the-scenes work. The telephone hardly stopped ringing when I visited Mr. Vic Bodsworth, section manager for the Waterways Board, and responsible for an area of about 50 miles of canal from his busy canalside office at Thrupp. Boat traffic increases from about 40 craft a week to nearly 30 a day during the summer season, and many of their captains are more enthusiastic than skilful, like the two boats with a party of Australians on board which tried to turn in shallow water near Cropredy a couple of years ago, and which ended up totally blocking the canal from side to side.

Trying to keep within a strict budget, and to play fair by all those who live and work on or near the canal, is no easy task. It means, for instance, that an ancient bridge can only be 'patched up' rather than properly repaired – but some repair work has to be done, so that a farmer could continue to have access to his harvest fields. The towpaths have to be regularly scythed free of brambles and undergrowth so that visitors can walk along them, but sometimes botanists then complain at the loss of a rare plant. Mr. Bodsworth has to find the compromise answer to all these problems. Even in the winter there is sometimes no respite. Some boat-hire firms offer off-peak bargains even over Christmas, forgetting that a peaceful winter would give maintenance workers a chance to repair banks, clear drainage ditches, and fit iron struts where a towpath is in danger of collapse.

The canal has long been attractive to fishermen. Aubrey Giles of Flight's Mill had eel-traps, and his son Laurence on one occasion caught a hundredweight in one night! The stretch of water near Washford Pits is particularly fruitful. Here lurk plentiful roach, and the small greedy gudgeon, but to catch fish here does require a skilful angler. Downstream towards Three Pigeons Lock there is a good chance of getting the cautious, watchful chub. Perhaps the most ferocious and deadly British fish is the pike. Lord Valentia's chauffeur caught one once, and it was put on display in the *Dashwood Arms*, Kirtlington, for some time. The British Waterways Board lease fishing rights to various fishing clubs, like the Coventry Anglers, and the season is from 15 June to 15 March the following year.

The botanist too can find much of interest on the canal. Dr. Eustace Jones, who is a great authority on the flowers and plants around Kirtlington, says that the yellow meadow rue, the bitter cress and the water aven still grow near the canal, but the small Venus looking glass, the lesser toadflax, and the danewort are now rare. A lot of the wild flowers once found round here depended on the growing of peat, when it was used for fuel before coal arrived on the canal boats. This has meant the gradual disappearance of the bog rush, marsh hellebore and parnassus grass. Not far from the canal the rare and beautiful bee orchid can still be found: but its exact location is known to only a few Kirtlington people.

The work of canal builders like James Brindley continues to be of value today. There is still a need for our waterways and the boats that use them. In the words of the old rhyme:

> There's a boat coming up,
> There's a boat coming down,
> There's one in the lock,
> And another in the pound.

May this always be the case on the Oxford Canal!

CHAPTER FIFTEEN

The Oxford Portland Cement Company

Fig. 35. Trade mark of
the Oxford Portland
Cement Company.

The founder of the Company was Major A.H. Dillon, whose family seat was at the Palladian mansion Ditchley Park. His mother Ellen was Sir Henry William Dashwood's daughter, and it was doubtless through this connection that Major Dillon was able to lease the quarry and the land for the cement works. The magazine *The British Clayworker* reported the opening of the new firm in July 1907, commenting on the 'very modern' machinery which had taken 18 months to erect. At that time, the works were under the management of Mr. A. E. Turner. Until about 1928, the Major and his family lived at the Manor House in Kirtlington, and often rode down on his well-turned-out hunter to inspect the work in progress. 'He looked the perfect picture of an English gentleman of the 1920s' according to Ernie King: 'he was a likeable man, always immaculately dressed, and smelling of some expensive cologne', but he was a thoughtful man, who took a great interest in his workforce. Mrs. Dillon also lent her support; during the First World War she worked alongside the quarrymen with a number of other Kirtlington women, working and loading stone, and packing cement.

The beds the quarrymen had to work were of cornbrash, Lower Forest marble, and the Great Oolite, and these layers of clay, hard limestone and cement stone alternated very conveniently for the manufacture of cement. Before blasting could take place, the topsoil had to be cleared away by workers above the quarryface, using the strong elm wheelbarrows made by the quarry carpenter, Jack Gillam. It was then the job of the stonebreakers, whose foreman was Walt 'Nobbler' Jones, to wield their seven- or 14-pound sledgehammers and reduce the stone which they had hand-dug from the quarry walls to a workable size. The clay beds were also hand-dug.

After breaking-up and digging-out, the stone and clay were loaded into separate 'Jubilee Skips', each holding about a ton of material. The ratio of stone required by the chemists was usually about 5-1 or 5-2: These skips ran on a narrow-gauge track, but had to be hand-pushed down a slope to the processing plant, and then back again for reloading. This work was also hard and dirty.

Once the skips had been unloaded, the intricate processing began. The stone was crushed, and the clay put through 'clay rolls' for later mixing with the crushed stone. It was then fed into a kiln fired by pulverised coal. This caused rings of ash deposit to form, which had to be broken away every 24 hours, while the kiln was still operating. The resulting blue-black clinker was then ground by a ball mill, finished by a pebble mill, and then mixed with a small percentage of gypsum to control the setting time of the cement. The finished product was kept in bins and later hand-packed into sacks, 11 of which amounted to a ton in weight when full. In later years the finished cement was stored in silos and packed by machine.

Considering the very limited access which the company had at the Washford Pits site, their production figures seem extremely good. Local deliveries by canal boat to Oxford took a day to complete, but a round trip to Coventry and Birmingham could last from five to eight days, which meant that stabling for the horses had to be arranged, and bags of chaff stored on board, which were cut and prepared in the two-storey building still to be seen in Mill Lane. Each of these boats – and at one time there were as many as seven – could carry a 25-ton load.

The company's boats had local names (like 'Kirtlington') and an official number, and under the terms of the Canal Boats Act of 1877 had to register with a local authority and pass regular inspections. Skippers like Thomas Brammidge and Lewis Grantham were obviously proud of their immaculate blue and white boats, and George James Dew recorded their condition as 'good' when he made his inspections between 1910 and 1919. It has been difficult to obtain any information about these boats, and no details of their ownership after 1929 have been discovered. However,

in August 1982 the magazine *Waterways World* published an interview with Mr. Herbert Tooley, of a long-established family of boat-builders at Banbury. He recalled that the last boats they built were for the Oxford Portland Cement Company, during the late 1920s. Although two were delivered, the third was cancelled 'around 1928' in the course of construction, and the makers were later able to sell it elsewhere for £250.

Unloading a boat was hard and dirty work, and with wheelbarrows and shovels only, it took four men most of a working day – between 7 a.m. and 4 p.m. – to deal with 52 tons, which was about two boatloads. There were also cargoes of sand and gypsum to be dealt with, as well as the cement itself.

Apart from the vital canal link, their only road route was down the stony Mill Lane, which must have been hard on the horses' feet in the early days, and on the tyres of the

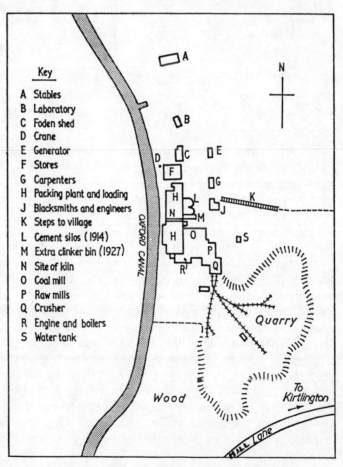

Key

A Stables
B Laboratory
C Foden shed
D Crane
E Generator
F Stores
G Carpenters
H Packing plant and loading
J Blacksmiths and engineers
K Steps to village
L Cement silos (1914)
M Extra clinker bin (1927)
N Site of kiln
O Coal mill
P Raw mills
Q Crusher
R Engine and boilers
S Water tank

Fig. 36. Plan of the works, 1907-1929.

new Foden wagons which came into operation to distribute the firm's products after 1925. Access for the workmen was also difficult in the early days. When the works first opened, they had to use the path by the Rifle Hut, and then clamber down part of the rockface to the quarry floor.

In spite of the many inconveniences, there was a good spirit amongst the men. Most of them came from Kirtlington or the neighbouring villages, and they knew each other well. Many had gone to school together, were related by marriage, or could boast another relative who also worked for the company. They also had a gift for nicknames: William Walton, a cement process worker and also the landlord of the *Oxford Arms*, was known as 'Baggy', Mr. Rogers the village barber, and a cement packer and loader, as 'Puggy'. 'Mailman' was Mr. Hemmings, a former post office coach driver.

Compared with today's wages, those received by the quarrymen naturally seem low, but they were quite reasonable at the time:

1914

Foreman engineer	...	...	...	£3.	0.	0. per week
Quarry foreman	...	...	...	£1.	8.	0. per week
Mechanic	...	...	...	£0.	0.	7. per hour
Mechanic's mate	...	...	...	£0.	0.	4½. per hour
Engine driver (stationery)	...	...	...	£0.	0.	7½. per hour
Stokers	...	...	...	£0.	0.	6½. per hour
Pit foreman	...	...	...	£0.	0.	6½. per hour
Millers	...	...	...	£0.	0.	6½. or 7½. per hour

Despite their somewhat remote siting, the firm became better-known after exhibiting at the Oxford Agricultural Show in 1911. Their stand featured samples of raw material in various stages of processing, and an example of a cement balustrade, of the type used in Roman Catholic churches.

In 1925 the firm acquired a new employee. It was Ernie King, who was 14 years old, and had just left school. His wages were 7s 6d a week, and out of this he gave his mother 6s and kept the rest for pocket money and new socks. The duty chemist in the firm's laboratory where Ernie was to become the 'sample lad' considered he was small for his age, but Mr. Lidgey, the manager, assured him that 'there was plenty of room down here for him to grow'. One of the most important jobs for the three chemists who worked there was to control the clay/limestone ratio, and to check the soundness and quality of the cement clinker, and this required regular liaison with the head millers in the plant. The young 'sample lad' arrived at 8.30, and his first jobs were to make up the fire, check that the laboratory utensils and safety equipment were clean and tidy, and then to break up the briquettes, which were made up every day to test the tensile strength of cement and concrete. There was just enough time before going home for lunch to put the 'boiling pats' and expansion test pieces on to the fire in their containers. These tests were carried out on the day's product, and on that produced by the night shift, at six in the morning and six in the evening.

After lunch, the cement and other raw materials had to be tested for 'fineness', to ensure that the crushing carried out at the plant fulfilled the standard required by law. Before going home for tea at five, the fire had to be restoked, and a supply of coal brought in for the night-shift chemist. He was often called on to carry out other less official duties – one of the duty chemists insisted that his newspaper should be opened and warmed for him, and when he was on night shift, he gave Ernie love letters to deliver to his sweetheart at Bletchingdon. Ernie must have felt his role of Cupid had been worthwhile when the couple later got married.

In the 1920s, the quarrymen usually wore strong boots or shoes and corduroy trousers held up by belt or braces. Their trousers were tied in just below the knee with a length of twine to prevent wear on the knees and hem. Their thick cotten or wincyette collarless shirts were set off with a coloured scarf, and worn under a waistcoat or sleeveless pullover, whilst jackets were usually tweed or twill. Their headgear was invariably a weathered trilby or cap. At one time in Kirtlington it was the 'fashion' for some of the older womenfolk to wear an old cap belonging to their husbands.

The quarrymen found it difficult to dry their clothes in wet weather, as the only form of heating they had was the coke stove in their rest hut, where they also kept their picks and shovels; but in spite of this, there is no record of any serious illness amongst them. St Barbara, patron saint of gunners, miners and quarrymen, must have taken good care of them. They were not allowed to smoke, but quite a few chewed tobacco. The village store displayed rolls of twist in two thicknesses on the counter, and would cut off any length required. It is interesting to compare the wages paid at this time with those of 1914:

1925

Foreman mechanic	...	...	...	£4.	7.	0. per week
Carpenter (no bonus)	...	...	...	£0.	1.	1. per hour
Foden driver	...	...	...	£0.	1.	2¾. per hour
Foden mate (no bonus)	...	...	...	£0.	0.	11. per hour
Stokers	...	...	...	...	£0.	0.	10. per hour
Chief Miller	...	...	...	£0.	0.	11. per hour
Foreman cement packer	...	...	£0.	0.	11. per hour
Sack repairer	...	...	...	£0.	5.	4½. per 100 sacks
Quarry foreman	...	...	...	£0.	0.	10. per hour
Quarrymen	...	...	...	£0.	0.	10. per hour
Quarry truckmen	...	...	...	£0.	0.	10. per hour
Crushers	...	...	...	£0.	0.	10. per hour

Between 1925-9 there was in addition for most employees a bonus system of 1d per ton of cement manufactured each year in excess of 300 tons. In 1922 17,287 tons were produced; after the introduction of the bonus scheme production rose to almost 20,000 tons a year.

The men usually received a week's paid holiday a year, and their Christmas break was a very short one indeed, as the following notice reveals:

CHRISTMAS 1913

The works will close from 6 a.m. on Thursday December 25th until 6 a.m. on Saturday December 27th.

WAGES: The Office will open at 4 p.m. on Wednesday December 24th, for payment of wages to date. Foremen are hereby instructed to make up their Time Sheets and pass them into the Office before noon, tomorrow, Wednesday December 24th.

Dudley W. Morse, Secretary

Ernie himself never became a union member, but the National Agricultural Labourers' Union operated at the quarry for some years, and he remembered an incident from his childhood, when he heard someone say 'The quarry is on strike!' Not knowing what a 'strike' was, he rushed down Mill Lane to find out what it was all about – but by the time he got there the dispute had been settled!

The First World War brought the company new prosperity, with over 50 per cent of the company's products being sent to government departments, like the Admiralty and the War Office, for use in munition factories, and for wartime building works. Their goods were also in demand by canal companies, city and county councils, hospitals, sewage works, tram companies and railways. However, like many other firms, they were adversely affected by the General Strike in 1926, when coal for their processing plant became scarce and expensive, and by 1928 it was decided to move to a new site at Shipton-on-Cherwell, where distribution would be made by railway and lorry. There were other factors encouraging Major Dillon and his co-directors to move. The plant was practically worn out, and the quarry virtually exhausted, despite the skills of the chemists, who were always trying to find new and more economical ways of using the raw materials available. An additional factor was the poor road access.

The machinery was gradually dismantled, and some of it found new homes. The Marshall steam engine travelled to India, where it powered a cotton-mill until 1936. The Krupp gear wheel went to Flights Mill, where Laurie Giles' grandfather installed it, and until the property changed hands recently, it was still being used to generate electricity during power cuts. A great deal of the remaining equipment was sold as scrap, although for about a year after cement production had ceased, the company tried to run a smaller enterprise on the site and produce roadstone and chicken grit. This project was eventually abandoned, however.

Their boats and horses were sold, and Washford Pits, once a scene of bustling activity, became once more a peaceful haven for wild life, visited for its wild flowers, and by the occasional fossil hunter. The Blue Circle Company, now the owners of the quarry, discourages trespassers because of the danger of falling rock.

Shipton-on-Cherwell is about two miles from Kirtlington, in the Wootton Hundreds. It was known in earlier days as 'Sciptone' meaning 'the sheep farm'. It was here, on just over 200 acres of land owned by Major Dillon, that it was proposed in 1927 to 'exploit the Great Oolite' and establish a new cement works.

The men working to excavate the site were surprised to discover that others long before had found the site to their liking. In the second century A.D. there were Romano-British people living on the heights above the river. Some of their coarse pottery cooking pots, and fine Samian ware, were found, and perhaps the most valuable find was a sheet-bronze cauldron, which may have been thrown into the river to placate a pagan god.

The new company was to be called, according to its prospectus issued in 1927, 'Oxford and Shipton Cement Ltd.', and included amongst its six directors Major Dillon's father-in-law Sir John Brunner, and also Lord Iver Spencer Churchill.

Twenty-three workers were transferred here from Washford Pits. By 1929 the firm were producing quality cement for a steadily-increasing number of clients, who paid about 2s 6d for a hundredweight bag. They now employed 280 men, and the works manager was Mr. Percy Lidgey, from the former Kirtlington quarry. He was still living at one of the three houses leased by the cement company in Kirtlington. Two of the former directors of the cement company – Sir Lucas Tooth and Mr. Tindall Wildridge – had also lived in the village during the early 1900s.

In 1934 the Oxford and Shipton Cement Company became part of the large Alpha Cement Group, which in turn was taken over by Associated Portland Cement Manufacturers in 1938.

With the coming of the Second World War, the company's work was once more of vital importance for the nation. Work went ahead during the night, with the only light coming from shaded blue lamps and pocket torches, because of the blackout. It was ironic to think that only a few years earlier in 1935-6, some of the firm's new plant had been bought from German manufacturers, and installed by German engineers!

The company continued to prosper after the end of the war, and its 250-foot high chimney is a well-known local landmark, even if it has sometimes aroused hostility from some, like W. H. Black, who wrote to the *Oxford Mail* in 1953 that it was in his opinion 'the only eyesore' on the 20-mile stretch of canal between Oxford and Banbury.

In 1977 the works at Shipton again changed their name when they became part of the Blue Circle Industries PLC group. It is pleasing to know that Blue Circle sponsor a living memorial to the early days of the cement industry, in the form of *Mirosa*, one of the finest and oldest 'spritsail' barges still in use. She still competes in racing events on the Thames, and is also much involved in publicity and promotional exercises for the company. The narrow boats of the Oxford Portland Cement Company can no longer be seen on the canal near Kirtlington, and the deserted quarry at Washford pits bears little trace of its past – but not far away, on

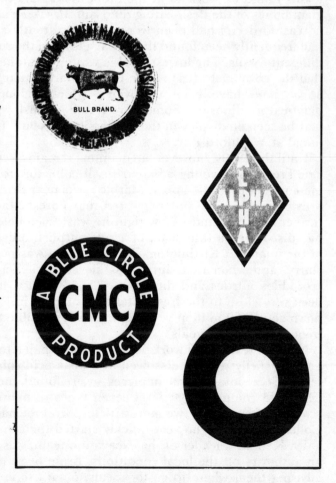

Fig. 37. Previous and present trademarks.

the River Thames, there is still a reminder of those early days, and the hard and dirty work which was the daily lot of many Kirtlington villagers.

* * *

Shrews, Dinosaurs and the 1976 dig: a footnote to the history of the quarry – or a starting point?

When Ernie King settled into retirement in 1977, he had no idea that his involvement with Washford Pits Quarry was by no means over. Academics and amateur fossil-hunters have long been aware that many spectacular fossil finds have been made in the quarries of Oxfordshire. In the 17th century, Robert Plot, first keeper of the Ashmolean Museum, described the 'formed stones' which were frequently found, which the country folk called 'fairystones', 'devil's toenails' and the like.

William Buckland, first professor of geology at Oxford, did much to put the study of fossil remains on a scientific basis. In 1824 he published his observations on some fossils found by workers in the Stonesfield slate quarries. Amongst them were the giant bones of the flesh-eating dinosaur *Megalosaurus*, and small mammal jawbones.

Washford Pits had been worked intermittently since medieval times, and bones had frequently been found there. Each level of the rock strata in the district produces different fossils. The lowest level is white limestone, then Forest Marble, and above that the cornbrash. It is in the Forest Marble that even larger bones than those of *Megalosaurus* have been discovered which belonged to the huge *Cetiosaurus*, a plant-eating dinosaur. Some were found at Enslow, a hamlet of Bletchingdon, and may be seen on display in the University Museum, Oxford. In the 1920s, others were found at Washford Pits.

Until the 1970s, however, no mammal remains were found at this site. At this time, Eric Freeman, a young amateur fossil collector from London, found a single worn mammal tooth in the Forest Marble rocks near Bridport in Dorset. He wrote a short article on this find, and suggested that Forest Marble might be a likely strata for further mammal finds. How right he was! Even before the article was published, he had discovered a thin seam of a soft purplish-brown clay, tucked away in a corner of the quarry at Kirtlington. When the clay was put into water, it readily formed a slurry, and when this slurry was sieved, it left a residue of bones and teeth of crocodiles, turtles and dinosaurs! This evidence showed that dry land must have been very close to the freshwater lake or river in which the clay was originally laid down some 160 million years ago. Was it possible to prove that this land had been frequented by mammals?

Now the really hard work began, as about half a ton of clay was washed and sieved, and the shelly residue dissolved in a weak acid solution. Eventually some mammal teeth – some intact, some in pieces – were found, most being smaller than a pinhead. They had come from at least seven types of mammal, five of which were new to science. After writing two more articles, Mr. Freeman 'donated' the site to University College, London, who very quickly started their own larger-scale 'dig'.

Dr. Kermack, leader of the excavation team, was put in touch with Ernie King as an authority on the local conditions. Ernie became deeply interested in the work, advising them where to go for meals, obtain rope or tools, and helping them find local labour. He made many friends during this 'dig' – but the thing that interested him most was the enthusiasm shown by University College. When they got to the small bed of clay they required 'they were so excited, I thought we must have found gold!' he recalled.

Ernie was suitably rewarded for his valuable help, as one of the new species which had been found has been officially named *Wareolestes rex* – *rex* being Latin for 'King'!

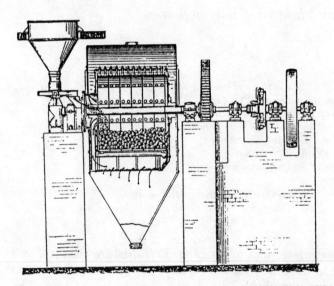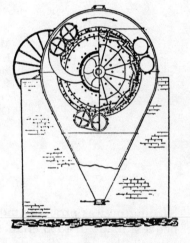

A ball-mill, *c.*1901.

CHAPTER SIXTEEN

The Schoolchildren of Kirtlington

Mr. Austin is a very good man,
He tries to teach us all he can,
He never forgets to give us the stick,
When he does he makes us dance
Out of England into France –
Out of France into Spain –
And out of Spain back again.

The unofficial school song, c. 1900

Kirtlington was probably more fortunate than many other Oxfordshire villages, as a bequest made in 1593 enabled it to have its first school in 1603. The benefactor was John Phillips, a woollen draper, who owned two adjoining houses in Woodstock. The rental of the houses amounted to a pound a year, which was to towards finding a schoolmaster for Kirtlington, 'if it fortune any school to be built or erected there'.

A schoolmaster (one William Albright) was found, but there appears to have been no special school building, and the 32 children who attended in the first year probably had their lessons in the tithe barn. No doubt they learned their alphabet by means of a hornbook, hung round their necks by a ribbon attached to the handle. Ten years later, in 1613, there was still no school building, and it was decided to use the church house as a 'schoolhouse, court-house and town-house'.

By 1702 the property in Woodstock, which had now been converted into one building, was too 'decayed' to yield any rent, and was no doubt demolished. It was at this time that a remarkable young man, John Sandford, was achieving considerable fame in Kirtlington. Born in 1683, he became the parish clerk at 11, and on 7 January 1702, 38 'principal householders' of Kirtlington voted that he should become the schoolmaster (at the ripe age of 19) and he was to hold this position until 1747. On 7 October 1705 he married Elizabeth Padgett, and they had five children. After her death, he married Martha Bucknell, in 1722. His memorial records the central role he played in village life for half a century:

IN MEMORY OF JOHN SANDFORD – WHO WAS CLERK OF THIS PARISH 54 YEARS – TAUGHT IN THE SCHOOL 45 YEARS – DEPARTED THIS LIFE JUNE 21ST 1750 AGED 66 YEARS.

In 1759 the school actually closed down for several years, no doubt for financial reasons. It must also have been extremely difficult to replace John Sandford.

A relic survives from the last years of this first Kirtlington school, in the form of a book containing samples of the children's needlework betwee 1760 and 1836. The East family are the fortunate owners of the fascinating glimpse of long-ago Kirtlington schooldays.

In 1774 the 'Charity School' began a new chapter in its history. Sir James Dashwood and the vicar, the Reverend Ashton Thorpe, were the governors and trustees of the charity. Apparently Sir James successfully negotiated with the duke of Marlborough for a 'building lease', whereby the plot of land at Woodstock was to be let to the Duke at four guineas a year. Seventy years later, when there were four houses on the site, the yearly rent was as much as £70, but there were heavy expenses for repairs, which reduced the average annual income available to the school to £23.

In 1781 several school rules were instituted, which reveal the strict pattern of behaviour expected from the pupils.

> The boy and girl that throughout the week behaves best to sit upon the two single stools. That to be decided by a paper being wrote and hung up in the school with all their names, and for each fault a dot made. Of course the child that has the fewest number of dots annexed to their name to be rewarded.

Lying and swearing were punished by the child not being allowed to wear its uniform at church on the following Sunday, and if they did not attend school regularly, unless their parents had good reason to show for it, they would be expelled. Religious instruction was an important part of school life. At the end of their first year's schooling, a child was expected to be able to repeat the Lord's Prayer, the Catechism, and the Creed. On Sundays, pupils were expected to walk up to Kirtlington Park and repeat the Collect which they had supposedly learnt the previous day to Lady Dashwood. This Sunday visit was obviously looked on as a treat, however, as the rules stipulated that 'if any child is found incorrigible, or in any degree obstinate, it shall be deprived of the above benefits, until such time as they are reformed'.

By 1808, with the original Phillips endowment supplemented by the generosity of the Dashwood family, there were 30 pupils, 22 of them being free scholars. The village at that time had a total population of about five hundred. Boys and girls were taught to read, but girls were additionally instructed in plain sewing.

By 1833 the school had come under the control of the National Society, which had strong Church of England connections. It had absorbed two other establishments and had 40 pupils – after the amalgamation, in 1834, it had 138 children. Parents were informed that 'You have brought your Child to be placed under our protection in this School, we shall receive it gladly, and you may rest assured that the greatest diligence will be used to train it up in the way it should go'. In May 1834, a separate infant school was established.

However, this was not the only educational facility available in Kirtlington in the early 19th century. There were two 'dame schools', one in a cottage near Kite's Pond, and the other somewhere in Crowcastle Lane. Here small groups of children were taught their first lessons, often by an elderly woman in her own home. Little is known of them, but one incident lives in village memory. The children were seated round an open hearth, listening to their teacher, when one lost his balance and fell into the fire. The resourceful 'dame' quickly bundled him up in her voluminous skirts, and extinguished the flames.

The charges at these schools were usually three or four pence a week, but even these modest sums were too much for some Kirtlington parents with large families, particularly as a child in full-time employment could earn three or four shillings at nine or ten years of age. From the census returns of 1841, we learn that nine-year-old Edmund Cato was employed as a toll collector, and ten-year-old Harriet Hounslow was an agricultural labourer. In 1881 12-year-old Joseph Coxhill was an agricultural labourer, and Ada Rogers, the same age, a general servant.

In 1875 the Agricultural Children's Act was introduced, which stipulated ten years as the minimum age for full-time employment. A further act in 1880 made it compulsory for all children over five to attend school. By 1893 additional legislation made school attendance compulsory for children until they were 13 or 14 years old, unless they could pass a 'leaving examination' in the three Rs.

Not a great deal is known about the Kirtlington schoolmasters between 1841 and 1881, apart from the bare details recorded in the census returns. In 1841 John Trafford, a married man with five children, was a schoolmaster, as was the 35-year-old William Walker. In 1851 Henry Gilbert was the headmaster, assisted by Henry Cramp from London. In 1853 we can gain a more personal insight into the life of James Phillips, from a rather unexpected source – the 'Bread Book' of Charles East, baker and carrier of Kirtlington. He not only supplied goods, but also carried out shopping commissions for fellow villagers when visiting Oxford or other large shopping centres. In that year, Mr. Phillips bought a pair of clogs, some blotting paper, a pair of gloves, a broom, two 'coppey books', 100 faggots and three bundles of sticks, as well as a regular supply of tobacco. The 1841 census reveals that there were schoolmistresses as well as masters. Sarah Nash had three daughters, and was apparently a widow, as no other 'head of household' is listed. By 1851 she had been joined in the school by her daughter Caroline, who taught the infants. A series of lady teachers succeeded them, but it was not until September 1899, when Miss Nellie Fruin was engaged, that the school enjoyed a really long period – almost a lifetime – of service from one of its female staff. When (in 1918) she married the son of the local wheelwright and undertaker, and thus became Mrs. Bunker, the school celebrated with three days' holiday!

In spite of the increased attendances, and the appointment of better-trained staff, there were still problems, and one of these was money. The endowment of about £40 annually from the Woodstock properties was still being supplemented by the Dashwood family. Sir Henry continued his family's involvement, being Manager, Correspondent and Patron until his death in 1889. The accounts of the school for 1890 show that his son, Sir George, had to pay a balance of £54 14s 9d to keep the school's expenses straight:

	£	s	d		£	s	d
Grant	102	12	6	Salaried teacher	120	0	0
Endowment	39	1	3	Assets	74	0	0
Pence a/c	40	13	10	Books etc. ..	7	13	8
Pence a/c		1	8	Fuel/light ..	8	13	9

Articles sold	..	..		2	5	Cleaning	..		19	0
Balance paid by						Rent	..	..	26	0	0
Sir George	..	..	54	14	9					
			£237	6	5			£237	6	5

The school fees paid by the children varied enormously in the years before 1891, when education became free. In 1889 there were three classes of payment:

1. Children of tradesmen, who pay 4d. for the first child, others - 2d. each.
2. Children of those earning above 1 gn. a week, who pay 3d, thereafter 1d.
3. Labourers, paying 2d. for their first child, and 1d. for the others.

Providing the weather was good and there was no illness about, attendances were generally good, and the school fees made a major contribution to the prosperity of the school; but it was a different story when the temperature dropped, and there was snow or heavy rain to contend with. Unless the poorer children were kept at home, they were forced to sit for most of the day in wet stockings and leaking boots or shoes, with only the prospect of bread and lard sandwiches for lunch. The kindly Dashwoods did what they could to alleviate these hardships, and provided hot soup 'twice a week' and cocoa 'three times a week' for the children who had to walk in from Northbrook or the outlying farms.

Although boots only cost about 2s 6d a pair, and were reinforced with hobnails for boys and 'spriggs' for the girls, repairs cost 4d or 6d a time, and if money was short, they had to be left. It is not surprising that a new pair of boots was an occasion for display and celebration, and the lucky child was expected to walk up and down the classroom, to show them off to the teacher and the other children. Woe betide the child whose new boots squeaked, however, for traditionally these meant that they had not been paid for!

By 1881 the school appears to have been most competently run, by the new headmaster, the 28-year-old Arthur Austin from Staffordshire, who was a 'certificated schoolmaster' and who was helped by his wife Ann, who was 30 years old and had an assistant teacher's certificate. Their two young children were looked after by Hannah Wickson, 14 years old, and they were helped in the school by Mary Parker, an unmarried young lady of 26, living at home with her parents, and the sewing mistress, Sarah Green, who was 47 years old. It is interesting to see the difference in the wages paid to a 'certificated' and an unqualified teacher: Mr. Austin received £120 per annum and his wife £50, but Miss Parker's wage was only twenty-four pounds.

Mr. Austin was also a member of the church choir, and had been the enumerator for the 1881 census, in company with the district registrar, the formidable George James Dew. Mr. Dew was relentless in another of his duties, that of school attendance officer, tracking down erring pupils and reprimanding them and their parents with equal vigour. ' 'E were a tough 'un', many villagers have recalled.

One of the most important records of any school is its log book, and the one for Kirtlington commences on 18 April 1887, when the children returned from their Easter holidays. The log book notes the attendance level ('May 9th, 1887. Thin attendance – cricket match in village') and notable events, both local and national (on 21 June 'Rejoicing in the village, in honour of Her Majesty's Jubilee. Holidays

Kirtlington Industrial Exhibition.

Easter Monday, April 14th, 1884.

The Committee beg to announce that the next Annual Exhibition will be held in the Schoolroom on Easter Monday, April 14th, 1884.

CONDITIONS UNDER WHICH THE PRIZES WILL BE AWARDED.

1. Every article must be the BONA FIDE work of the Exhibitor and made after 1st October, 1883. Needlework must be shown unwashed.

2. An entrance fee of 1d. will be charged for each exhibit.

3. No one will be permitted to compete in any work connected with their particular trade, or to take more than one prize in each Class.

4. Exhibits with a piece of paper, bearing the name of the Exhibitor, the Divison number and Class letter, attached, must be brought to the School not later than 9-30 a. m. Exhibits must not be removed before 6-30 p.m. All articles that are of a large size should be delivered at the School on the previous Saturday afternoon.

5. All intending Competitors should send a list of the articles they intend exhibiting to the Exhibition Secretary, not later than Thursday, April 10th, 1884.

6. The decision of the Judges shall in all cases be final.

7. The following prizes will be awarded—Classes in which there are—

    (1.) 9 or more Exhibits, 3 Prizes, 2/-, 1/-, 6d.   (2.) 5 or more Exhibits, 2 Prizes, 1/-, 6d.
    (3.) 3 or more Exhibits, 1 Prize, 1/-.

8. The articles in Classes in which there are less than three Exhibits will be grouped together by the Judges and prizes awarded on the same scale.

9. Any article offered for sale must have the price marked on it

The Exhibition will be open to the public from 2 to 7 o'clock. Admission till 5 o'clock, 6d. Afterwards, 3d. Exhibitors Free.

The prizes will be given away at half-past 5 o'clock.

Drawing, Map, and Writing Copybooks may be purchased from the Exhibition Secretary.

INDUSTRIAL EXHIBITION.

I. Division.—Needlework.
Over 14 years of age.

Class A. Making a *man's shirt*, or *lady's nightdress.*
Class B. Making a child's frock in calico, coloured shirting, or print.
Class C. Small boy's cloth suit.
Class D. Patching trousers or coat (patch to be at least four inches square).
Class E. Making a quilt.

Under 14 years of age.

Class F. Nightdress with frill, a baby's robe, or child's fancy pinafore.

Under 10 years of age.

Class G. Child's pinafore or flannel petticoat.

Under 7 years of age.

Class H. Any simple garment such as a child's pinafore, plain chemise, etc.

II. Division.—Knitting and Darning.
Over 14 years of age.

Class A. Knitting a pair of stockings, socks, or gloves.
Class B. Knitting a shawl, or petticoat.
Class C. Knitting a hearthrug.
Class D. Best specimen of darning (piece to be at least 1½ inches square.

Under 14 years of age.

Class E. Knitting a pair of stockings, or socks.
Class F. Knitting a scarf, or pair of cuffs.

III. Division.—Cooking.

Class A. A pudding (rice, sago, tapioca, or bread).
Class B. A plain loaf.
Class C. Half-quartern family cake (cost of ingredients to be stated).
Class D. Quart of clear soup made from vegetables only.
Class E. A Temperance drink.

IV. Division.—Washing and Ironing.

Class A. Man's shirt, baby's robe, or baby's fancy frock.
Class B. Two collars, or a pair of cuffs.

V. Division.—Penmanship and Drawing.

Class A. Illuminated text from Bible (design to be original).
Class B. Pencil drawing from nature.
Class C. Full drawing copybook.

Class I. Full map copybook.
Class J. Full writing copybook.

Age and other special circumstances will be taken into consideraton in awarding the prizes in these Classes.

VI. Division.—Composition.

Class A. Essay on reasons for total abstinence.
Class B. Essay on evening employment of working men.
Class C. Letter descriptive of any real or imaginary expedition, or outing.

VII. Division.—Handiwork.
Over 14 years of age.

Class A. Any useful article made of wood, sawing horse, seat for garden, stand for flower pots, short ladder, hen-coop, or similar articles.
Class B. Straw mat, beehive, or basket.
Class C. Bookcase, picture frame, or birdcage. netting
Class D. Model of any kind, specimen of wood carving, or child's waggon.

Under 14 years of age.

Class E. Specimen of carpentering (sons of carpenters not to compete).
Class F. Scrap-book filled with pictures.
Class G. Pincushion.

VIII. Division.—Gardening.

Class A. Three window plants (must have been in possession of exhibitor since Christmas, 1883).
Class B. Specimen plant (as above).
Class C. Collection of cut flowers (cultivated).
Class D. Collection of cut flowers (wild)

IX. Division.—Artizan's Work.

Artizans are cordially invited to prepare some specimen of their handicraft for exhibition only.

X. Division.

Any article which cannot be classified in any of the above divisions will be thankfully received for exhibition only.

XI. Division.—Patching by Men or Boys.

Sir H. W. Dashwood, Bart., desires to offer Special prizes for the best patch (at least four inches square) on coat, waistcoat, or trousers :

Class A. Boys under 14—First prize, 1/6 ; Second do. 1/-
Class B. Boys over 14—First prize, 3/- ; Second do. 2/-

ARTHUR H. AUSTIN,
Exhibition Secretary.

DEW, PRINTER, POST OFFICE, HEYFORD.

Fig. 38. The Industrial exhibition, 1884.

in consequence' and on 14 July 'No afternoon school. Church of England Temperance Fete'). Sometimes the reasons for absence, either of a pupil or entire groups of children, were less happy: in November 1888, the Wilkes children had scarlatina, and the whole school was closed for two weeks, and in September of the following year, James Edgington was 'dangerously ill'. Unusual school activities were recorded as well: in July 1900, perhaps inspired by the Boer War, the boys had their first lesson in military drill, and in 1942 half a ton of conkers were collected and sold.

Soon after the introduction of the log book, we are fortunate in gaining the insights of another source – the diary of the Reverend James Deane, kept between 1890 and 1894. His descriptions of events are often enlivened by his personal reactions, perhaps the most frequent concerning the less well-behaved village boys who sometimes caused havoc during a magic lantern show, or during a meeting of the newly-formed Church of England Temperance Society. One of the highlights of the school year was the 'Tea Treat' usually held at the 'Big House'. On 14 August 1890, for instance, the children 'marched up to the Park at 3. It was fine weather until tea at 4 p.m., which was set out in a large tent, and shared with the Mothers, who had just finished their meeting ... After tea it started to rain, but there were races and games of "tug-of-war" in the tent'. Then everyone was mustered for the prize-giving. There were rewards for good conduct, the 'Diocesan prize', and perhaps most valued, awards for good attendance, when fortunate children who had never been late or absent during a whole year received a school medal. Those special few who could claim five years' perfect attendance had an engraved silver watch, a prize for the child to treasure for ever.

Another less happy event of the school year, which was greeted with dread by staff and pupils, was the inspector's visit. The annual grant depended in part on how well the children performed in a basic test. When the inspector called on 27 June 1894, he found the total number of children included:

    50 boys over the age of seven
    24 boys under the age of seven
    62 girls over the age of seven
    20 girls under the age of seven.

The average attendance figure was 121, and the average age of the first class was 11 to 12 years old.

'The children in each class showed a great interest and intelligence in their work' the Inspector reported. The religious side of the school also met with his approval. He concluded that the school was in 'a very fair state of efficiency' although 'reading was rather a weak subject', and order and discipline had been well maintained.

Until the village institute hall was built in 1922, the school was used for lectures, dances, the lamb ale feast, parish council meetings, and as a temporary church during rebuilding work on St Mary's. Once a year the school concerts were held: on 18 January 1911, the programme included duets by A. Lamborne and W. Norridge – 'Fall in and follow me' – and 'What are the wild waves saying', which was rendered by Miss Millie Kirtland and Miss Adam. There were also piano duets, and a humorous solo by Mr. Enser – but the most popular item was the lively 'Hunting Song', performed by six schoolgirls trained by Mr. Austin himself.

In those days the infants found it a long day at school, as they stayed until 3.30, but the three to four year olds were allowed to rest in the afternoon, when the desk tops

Oxford Diocesan Inspection of Schools.

August 18 1909.

DEAR SIR,—I forward you herewith a copy of the Report I have made of my Inspection of your School. I am to ask you to consider it as confidential to the Managers and the Head Teacher.

I am, dear Sir,
Your faithful Servant,

CATHREW FISHER,
General Diocesan Inspector of Schools.

SCHOOL *Kirtlington.*

EXAMINED *July 7 1909*

SUMMARY MARK *T. S.*

REPORT.

This school is doing effective work on good lines; I think there is a little danger in the lower classes of the children depending too much on ~~their~~ answers committed to memory. I was particularly impressed with the singing which was most beautifully careful and reverent. The written work was above the average.

Bishop's Prize:-- Ivy Pratt.

Certificates:-- Frances East,Florrie Stockford,Ethel Walker,Arthur Keys.

Commended:-- J Brackley,E Coats,Cissie Warland,Percy East,R Woodley.

Daisy Bell,Lilie Tyrell,C Giles,A Allam,H William.

Mollie Gilbert,R Simmonds,F Herbert,O Pratt,L Collett,G Loft

NOTE—If you should see fit to enter this Report in the Log-Book, it may be useful for future reference. The ordinary Summary Marks are "Thoroughly Satisfactory" (T S), "Satisfactory" (S), and "Hardly Satisfactory" (H S). "Excellent" (E) may also be given to Schools of exceptional merit, either in the results attained or the conquest of special difficulties. "Unsatisfactory" (U) may also be marked if necessary. Summary Marks are included only in the Reports of the General Inspector.

Fig. 39. The Diocesan inspection, 1909.

were shut down and they 'slept' for a while with their heads on their folded arms. Even the youngest pupils, however, were not excused from observing the 'Good Rules of Health':

> Be polite when speaking – always begin and end with the word 'please'.
> When meeting your schoolmaster or mistress, always raise your cap as a mark of respect.
> When walking along the footpath or road, step aside for people older than yourself.
> Cleanliness is next to godliness. To be clean all over from head to foot is the best rule for health.
> Always speak the truth. Truth is brave, lying is cowardly.
> A liar is never believed – even when he is speaking the truth.

Although even in the 1920s, some children left school to start work at fourteen, like Ernie King, who joined the Oxford Portland Cement Company at Washford Pits Quarry, a number of others did manage to continue their education at various local schools, at Bicester, Oxford or Woodstock, and special school funds were available to help them with the cost of uniform and travel. Amongst those who benefited were Vera Norridge, William Walker, Polly Bunker, Jack East, Ernest Siggers and Olive and Joseph Pratt.

Perhaps the biggest upheaval in the school's history took place during the Second World War, when evacuees poured into the village. Fifty-nine children from West Ham set up a separate school with their own teachers in the village institute hall.

In 1956, Mr. George Ward retired after 37 years as headmaster, and was replaced by Mr. Porter. In 1959 the wonderful Mrs. Bunker, who was then 83 years old, finally left 'her children' after sixty years as a teacher in the same school, surely a record. She was noted for her ability to spot potentially bright scholars after teaching them for as little as a month. Although a disciplinarian, she had understanding and a sense of humour. One little boy decided after his first two days of school that he didn't want to go any more. Much to his surprise, one morning who should appear on his doorstep but Miss Fruin (as she was then) and the whole of the infant class, come to take him to school!

In 1962 Mr. Porter was replaced by Mr. Ashley, who arrived at the start of a period of change for Kirtlington School. The old school was demolished and the new one had, besides better facilities indoors, a larger playground. In 1972 this was expanded still further to include Pond Spinney, formerly the property of the Budgett family and out of bounds to the children.

The opening ceremony of the new school took place on 18 November 1966 and was conducted by the Bishop of Oxford, the Right Reverend H. J. Carpenter, M.A., D.D.

The present headmaster is Mr. David Mankelow. His pupils are very active in village life and take a bright, intelligent interest in everything around them, as the many essays, articles and poems they contribute to the *Village News* clearly demonstrate. Their current project will be of great value to pupils in the 21st century, as they are preparing their own version of the history of Kirtlington, and the school's part in it.

CHAPTER SEVENTEEN

The Days We Remember

Victor and May Tugwood

The historic village of Middleton Stoney is not far from Kirtlington. In the early 1900s the earl of Jersey was lord of the manor, and, like most 'model' estates in those days, there were a number of farm cottages included for the staff. One of these was occupied by Henry and Adelaide Tugwood, with their son Victor. He left school at 14, and his first job was as a poultry-plucker for Lady Jersey – 'she was a very good boss'. However, when the earl found he needed to take up the land occupied by chicken houses to provide extra stabling for his racehorses, Victor found himself without a job, at the age of seventeen.

Fortunately he was tall and strong for his age, and was soon able to find employment with a firm of Oxford builders working on the site for the Pressed Steel Company, as a bricklayer at 34s a week. Victor did not only find employment in Oxford, but also a bride – a pretty young girl called May, who was working as a parlourmaid for a deacon. They married in 1929, but unfortunately the 1920s and 1930s were years of slump and depression. Once again, Victor was unemployed. At the suggestion of friends in Kirtlington, Victor found work at Washford Pits quarry, then manufacturing roadstone grit. The family settled down in the village, with a comfortable house next to the school, which was to prove handy for their three children, Edna, Joy and Gerald. When work was over, Victor had plenty of hobbies, like playing cricket for the village team, following the Bicester Hunt, and enjoying the Brass Band concerts at Bletchingdon.

However, when it was decided to close down the roadstone grit manufacturing plant, Victor found himself out of a job yet again. Bill Scarrott, Mr. Hubert Budgett's gardener at the 'Big House', suggested that 'you come up here for six weeks – there's a vacancy'. This 'vacancy' led to 38 years of employment on Kirtlington Estate.

Apart from gardening, there was always work at the estate timber yard, and in 1933, a long-term project of planting and tree-felling was begun by the Forestry Commission, which led to Victor working in the forest and woodland with his old friend Bert Collett.

During the Second World War Victor served as a member of the Home Guard, and remembers seeing, from his vantage point on the roof of the 'Big House', the distant skies of London and Coventry lit up during heavy bombing raids. The war brought Land Army girls to work at Kirtlington. 'They were a grand lot of young women, and used to come down from their hostel at Chesterton and work in "gangs" of six, helping with the dairy-work, harvesting, and ploughing up extra land for growing food'.

Victor will never forget Jolly, the half-bred bay hunter, who used to draw the feed trolley for the sheep and cattle. He noticed that the horse would often slow down,

and when he leant down to see if anything
was blocking the cartwheels – there would be
a crouching rabbit, unaware that Victor had
the tine poised and ready to provide a
favourite meal. Although Jolly may have
been a natural poacher, he was not always a
very reliable ride. Any daredevil who fancied
their skills riding him bareback with a rope
rein and a headcollar would soon be carted
off at a cracking pace, particularly if he heard
the hunting horn!

Fig. 40.   Rabbit.

The Tugwood family had by now moved to
one of the park lodges at South End. With
free milk, no rent, and wages even during sickness, Mr. and Mrs. Budgett's
employees were well-treated. Another animal 'pal' who became a great favourite with
Victor was the black labrador/spaniel Towzer, given to his daughter Edna by Mrs.
Budgett as a puppy. He was a lively, intelligent dog who could gently retrieve any
bird, dead or alive. The only thing he could not pick up safely without breaking was
an egg! But even a perfect dog can have his faults: May Tugwood 'will never forget
the times he used to bring in a hedgehog, and I had to give him a good scrub down in
the bath to get rid of the fleas and lice'.

Victor Tugwood is a clever molecatcher, and his services are still in demand.

> Parson come to me the other day – 'Victor' he said, 'can you set a trap, I've got some moles on
> my lawn', so off I went. When I goes back a couple of days later to see if anything has been caught
> – there's no sign of the trap, so I takes a look around and finds it stuck in the hedge – it could
> have been a fox tried to take it. Now, another favourite spot for moles would be a field of kale –
> it was a sure sign they were there when you saw a lot of blackbirds flying around. We got 25 one
> morning before nine o' clock. Moles will always make a run towards water – if you put your foot
> down just behind the hill, the mole can't run back, and you'll be sure to catch them, as they breaks
> through the earth in front of you.

On several occasions, Victor has had strange encounters with animals who seemed
to embody the spirits of the recently dead. Shortly after his mother's death, a hen
blackbird flew right in through the open window, making herself quite at home. The
cat, who normally attacked any bird, took no notice at all. 'I reckon that's mother
come back to see us' they all agreed. On another occasion, the Bicester Hunt was
meeting in the village, and a young hound detached himself to sit at Victor's feet and
make a fuss of him. The huntsman remarked that he must be 'someone who knows
you', and was not in the least surprised to hear that Victor's father had just died.

Perhaps Victor's most unforgettable experience was one which resulted from an
accident, when he had a bad fall from a ladder whilst picking apples. For over a
month he lay in a coma, with May and his family keeping a constant vigil by his
bedside.

> I was floating, disembodied, in a borderline between life and death. There was this beautiful vivid
> green landscape, much brighter than anything I had ever seen at home. People were moving
> about, but I didn't recognise any of them. There was a wonderful feeling of peace, but I knew there
> was a vital decision soon to be made – I seemed to be approaching two paths – if I moved in one
> direction, I would live, if I went the other way, I would die.

To the joy of his family, he was guided along the right path, and made a good recovery. Victor Tugwood is a straightforward man, but it is plain that this experience has added a new dimension to his view of life.

Jack Talbot and the Reliance Dance Band

Jack and his brother Alf (often known as 'Turp') were the sons of Edwell Walter Talbot and his wife Florence. They were born in the village of Chilton, near Harwell, where their father was employed as a shepherd and their home was a cottage with a large barn attached. In the 1920s Walter Talbot came to work on the Kirtlington Park Estate, and he and his family moved to a thatched cottage opposite the gates of Park Farm.

Pocket money had to be earned in those days, by taking 'Lady', the Park Farm pony, to be shoed at the forge; or, when he was older, by helping his father with the flock. Some of this money went on his favourite pastime. On a Saturday afternoon, he would ride the ten miles into Oxford, and catch the first three-hour programme at the *Electra Palace*. When he came out, it was time for the second show at the *Scala*! The local fairs were another attraction: on one occasion he went to Chipping Norton Carnival with a friend, who tried in vain to win himself a coconut to take home. In despair, he suggested that Jack have a go with the remaining two balls of the 'four-for-a-penny' he had paid for, and with the second of these Jack was successful. A lady who had watched his performance asked him to throw a ball for her:

> I was ten years old at the time, and had no fear of failure, so I threw it and down went the coconut. The lady was so delighted she opened her purse and gave me sixpence. At the moment I felt not only rich, but a great sense of achievement. It may have been only a child's simple moment of happiness, but I have never been able to recapture it in later life!

Like many youngsters, he was fond of music, and longed for his own wireless set. To buy one new was far beyond his means, so with the aid of instructions from a magazine, he made his own. This led to making 'Mit-met' crystal sets for his friends, and later on to the construction of valve sets. By now Jack had built up quite a local reputation as a wireless mechanic, and he was often asked for advice and help when a set went wrong. 'There goes the Radio Doctor!' said his family, when he set off with a black bag full of tools to tend to another ailing wireless.

After Jack invested his savings in a piano, which cost £10 including delivery, the next step was to buy a course of lessons – 'Naunton's National Music System'. Later he bought a better piano for £34 and returned his first one to the shop.

Whilst pursuing his musical interests, Jack had found work driving a lorry, and very much enjoyed actually passing other vehicles at 20 miles an hour.

His real passion remained music, however, and in company with other young musicians, he decided to start his own dance band. In 1928 the Reliance Dance Band made its first appearance, after hours of careful practice and rehearsal. Eric Terry was the drummer, Phil Fiddler at the piano, Ken Taylor played the violin and Bill Reason later joined as a trumpet player. Jack himself performed on a rather unusual instrument – a beautifully inlaid 'zither-banjo' which had been lent to him by the carter from Park Farm. He learnt the basic chords from playing a ukelele.

The band dressed as smartly as they could, usually in dark suits, and the immaculate white starched cuffs and shirt-fronts were well worth the 6d a time it cost to have them laundered. Within a short time they had plenty of bookings at nearby villages, as well as wedding and birthday parties, and sometimes at the Servants' Ball at the 'Big House'. The band and their friends travelled to their bookings in Bob Casey's 14-seater bus 'The Mascot', paying one shilling apiece. The dances usually started after eight, and the name of the next tune to be played was displayed in a slot at the top of the 'shield' which had an emblem of a lion on each side of the word 'Reliance'.

The band played the latest jazz tunes, but were also willing to play the old favourites, for the Veleta or Paul Jones. The evening's entertainment would probably finish with a waltz at about two in the morning. The band charged only £2 10s for their services for an evening, which sounds like excellent value for money. It is sad that no photograph of the band in action seems to have been taken.

With so much of his spare time taken up in this way, it is not surprising that Jack found little time for girls. One evening, however, his mother told him 'some young ladies are coming round to see us later on'. 'I'm not interested – I'm going out anyway' Jack said; but just at that moment the visitors arrived, and Jack saw Ellen Woodley. That evening he did not, after all, decide to go out, much to his mother's secret amusement! Ellen, who came from Middleton Stoney, was the daughter of a shepherd, Ernest Woodley, and his wife Lizzie. Ellen has vivid memories of their courtship:

> We used to get up very early on a summer morning – about four o' clock, and cycle down to the canal, where we would walk along the towpath to find the right spot to fish, near Pigeon's Lock. Very often the first of the narrow-boats would be gliding gently downstream, and someone would be playing a melodeon. Often the tune would be 'I know two bright eyes' – those days were so lovely.

It came as no surprise to anyone when the young couple eventually married.

Unfortunately, about this time the Reliance Dance Band dispersed, as members moved away for reasons of work or marriage, but Jack maintained his interest in music whenever time allowed. He and Ellen moved to Wantage, where their son David was born, but they liked to revisit Kirtlington and join in the annual Lamb Ale Festival.

One of Jack's absorbing interests since he retired and moved to Abingdon has been visiting traction engine rallies, often in the company of his old friend Ernie King, and he is now completing meticulous work on a model 'Marshall' steam engine.

The East Family of Troy Lane

One of the earliest mentions of this family occurs in the Kirtlington Surveyor's account book, which records that William East was one of the Surveyors of the Highway in the year 1799-1800. These unpaid parish officials were expected to survey the roads within the parish boundaries three times a year, and organise the six days of labour on road-repair which they and all their neighbours were supposed to give annually.

In 1849 William's son Charles married Luesa Ann Avenal, daughter of a Kirtlington blacksmith. It was soon after this that the family bakery business was established in premises at West View – close to the present post office and stores – and from 1854 onwards Charles East is recorded in various Oxfordshire directories as a 'baker and carrier'. In his latter capacity, he called at the *Star and Garter*, Oxford, twice a week, and delivered bread as far away as Bicester, Shipton-on-Cherwell and Banbury.

Business was good, and Charles East decided to have a new house and bakery built on the corner of Troy Lane, opposite the *Oxford Arms*. The well-known Oxford firm of W. Lucy & Co., whose Eagle Ironworks still overlooks the canal in Jericho, supplied the large ovens, over 12 feet long. These would have to be lit at four each morning, in readiness for the first batch of bread and cakes to go in at six.

In the early days, the fuel was usually faggots, but in later years a special type of 'baker's nuts' was used. The room above the bakery held the stocks of flour, which came down in a shute to the waiting bins. The warmth from the ovens reached the top floor of the house, where one of the rooms was regularly used for drying the family wash!

Fig. 41. Detail from the smock of Charles East, master baker.

As late as the 1900s a smock frock was still a practical working garment, and it is fortunate that the beautifully-embroidered one used by Charles East is still preserved in the County Museum at Woodstock. The heavy linen or homespun fabric had an individually-designed smocking pattern, often with symbols of the owner's occupation; in the case of Charles East, however, there was a crown with the letters 'V.R.', no doubt in celebration of Queen Victoria's Jubilee. The usual form of headgear worn with a smock was a black top-hat, a billycock, bowler, or sometimes a soft round felt hat with a narrow brim.

In 1869 Charles East bought a pub in Troy Lane, the *George and Dragon*, formerly owned by George Cole. So began the family's involvement in the licensed trade. Between 1887 and 1895, Charles's son Walter was the landlord, but he later moved to the *Oxford Arms* with his wife and 11 of their 13 children. Charles and Walter brewed their own beer, which was stored in the cellars at the Red House. These old days have been vividly recalled by Albert East, who still lives in the house with his sister Frances. In 1948 the ovens were extinguished for the last time and this chapter in the family's history came to an end. Albert describes some of the secrets of the family's success:

You can't make a good loaf with English flour, it's all right for biscuits. What you need is a special flour like Ranks or Spillers mixed, and if you added a bushel of sieved potatoes, this would make a good keeping loaf.

In 1942 the firm received a diploma from the Ministry of Food in their National Bread Competition. During those war years, Albert would set out with a vanload of bread and cakes, but before he had gone far he would be stopped by English and American servicemen who bought up large quantities on the spot, which meant returning home to light the ovens and bake a fresh batch.

Frances East remembers the cottage loaves they baked, which were very popular, and rounds of scones at five for sixpence. Their sister Jessie used to make the dough cakes sold at 1s 3d, but when it came to hot cross buns for Easter, the whole family had to work through the night to satisfy the demand.

In their father's and grandfather's day, the horse-drawn carriers' cart served them well, and carried passengers, baggage, and even loads of hay and roadstone as well as bread. The driver was sheltered from rain by a large cart umbrella with a cane handle which fitted into a special socket by the driving seat. Eventually, however, horse-power had to give way to mechanisation, and Teddy, the fine chestnut cob, was replaced by a Model-T Ford van, the first in the village, in 1920. Like its horse-drawn predecessor, the van earnt its keep in many ways apart from carrying bread; it even carried coffins for John Bunker, the village wheelwright and coffinmaker. On happier occasions, it took the village cricket and football teams on outings.

Walter East's family of 13 was talented and hard-working. Albert, who is now approaching his 91st year, started off as a farmer's apprentice under Mr. Johnnie Hayens at Buckness. He worked with horses, sheep and cattle. He was an excellent rider, and on one occasion was able to show the clergyman's son who had failed to master a spirited chestnut horse, how to assert himself and improve his horsemanship. Two other animals must not be forgotten in any account of the Easts: Bimmy the golden cocker spaniel, who one day picked a sitting partridge off her nest, and replaced her on instruction – apparently without harm to hen or chicks; and Anson, a King Charles spaniel, given to them by Lady Astor when she was lady of the manor at Bletchingdon Park.

Albert's brothers Percy, Aubrey, Charles and Robert all served in the First World War. Jack worked for 30 years at Smith's gravel pits, Bletchingdon, eventually becoming a foreman, while Charles, when he left the army, became apprenticed to a tailor at Middleton Stoney who specialised in hunt uniforms. Jessie, the eldest daughter, won prizes for her cheese and buttermaking, and also ran the house, as well as helping make bread and cakes. Louie became a nurse, and Ethel and Dollie got married.

Since the early 1900s the family had added dairy farming to their other interests, specialising in a fine herd of pedigree Guernsey animals. They usually had between 18 and 20 cows. Walter had 19 acres of good grazing land at Mill Ground, and he was helped by his son Algernon, who did all the milking. For many years Algernon was a familiar sight driving his herd through the village, but increasing traffic in the 1950s eventually made this impossible.

Albert and Frances will always remember the hard work and the happy times in their lives, but it looks as though other Kirtlington villagers haven't forgotten them either. 'Why, it was only the other day that some of the older villagers came up and asked when we were going to start up the bakery again, as they missed our lovely bread', said Frances thoughtfully!

Postscript: history from a bread book

When Charles East founded his bakery business in 1850, he began to keep meticulous records of all his sales in his huge 'bread book', which is still in the possession of his family. With the aid of the information from the 1851 census, we can identify many of his clients. Amongst the first entries we find:

Sept.16 J. GODDEN: cask of beer, 9d.

Joseph Godden, a farm bailiff, was probably buying this for the Harvest Home celebrations.

Oct.18 HENRY HAWTING: 2 Quartern Loaves, 11d.

Henry Hawting was an 80-year-old 'Road Contractor', living with his elderly wife Sarah and their son and grandson, and was probably the brother or cousin of Anthony Hawting, the retired village wheelwright.

Oct.18 JOHN KIRTLAND: 4 Quartern Loaves. 1s 10d.

John Kirtland, the 44-year-old village blacksmith, and his wife Harriet, who was 41 in 1850, had ten children. John was a good customer, who made payments usually once a quarter.

Oct.22 HENRY TRAFFORD: 6 Loaves.

He was 39 years old, and a grocer, born in Kirtlington.

Three other regular customers in this first year were Mr. Scarsbrook, no doubt the saddler James Scarsbrook, whose family name first appeared in the parish register in 1726; George Wakefield, one of the village shoemakers, who had five children by his wife Ann, and two lodgers (John Morris, a journeyman-shoemaker and an apprentice, William Busby); and Mr. James Guillemard, the 43-year-old vicar, who had a young wife, Louisa, and four children. They had a large staff, consisting of a groom, two nurses, a cook and a housemaid. Mr. Turton, the curate, also bought his bread from the Easts and on one occasion also bought 18 pounds of 'plumbs' – perhaps he liked plum jam! The cost of half a loaf for communion was twopence-halfpenny.

In 1851 other customers appear: John Jessett, who was a branch secretary for the National Agricultural Labourers' Union in its early days; John Bunker, local wheelwright and undertaker, whose son later married Nellie Fruin, Kirtlington School's longest-serving teacher; and William Walton, who was the village hurdle-maker, and lived with his wife and four sons. Charles East, as we have seen, was willing to do shopping for his neighbours during his trips to Oxford and other towns, and in 1852 we find him buying nails, planks and piping on behalf of Edward Herbert, a carpenter, whose descendants still live in Kirtlington.

Charles East seems to have done his best to help customers who got into financial difficulties. One farm labourer, who was East's tenants in one of the cottages he owned at South Green, was allowed to owe rent for 45 weeks, and was also still supplied with bread and dough. Other customers could pay off a small amount each week, and carry the debt over. If circumstances were really bad, Mr. East lent them

Fig. 42. The village shoemaker.

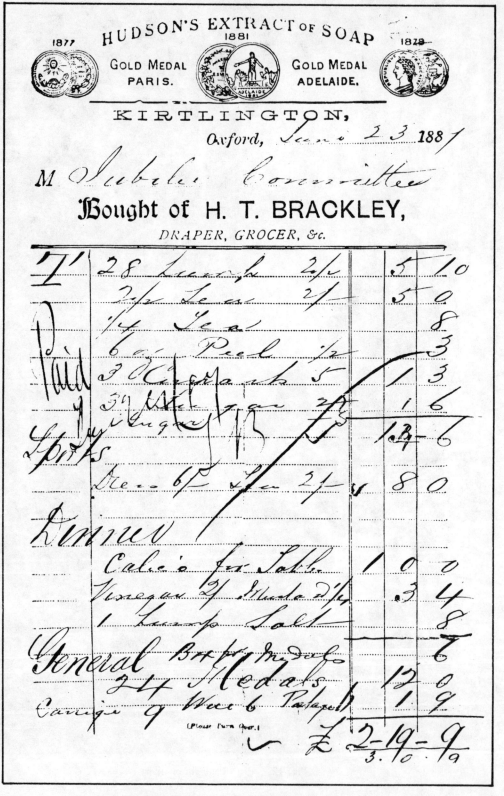

Fig. 43. An account from Brackley's stores, 1887.

small sums – anything from twopence to three shillings at a time – which in most cases were probably never repaid.

It is this sort of information which makes the 'Bread Book' a unique document, central to any study of the village in the middle of the last century. Both as a baker and as a carrier Charles East and his family made great contributions to the life of the community in which they lived. There is probably nothing which has quite taken their place today.

Bill Johnson: carter, pigman, hedger and ditcher

'I left school before I was thirteen, and used to dodge about helping Father on the farm – getting 2d for chopping faggots sometimes, but I could earn a bit more on hunting days, when I got sixpence for opening a gate!' Bill Johnson has mastered many other skills since those early days in the Oxfordshire village of Swerford, which lies between Bloxham and Chipping Norton.

His father, grandfather and great-grandfather were all farmworkers, used to ploughing, tending sheep and all the other jobs which crop up in the farming year. It wasn't long before Bill got his first regular job, helping a widow and her son with their farm. He looked after three horses and did the ploughing for 3s 6d a week. His employer was kind to him, making sure he had his tea before going home, and putting an extra piece of cake in his pocket for supper. When he had been there a few months, Bill was given a rise. He hurried home to tell his mother, and hoping that she would say he could keep it for pocket money, he held out his hand with the extra sixpence. 'Well, put it in the tin then, I'll get some clothes for Christmas for you,' said his mother briskly, getting on with the preparations for supper.

But life wasn't all work for Bill. One day when he was 18, he and some other lads were talking to a group of girls in the village street on their way home. It was then that he made a bold decision which changed his life. Leaning on his bike, he issued a challenge to the surprised young women:

'Now – which of you is going to walk home to Brackley with me?'

He waited, grinning mischievously, until the girls had finished their nudging and giggling, and one of them stepped shyly forwards. It was 16-year-old Ada Hawtin, who became his wife two years later. Ada was one of 13 children, and not only was she slim and pretty, she was also hard-working and a good cook. She had been in service and thought nothing of coming home at weekends to prepare two large roly-poly puddings.

In the early days of their marriage, the only outings were on their bicycles at the weekend, with the baby in a basket carrier, although sometimes Bill's employer at Steen Farm would allow them to borrow Daisy the pony and the tub cart and drive into Chipping Norton to do their shopping. In the late 1920s Bill and his family moved to Kirtlington, where he had found work with Mr. Henry Viner at Foxtownsend Farm in the Heyford Road. 'He was a good boss, full of useful sayings,' Bill recalls. 'One of them was "always look as far ahead as a waggon rope" '. Foxtownsend was quite a large mixed farm, with good sheep pasture and arable land, and plenty of work for the horses, one of whom Bill will always remember. This was Tucker, a black gelding of strong character and definite likes and dislikes. If he was left standing with a loaded cart while his driver went for lunch, he would sit down in the shafts, and it would be a difficult job to get him back up again without

Fig. 44. Off to market.

unharnessing him: but the funny thing was that he would never do it with an empty cart! On his way home Bill would water the horses at the pond which used to be in front of the *Granary and Barn* in the Heyford Road. This was eventually filled in and drained back to Foxtownsend well, and nothing can be seen of it today.

Ada and Bill now had three children (Mary, John and Jim) and had settled happily in Kirtlington, but Bill felt that much as he liked working for Mr. Viner there was little chance of promotion. He was glad therefore when a vacancy came up at Park Farm, then owned by the Budgetts. The flourishing Kirtlington Park Estate offered plenty of chances for a young man to learn more skills. Bill's first job was to take care of the heavy horse teams. There was also young stock to school. Most of the breaking was done in the stableyard, with the horse wearing a collar, crupper and a straight bar bit. A man on each side held a plough line, and another walked at the horse's head. After a couple of years in harness work, they could be sold as useful six-year-olds.

Bill took a great pride in his animals, and looked after their every need. If he felt they needed conditioning, he would buy some powders from the chemist to mix into a warm bran mash with some treacle and carrots. To keep the dreaded 'grease' at bay, he would wash their feet and legs in a wooden tub with some disinfectant in it, and dry them off thoroughly afterwards. 'That's the trouble with Shires, all that leg feather. You don't get it so much with the Clydesdales – they are a nice sort of horse, but I think the best of all are the Suffolk Punch, they're clean-legged, and they pull well'. His dedication brought him rewards at the local ploughing matches held by local Young Farmers' Clubs and Bill came home many time with cards and prize-money for the 'best turned out horse'.

No doubt the dedication he gave to his animals was apparent in his working life as well. The horses were fed about five o'clock, and out in the fields by seven in the morning. In a double-plough three horses were needed, and they could work as much as an acre and a half in summer, or as little as half-an-acre in bad winter conditions. Not all horse-teams were equally easy to handle. 'Sometimes you would get youngsters who played up when they worked together, like the couple of greys Mr. Budgett had got from the market at Banbury. We used to split them up and hitch them to an older, steadier horse'. At nine-thirty there would be a lunch break, and they would finish work and be home by three in the afternoon. The horses were then rubbed down, watered and given hay, whilst the men went home for a meal. Back again at six, the horses were bedded down, fed and watered, and the men were finished for the day.

Change was inevitable, and became more rapid with the outbreak of the Second World War. Gradually the horses were sold off, and Bill took up tractor-driving. 'I shall never forget when I took my test: there was the examiner standing behind me on the machine. I had to turn left, then right, stop and start, circle round a bit, and then I was told I had passed!'

After the war Arthur Budgett became established as a racehorse trainer, and later when he moved to a new centre at Whatcombe, he used to bring yearlings down to Park Farm for running-out. Park Farm also housed a breeding-unit of between 80 and 90 sows. The Budgetts favoured Large Whites and used the long-bodied Landrace boars. Instead of horses, Bill became dedicated to pigs and the unit prospered. The animals were watched over like children, and Bill would sit up all night with a farrowing sow. He believed in good deep straw beds, a small light in the corner of the sty at night, and sows and pigs separated when not feeding, which minimised the risk of sows rolling on their piglets.

With so many pigs, extra housing was often needed, and Bill turned his hand to masonry and carpentry to convert old cowsheds. He was allowed to keep some pigs of his own, and one Christmas he had one weighing nearly 20 stone. 'It nearly broke the beam when we hung it up'.

In the late 1960s Bill reluctantly faced retirement, but that didn't mean he stopped working. There was still his large allotment in Crowcastle Lane, the vegetable patch in his garden and the 'delivery service' with a hand-barrow which he continued to maintain around the village. Sadly, Ada died after a period of illness shortly before their 60th wedding anniversary.

Bill is now 83 years old, lives alone, but is rarely lonely. His sense of humour and cheerful outlook make him a popular member of the Welcome Club, and good company for his children and grandchildren. He still manages to 'dodge about' and no doubt if the chance arose to 'tickle along' with a horse in harness, he wouldn't miss the opportunity!

Mrs. Edith Georgina Chandler: *former midwife of Kirtlington*

Edith Davies grew up in Walthamstow, London. Her father had been an expert French polisher and worked as a furniture restorer. They were a happy family – five girls and three boys – but life was not easy for them after Mr. Davies died. His widow was able to earn some money acting as an agent for their grandmother, who ran a secondhand clothes shop, and when the First World War broke out, there was work for her at home sewing bandoliers for the army. For a while Edith went to live with her grandparents who had a house near the canal at Hoxton, where her grandfather had a small business as a boot-and-shoe repairer.

When the time came for Edith to leave school, it was suggested that she might go into service, but her mother flatly refused, knowing as she did how much her daughter longed to become a nurse. This ambition, however, was not immediately realisable. By this time the family was living in Nottingham, and Edith found work at a greengrocer's shop. Her employer was well aware of her burning ambition, and one day told Mrs. Davies that he knew of 'a very nice lady' who wanted some help – and so Edith began a new job as nanny to the two young children of a Sunday School Superintendent. Much as Edith liked the family and enjoyed the work, it was still not really nursing.

In her spare time, she studied any medical books she could get hold of, but she knew the complicated diagrams and Latin words were beyond her understanding without expert help. It was obvious that she must pluck up the courage to approach the matron of a hospital, explain her situation, and ask if there was any chance of her being accepted for training. Perhaps her obvious determination to succeed despite her lack of money and a higher education made a good impression: she was able to persuade the matron of the Fever Hospital in Edmonton to give her four weeks' trial at the very bottom of the ladder as a ward maid.

With this experience in hand she was able to get further employment at the Home for Incurables in Leamington Spa, and later at a hospital in Birmingham. At last she was accepted for training in Hammersmith, and then went on to become a probationer at a Portsmouth hospital, but the strain of long hours of work and study took its toll, and illness forced her to take a month's convalescence at the Edith Cavell Rest Home. Her next post, when she was well enough, was at Wellingborough Infirmary as an assistant nurse, earning £30 a year.

In the years before the introduction of the National Health Service, there was an organisation called the Nursing Association, which arranged for the appointment of village nurses who were paid either through a subscription system, or at the time of treatment. In 1924 Kirtlington, together with Bletchingdon and Tackley, decided to avail itself of this system. Miss Annesley (daughter of Viscount Valentia) purchased a small house to be let at a reasonable rent to the new nurse and organised the subscription system. A nurse's visit cost a subscriber only fourpence – otherwise it was a shilling – and the cost of her attendance at a confinement was £1 10s. The successful applicant for the new post was none other than Miss Edith Georgina Davies, newly qualified nurse and midwife (registered number 59300 at the Central Midwives Board).

Her first task was to learn to ride a bicycle: she often had as many as 15 visits to make in a morning, with others in the evening as well. During one heavy flu epidemic, she was so exhausted that she fell off her bicycle on returning home.

Some of Edith's patients in Kirtlington were families from the narrow boats who worked the Oxford Canal, and moored near Pigeons Lock and the historic Flights Mill. The owner of Flights Mill had a son, who worked in the family timber business and was often to be seen in Mill Lane driving the two-horse waggon with its heavy load. His name was Aubrey Giles. It was not long before he began to pay attention to the new village nurse, and soon they were known to be courting.

After their marriage in 1927 the young couple managed to rent two rooms in Kidlington as their first home. Edith was very proud of all their new possessions and wedding presents, but most of all perhaps the beautiful Axminster carpet and their bed, which had cost far more than they could really afford. It was not long before it was Edith's turn to become a mother, but two rooms were not really enough for bringing up a family. In the hamlet of Northbrook were two cottages housing a farm labourer and his abundant family – Edith had delivered his 15th child. When they moved elsewhere Mr. Eeley, who owned the cottage, agreed to rent it to Aubrey and Edith.

The cottage was surrounded by elms – hence its name 'Elm View' – and Edith remembered having to push the babies to and fro from Kirtlington for shopping. She had an especially vivid recollection of the night Aubrey fell into the canal, complete with bicycle! When Aubrey's father died, his son's family were able to move into Flights Mill. It was a much bigger house to look after, and some of the rooms had cold stone floors, but there was much more space for their six children. (Edith, however, could boast with a twinkle in her eye 'I've had 300 babies, you know!' which may be a record for a midwife.)

The years passed full of activity and events and Edith and her husband were preparing to enjoy retirement together when their children were off their hands – but sadly Aubrey died in 1963. When a cottage at the south end of Kirtlington became vacant in 1965, Edith decided to move there and live on her own. Just a few doors away was the small Methodist Chapel which she sometimes attended. One lay preacher who particularly caught her attention was Albert Chandler, and one evening they fell into conversation. She invited him in for a cup of tea and this invitation led to seven happy years of marriage until Edith was widowed again in 1974.

During our conversation in 1982 I was struck by her expressive face, and by her warm smile. She will be remembered for many reasons by her family and friends, but not least for the self-discipline and courage, as well as personal charm, which were manifest throughout her life.

Mrs. Esmé Faulkner: tales of a remarkable grandmother

'I should love to have worked in the theatre, and in the best romantic tradition, to have been "discovered" whilst understudying for the leading lady who had been taken ill; but perhaps my mother was right, and I did like to show off a bit – like the episode of the green coat', Esmé says. Her mother Sybil had been given a green coat with a green and yellow patterned silk lining which she altered to fit Esmé. Unable to resist the temptation, the little girl unfastened the belt so that the coat swung open and displayed the lining. 'I saw you showing off', scolded her mother when she got home: and Esmé was roundly told off for vanity.

Esmé's theatrical ambitions were given some vent when she took part in the pageant written for the village by the then vicar, the Reverend Reginald Ward Bennett, a story woven around the dream of a man in an office pursued by 'fairy' and 'nightmare' characters. Rehearsals for the fairies, of whom Esmé was one, took place at the former vicarage, now known as Stonehaven.

> I shall never forget the joy of those occasions ... the beautiful garden with its neat lawns and well-stocked flower beds ... and the atmosphere as you stepped into the cool entrance hall, where you were met by a trim maid, with be-ribboned hat and starched apron setting off her neat uniform. The floor was beautifully polished, and gleaming silverware and fresh flowers were tastefully arranged on the elegant furniture – it was like going into a different world.

It is pleasant to record that the dainty colours of the costumes, the music, and the overall charm of the performance reduced Esmés father, Will, to tears when the pageant was performed.

There were other occasions when Esmé's acting skills were in demand. Sybil and Will Scarrott must have been very proud as they watched the eight-year-old star of 'The Water Babies' and 'Crying for the Moon', performed at the Kirtlington School Christmas Concert. She could also be relied upon to sing a duet with her friend Mildred Palmer if called upon. Their particular favourite was 'Red Sails in the Sunset'.

Esmé looks back with gratitude to her childhood with sister Enid and brother Arthur:

I don't remember ever feeling cold, hungry or miserable. We had a well-ordered life, with meals always on time. Our clothes were neat and tidy, and we had a warm and comfortable house [a cottage on the corner opposite the Manor House on South Green] to live in. On Sunday we were involved in Church activities for most of the day, with father bell-ringing, and the three of us at Sunday School. In the evening, we attended the service at St Mary's together.

After gaining a scholarship, Esmé went on the County School in Bicester. The list of uniform and equipment required seemed formidable, but the family managed to provide everything needed and Esmé thought it was wonderful to have so many new clothes all at once! Not only did she have new clothes, she also had a bicycle as part of her scholarship, which meant that she could cycle into Weston-on-the-Green to catch the bus to Bicester.

When the time came for her to leave school, it was settled that she should become an office clerk, but for her, as for many other young people, the outbreak of the Second World War in 1939 meant a change of plans, and she joined the Land Army. All the recruits in Kirtlington were put through a training course of about six weeks, including instruction on milking and dairy work. It is certain that Esmé had no idea that she would one day be living in a modern home on the site of the old milking parlour!

One member of Esmés family with a special place in her affections was her grandmother, Martha Scarrott, whose husband Jack was the estate's gamekeeper. 'The Soldier', as she was often called, was a familiar figure as she strode about Kirtlington or its neighbourhood on her errands of mercy to help a fellow villager in trouble. It was not unusual for her to spend the night with a dying person to give their relatives some rest, or to lend a hand with other nursing. She was also a leading light of the Mothers' Union and the Women's Institute, and a great organiser of wedding receptions, funerals, teas and dances. She also oversaw the preparation and serving of cricket team teas, at which Esmé would be called to hand round cups and plates. She loved to have her own grandchildren to tea, and encouraged them to eat as much as they wanted, whether of new bread or sticky fancy cakes.

During the war Granny Scarrott found time to do washing for R.A.F. officers stationed at Slade Farm Camp, become a champion flagseller for the British Legion, and look after a houseful of evacuees, while continuing her other 'duties' as before. When the mother of two evacuees died, she kept them with her until they were old enough to earn a living.

The wartime period saw her son Will promoted to head gardener at Kirtlington Park, and later to foreman at Park Farm. He had become farm manager by the time he retired at 65, and 'helped out' after that for another five years.

In 1948 Esmé got married, and went to live in a pretty cottage on South Green. When her first child was born, Granny Scarrott was there to help with the confinement, and to do the washing and ironing for her. This remarkable grandmother lived to the age of almost ninety-nine. It is certain that if she had reached her 100th birthday, she would have insisted on organising the whole affair herself!

Miss Edith Mary Viner

The Viner family lived at Foxtownsend, a three-storeyed 17th-century farmhouse in the Heyford Road. It is one of the oldest houses in the village, and had over 200 acres of land which included a sheepfold at Brian's Hovel nearby. Inside the house is a 16th-century staircase, thought to have come from the old manor of Northbrook. As early as the 12th century the farm appears in charters as 'Foxtoneshull', which could perhaps be interpreted as 'farm by a hill frequented by foxes'. The '-townsend' incorporated in the present name undoubtedly refers to the fact that the building faces the Town Green, which provided common grazing for the villagers' cattle and horses before the 1811 Enclosure Act.

Edith Mary was the daughter of Henry and Edith Viner, who also had a son, Bob. Their father, although stern when the occasion demanded it, was devoted to his children, and always thinking up little ways to give them treats and extra pocket-money. One of these arose from the fact that the Kirtlington football team played in Dairy Field, which belonged to the Viners. During each game, a player or supporter would go round collecting from the spectators towards the two-shilling hiring charge for the field – which was given later to Mary and Bob!

Mary was something of a 'tomboy' as a child, and her determination to join in the same sports as her brother and his friends could lead her into trouble, like skating on moonlit nights, and the time when she was climbing the drawbridge round Bletchingdon Lock and got her petticoat caught up. As usual, the boys ran off somewhere, and she was left to struggle free on her own. One of Mary's special friends was Peggy Broadbent, the stepdaughter of Major Dillon, who owned the cement works, and Peggy's governess often brought her over for tea. As soon as possible, the girls would escape from adult supervision and accompanied by Mr. Viner's fox-terrier, they would embark on great mouse-hunting expeditions in the barn or the hayrick. Even if she found herself in disgrace and banished to bed, she loved to look out of the window at the beautiful monkey-puzzle tree just outside, and to listen to the natural sounds of the countryside – the distant hoot of an owl, and the quick sharp bark of a dog fox.

Following a tradition which had probably remained unchanged for centuries, Mary, like a number of other young children, was given a special present of a lamb; if one happened to be born on 13 January, it was given to her, and Shepherd Pratt would make sure it had special handling and attention. He would feed it tit-bits, and very often taught it to pull a small wooden cart. When it was six months old, it was usually sold, and Mary would be given the money; she still treasures a handbag bought with the proceeds of the last of these sales.

While Mary would be cuddling her pretty lamb, her brother's sow was probably giving birth to piglets. One of these was born with only one ear, just smooth skin where the other should have been. In all other respects it was fine, and lived happily with the Edgington family, to whom Bob gave it.

Mary has vivid memories of food in her childhood, particularly on special occasions. On Whit Sunday, for instance, the Viners always had roast lamb, mint sauce, and a pudding of stewed gooseberries. The delicious wine which accompanied the food had been brewed by Mrs. Ted Kirtland, from potatoes and barley grown at Foxtownsend Farm. Mary also remembers the 1911 Coronation celebrations, which were held on South Green. Tables were spread with clean cloths, plates were piled high with an assortment of good things, and a crowd of expectant villagers sat waiting for Henry Viner to finish carving – but not all eyes were on him. An elderly lady who had come over from Northbrook hamlet for the occasion was furtively removing pieces of cheese from one of the plates, and stuffing them into the umbrella at her side. Unable to contain her amazement, Mary rushed up and told her father, who grinned and remarked 'That's all right my dear, let her get on with it, and good luck to her', and calmly resumed carving!

Mary's childhood had been a happy one, and provided a solid foundation for her adult life, which was also to have its highlights, such as the day when she successfully completed her teacher-training course, and her appointment to a post at a school in Bicester. Her brother Bob, meanwhile, decided to leave the village and study farming methods in South Africa for a while. Eventually, however, he returned to Kirtlington to farm. After he had retired, he used some of the land near Brian's Hovel sheepfold to build a bungalow, and this later led to the construction of further properties in a modern development called 'Akeman's Spinney'. In 1933 Mary herself invested £500 to buy her own house at the south end of Kirtlington. Its name – Gossway – is a derivation of the 15th-century name 'Goshay' or 'goose enclosure'. In 1953 her mother Edith died, sadly just a few years before the celebrations which took place to mark Henry Viner's 100th birthday: he was especially delighted with his congratulatory telegram from the Queen. 'It was a happy day for us all,' Mary remembers, 'but it was a great pity that he was within two months of his 101st birthday when he died'.

Looking back on the happiness of her childhood, Mary Viner recalls one of her father's favourite quotations, from Wordsworth, 'Heaven lies about us in our infancy', which sums up her feelings exactly. Mary Viner is a fortunate woman, with the rare gift of being able to find happiness not only in memories of the simple everyday events of her childhood, but in those of all the years which have passed since then.

The Kirtland Family: life and tradition at the forge

There was no doubt a forge in Kirtlington in the Middle Ages, when the blacksmith might be required to fashion a sword, as well as fit new shoes to a knight's horse. The 16th-century Kirtlington blacksmith John Hawle would have cared for the animals belonging to the Arden family, as well as those of farmer Thomas Woodward. John Bath, another 16th-century smith, had 13 children, and was succeeded by his son Richard. In the late 18th century the Enser family, beginning with James Enser, were involved in village life not only as blacksmiths, but as horse and cattle dealers. It was James's son Joseph who was first described as a 'farrier', in 1836.

In the early 19th century there were several blacksmiths in Kirtlington – Henry Kirby, Joseph Walker, and the Avenal family among them – but the family whose tenure of the forge lasted the longest was the Kirtlands. The family business was begun by John Kirtland and taken over by his son Edwin in the 1870s. His son Leslie took his father's place in the 1920s, but sadly, although Leslie's children Arthur and Marion still live in the old forge, it proved impossible to continue the business for a fourth generation. The Kirtlands still treasure the family's account books, however, and have many memories of the days when their quiet home was a bustling workplace.

The site was previously occupied by another building used as a forge, but the premises were rebuilt by the Dashwoods in 1878 and leased to Edwin Kirtland. The new building, however, faced east rather than south, which as Marion Kirtland says, would have been 'more comfortable for humans and horses'. The smith's shop has changed very little since the days of Edwin and Leslie Kirtland. The forge fire was made by Charles Grey of Stamford, who also supplied the wooden boxes of horseshoe nails which are still on the shelves. Arthur remembers having to blow the bellows for his father when he came home from school, and during weekends and holidays, and Marion recalls evenings spent holding a lantern or candle for Leslie when he worked at night. It was often nearly dark when carthorses were brought in for shoeing, straight off the ploughed fields.

With a large number of sheep in the area, clucket and canister bells were often needed, and scissors and shears were also made and maintained. The tail-docker lying discarded on a shelf is a reminder of more barbaric days; when the tail had been cut off with this implement, the stump was seared with a hot iron. The tail could also be 'nicked' to make it stand upright. Branding-irons were used on sheep or cattle. The farrier was traditionally supposed to have some medical knowledge. A child with a stye would be sent to the forge, where the farrier would tell them 'just wait a minute till we finish this shoe': by the time that was done the heat and the steam would have caused the stye to burst of its own accord, and a painless cure effected. The farrier could help in other ways too, like the time when 'Chummy' King's wife came round to Leslie with a ring that had become so tight that her finger was badly swollen and extremely painful. Slowly and carefully he was able to saw it through and she went home full of gratitude for his skill.

The forge was not only a popular rendezvous and centre for gossip, but also an excellent place to get advice on buying a horse. A farrier who had shod the neighbourhood's horses knew all about differences of temperament, and when he rasped a sharp-edged tooth, would note the animal's true age!

The forge account books give many interesting details about the village as a whole, as well as the business. When Edwin Kirtland first began to keep his accounts, in 1883, he was 31 years old, and employed one man, Jonathan Davis. The lord of the manor was then Sir Henry William Dashwood, and it is interesting to see the economy with which even the 'Big House' was run. Edwin was often called in to repair household objects – a watering can or a bucket – or to refurbish an old item, like the dog irons he altered in December 1885.

We can also see the many incidental tasks which a farrier was called on to perform, paring a cow's feet, or providing rings for the noses of 19 pigs. In 1884 and again in 1886 we find the note 'burning horse's mouth for Lampers'. 'Lampers' or 'lampas' is a swollen condition of the roof of the mouth, and young horses changing their incisor teeth can often suffer from it. Horse shoes came in many different shapes and sizes, some made for particular purposes, like 'bar' shoes, which were used if a horse had weak heels and was suffering from corns. The design of the shoe transferred the horse's weight to its frog. In 1885 Edwin fitted a carthorse with 'Charlier' shoes, where the shoe is sunk into the wall of the hoof, using small nails but no clip, so the frog has contact with the ground. When the icy weather came round, he would fit frost-nails to existing shoes to give horses a better grip on the slippery ground.

Entries in the forge account book during Leslie Kirtland's time were different, now that farms were becoming more mechanised, and there was less demand for a blacksmith's skills. There was still no piped water supply to the village in the 1930s, however, and most people relied on their own garden wells or the several village pumps. 'New leathers and bottoms' were still needed for their buckets. There were some pieces of machinery which Leslie felt competent to deal with, however, and he did a lot of work repairing bicycles in this period.

Leslie Kirtland had seven children, of whom six are still alive. His wife, who was Miss Annie Boddington before her marriage, came from Weston-on-the-Green, where her family ran a well-established wheelwright's business. Apart from his work at the forge, Leslie found time somehow to be a churchwarden and ring the tenor bell at St Mary's, to be school manager for a while and also get involved with the Whicker Charity, which gave small sums of money or supplies of coal to the poorer villagers at Christmas. He also enjoyed sport, playing cricket and leading the Kirtlington Football Team to victory in the 1911-12 season, when they won the Jersey Cup.

In 1928, however, a tragedy occurred: a horse-hoe share flew out of a vice as he was working on it, and he lost the sight of one eye. Worse was to come in 1934. He had been having a lot of pain in his leg, and when it was X-rayed it was discovered that constant taps and blows from the hammer, as it slipped off the shoes he was fitting, had damaged his knee-cap beyond repair. His leg had to be amputated. For a while, he was helped in the forge by three or four assistants; whilst he made the shoes, they fitted and nailed them on.

Soon after this the Kirtlands went into the dairy business, and the children helped with the twice-daily deliveries before and after school. When Marion left school, the dairy provided her with ready-made employment – 'There's nothing like good Guernsey milk in a sparkling clean bottle' she says – and deliveries became much easier for them when in 1953 they acquired their first motor van, a little green Ford.

In the spring of 1969 Leslie Kirtland died, and with him ended the Kirtland's long family tradition as village blacksmiths. There is a memorial to him in the church in the form of two wrought-iron candleholders. Although the Kirtlands continued to run their dairy until 1975, they ceased to do milk deliveries some years earlier. Today they are involved in the breeding of beef cattle, mainly Herefords, and these animals still enjoy the lush green grass of Sheep-Walk Field.

Frederick Blake: the gamekeeper and his place in Kirtlington's history

The lords of the manor through the centuries have always needed good keepers to protect their game, not only from the professional poacher, but from villagers who had fallen on hard times. Sometimes they may have been strangers to Kirtlington, like the navvies working on the Oxford Canal in the 1780s, or later the crew of a narrow boat.

The keeper was more than just a guard, however: in 1829 young Henry William Dashwood wrote home from Eton to ask his father to 'tell Guyatt that if he finds any Merlins, Cestrels, or Hobbys nests – to take a couple and keep for me'. The skills of falconry could be of great assistance to the hunter. The Hampshire-born William Guyatt had been appointed gamekeeper to Sir Henry Watkin Dashwood in 1804, and no doubt lived at 'The Bushes', which was the traditional home of the estate's keepers for many years.

The deterrents applied against poachers at this time were often extremely harsh by our standards, like the 18th-century man trap, and the spring gun which fired an iron bolt at an intruder's leg if the trip wire was moved. Offenders could be sentenced to hard labour, whipping, imprisonment or deportation, depending on the severity of their crime. However, the punishments issued by Bicester magistrate's court in the later 19th century were mild. Anthony Williams had to pay 16 shillings and 14 shillings costs when he was caught on Sir George Dashwood's land in 1850, and Lewis Taylor was fined eight shillings with 12 shillings costs in 1855. Some poaching offences were even dismissed, as the cost of bringing witnesses to court could be greater than the fine or the value of the poached bird or animal.

During the 1900s, there were informal pigeon shoots in Kirtlington, which took place usually on a Saturday between February and March, and provided many good pies for village families afterwards. On 12 May each year there was the great Rook Shoot, using .22 rifles and shotguns, which many considered a bit of a carnage. Despite this, a survey of rooks' nests carried out between 1928-32 by the Oxford Ornithological Society revealed that the nests in Kirtlington were 'well established'.

Very few details of the gamekeepers' private lives are known until 1932, when Frederick Blake from Berkshire was appointed as Mr. Hugh Budgett's gamekeeper. He had served in the R.A.S.C. during the First World War. His wife Edith was a gentle affectionate person, who was skilled in rearing young birds or egg hatching – but still not as dedicated as her husband, who would tuck the eggs inside his flannelette shirt to incubate if no broody hen was available.

Their daughter Winifred found work as a shop assistant in Oxford, and when she was at home was kept busy with errands for her father, like collecting a new springer puppy from Farmer Parrott. These dogs were never household pets, and were kept in their own kennels when they were not working. In 1935 Winifred acquired a new sweetheart, whom she was eventually to marry. Ernie King proved to be a valuable part-time assistant to his father-in-law, finding out which farmer could sell Frederick a broody hen, or having a day out at Cruft's Show to visit the trade stands and choose suitable products for use against the wily fox.

Frederick was really in his element during night work. He taught Ernie how to go long-netting for rabbits, and the way to handle a ferret properly, but it was Frederick's skill in whistling up a stoat from his hole which really impressed his young companion. One night the two men heard a distant gun shot. 'Fred went through those woods like a dog', Ernie recalled. 'He was as quick as a flash, and there was I, a younger man, stumbling and tripping along, hardly able to keep up with him as he moved so fast'. No evidence was found that night, but some time later the same suspect was caught red-handed in a nearby village.

Night-work could be dangerous, however: on one occasion Frederick was struck by lightning and thrown to the ground during a storm.

Victor Tugwood (see above) was more than once called in to search out sitting game-birds with his clever dog Towzer, and on one occasion he was asked to help Fred trap a badger. 'Don' leave 'un bite me – I 'avent got me gaiters on!' Fred pleaded anxiously. Sadly this partnership was brought to an end in 1939 when the outbreak of war meant a complete reorganisation of the estate, and the end of shooting parties. When Frederick and his wife moved to a house at Weston-on-the-Green, he turned his hand to breeding ferrets and rick-thatching for local farmers. After Edith's death, Frederick moved in with Ernie and Winifred.

Today 'The Bushes' is still occupied by a gamekeeper: Jim Churchill hails from Dorset. The modern poacher may be more sophisticated in his methods, but he still has a force to reckon with. Jim can proudly claim to have the combined skills of three generations of gamekeepers behind him!

CHAPTER EIGHTEEN

Ernie King: the Boy who had Room to Grow

Ernest James King was born in Kirtlington on 9 April 1911, the youngest of the six children of Thomas and Beatrice King. Although money was short, as for many village families, he remembers his childhood with pleasure. His elder brother Harry, 15 years his senior, made him something of a favourite, and gave him small treats, including his first puff of a cigarette – at the age of five! He also took him 'clap-netting' for sparrows, and rewarded him with sweets and pocket-money. As the youngest he was always been sent to run errands for his brothers, but some items were easier to find than others, like the pint of pigeon's milk he was asked to get from the dairy. When pocket money was short – as it usually was – Ernie and his friends looked about for a job to do to earn a few pence. Mr. Coates of the *Dashwood Arms* kept his cows down at Mill Ground, near the canal, and after they had been milked, Ernie would drive them back to their field, stopping by the grass verges in Mill Lane to let them graze, and for this he earned himself 6d a week. In the spring, bird scaring with a pair of wooden clappers could bring in the same amount, and later on, some more money could be earned by picking strawberries at 'The Nutlands' down at South End for Mr. Scarsbrook. Perhaps the least pleasant job Ernie undertook was roping bullocks for Stockfords the butcher's on North Green, in readiness for the pole-axe.

Like many other villagers, the Kings had a large allotment, in which the children were expected to lend a hand. Very often, Ernie needed a little persuasion to come and do his share, so Charlie or Joe would rush in to announce 'We've seen a blackbird's nest up there – come on!' and their younger brother would be off in a flash, only to discover when he reached the allotment that it was only a ruse. If he showed his disenchantment with gardening too clearly, his father would get hold of a brussel-sprout stalk, a weapon which could give quite a hard whack – if the intended victim could be caught.

Often his brothers found him too cheeky for their taste, and would gang together to duck him in the rainwater barrel, or tie him to a tree or lamp-post, leaving him to struggle free or wait for help. One day, however, Ernie saw a chance of revenge. Harry had come home to convalesce after being wounded in the First World War, and was confined to bed. He asked Ernie to give him his bed-pan, only to be told 'I will, if you give me sixpence!'

Some village boys were rather more of a handful than Ernie and his brothers, however, and sometimes the village policemen had to take a hand. 'There was a Mr. Adams, a Mr. Page and a Mr. Woodward' Ernie remembered. 'They appeared to keep themselves a bit aloof from the rest of the villagers, but they could usually control the more troublesome lads'. The 'bobby' also had to check that sheep dipping was carried out properly, issue summons to people riding bicycles without lights, and check that the public house closed at ten o' clock. There was more traffic than there had been, and the policemen had to try and stop children from playing freely in the roads, as they had been accustomed to do.

The village saw visitors from time to time, many of them vagrants like Old Dick and his wife, travelling to and fro from the various local workhouses, or the gypsy knife-grinder with his donkey and cart. One of the most distinguished visitors must have been Mr. Spencer Jones, the Astronomer Royal, who was a relation of Miss Jones, who ran the post office and general stores. He was instantly recognisable from his habit of walking down the village street gazing heavenwards, quite oblivious of what was happening around him.

No doubt Mr. Spencer Jones would have been interested in Ernie's experience when 'leazing' for wheat with his mother one day. The peace of the summer afternoon was suddenly disturbed as a freak wind or 'whirlygig' erupted, scattering wheat and hay stalks in all directions.

This sort of excitement, however, was extremely unusual. The red-letter days which the village children looked forward to were generally Club Days, special outings, or family weddings. Not many families could afford to have 'Sunday best' clothes, but they made do with everyday things well-brushed, like a clean dickey over a working shirt, or a spotless white pinafore for the girls. Many families looked forward to the familiar pleasures of a Sunday, with a roast lunch and all the household together at leisure. One of the girls, Emma or Eva, would take a pan of meat and Yorkshire pudding down to Wakefield's, just opposite the hollow tree on South Green, where for 2d a meal would be cooked and waiting for you by the time you came out of church. There were always villagers to be seen scurrying homewards with a succulent dish covered by a white cloth. On Sunday nights the bakers would pop a dish of fruit cake mixture into the ovens they were warming up for Monday. Ernie usually went to Sunday School or chapel. When the time came for him to be confirmed, the Reverend May asked him 'Are you earnest in being confirmed, as well as Ernest in name?' 'Oh yes, sir!' came the reply. No games were allowed on Sundays, and Ernie generally settled down with his *Boys Own Paper*, while older members of the family might leaf through *Reynolds News*, delivered on Saturday evenings; but there was a chance sometimes to sneak off to join his friends at Cuckoo Bank, with a cricket bat or stumps concealed down his trouser legs.

Christmas celebrations were simple, with beef for lunch, and no Christmas tree, but the children looked forward to stockings, which usually contained an apple, an orange, some sweets, a colouring book and some paints. However, there was one year when the contents of Ernie's stocking were a little different. When he had been in Oxford shopping with his mother, he had seen a brightly-painted tin lorry, but it cost 1s 11d, which was quite a lot of money. Although it meant scrimping and saving, and going without sweets for a while, Ernie was determined to have it. When he eventually had enough money, he asked his older sister Emma to buy it for him, and put it in his stocking!

Treats sometimes came unexpectedly, however, like the time when Ernie and his friends, travelling back from woodwork classes, which were held at Bletchingdon School, cadged a lift home from Carlo the fish and chip man. The van was stopped by a distinguished-looking stranger, who asked 'What are all those boys doing in your van, Carlo?' On hearing that they were Kirtlington boys on their way home, the stranger – who turned out to be Lord Valentia of Bletchingdon Park – bought them all a bag of chips!

Looking back on village life in the 1900s, it seems that every part of Kirtlington was known and enjoyed for specific reasons, like the secluded places where sweet chestnuts could be found after the first winter's frost; the best trees to climb for apple scrumping; and the favourite spots where blackbirds nested. 'I think all villages were a close-knit community in those days' Ernie reflected. 'Everyone seemed more willing to help than to push anyone down, and if you did not help each other, there was very little assistance from elsewhere. Everyone knew each other, and there were few secrets to be kept – even from the village policeman and schoolmaster! The parson, I think, played a bigger part in village life than he does today.'

There was another aspect of life then which Ernie didn't mention, but which comes through clearly from his reminiscences, as from those of his contemporaries. People were instilled with respect for a firm routine, and for discipline, both in the family and at school.

After Ernie had grown up and gone to work at the cement works (see Chapter 15 above), like all young men, he began to appreciate new pleasures. At the *Old Swan* inn in Bicester, a half-pint of beer was only twopence, and a hot potato cost a penny. At these prices, Ernie and his best friend Billie Warland could afford a good night out on a Friday or Saturday. 'We used to feel like millionaires as we cycled home' he recalled.

The key to freedom was the possession of a bicycle, even if it was a bit rickety and handed down from another member of the family. With Oxford only ten miles away, it was a common practice to cycle the mile or so to Bletchingdon, leave the bicycle at the station, and get in the 'Woolworth Flyer' which cost only 6d return after four in the afternoon, and this gave you plenty of time before the last train home at nine-thirty. According to Ernie, the city's attractions were not expensive. Admission to the ice rink, where he went occasionally to watch the skaters, was 3d, a 'floor ticket' 6d, and to hire skates cost a further 3d. Unfortunately the rink closed after the Second World War.

Kirtlington had its own 'Lamb Ale', and there were fairs at Bletchingdon and Tackley, but St Giles Fair at Oxford, held in September, was a great attraction. The first Oxford cinema had opened in 1911, the year of Ernie's birth, and it was usual for village outings to consist of a visit to the 'Electric' or the 'Scala', followed by tea, often at the cafe owned by Amos George, a Kirtlington-born former mayor of Oxford. During the last years of the First World War, and the early 1920s, dance styles changed rapidly: ragtime was suddenly all the rage. Gramophones and records became easily available. The Kings decided to hold a dance one Saturday night. The furniture was moved back, and a few records bought for the prized new gramophone. Emma and Eva and a couple of their friends had been practising their steps well beforehand, helped by Harry, who owned a mouth-organ and could play the latest hits for them. This was an evening which Ernie will always remember, watching the dancers doing the new fox-trot as well as the old favourites – the valeta, the waltz and the lancers. The records were to be played over and over again, sometimes attracting an audience of village lads, who would stand outside the cottage to hear the music – until the evening when Harry bribed Ernie with twopence to throw a bucket of water down on them from his bedroom window!

The gramophone was not confined to the parlour. On fine days, it was taken into the park, and the young couples would laze on the grass, listening to the music. In 1928, *Jackson's Oxford Journal* listed the current hits: *Serenade–* by Toselli; *Joshua*; *The Trail of the Tamarind Tree* by the Sunny South Dance Orchestra; *Who is Sylvia?*; and *Can't help loving dat man*. This exciting new music had been inspiring a young man from

Kirtlington to a new venture. Jack Talbot started the Reliance Dance Band in 1928, and it soon developed a great following in the area. Jack created many happy and romantic evenings with his well-rehearsed numbers and stylish presentation.

Meanwhile at the Oxford and Shipton Cement Company, Ernie had been promoted first to tester and then to gauger. It was responsible and exacting work, but he enjoyed it, and also appreciated the excellent sport and social facilities the firm provided. In spite of having to fit in with the three-shift system, there was always time for football and cricket matches, a weekend 'hop' or a country or morris-dancing session. It was at none of these, however, that Ernie and his future wife, Winifred Blake, the gamekeeper's pretty daughter, established their relationship, but during the Jubilee Celebrations of 1935 for King George V and Queen Mary. In 1939 they were married. The heavy demands which wartime made on the cement works and his Home Guard duties meant that Ernie was away for many long hours, and Winifred was left alone with their baby, Ivor. Always a skilled needlewoman – she had made her own white pinafore for school – she whiled away the time knitting and making clothes to save clothing coupons.

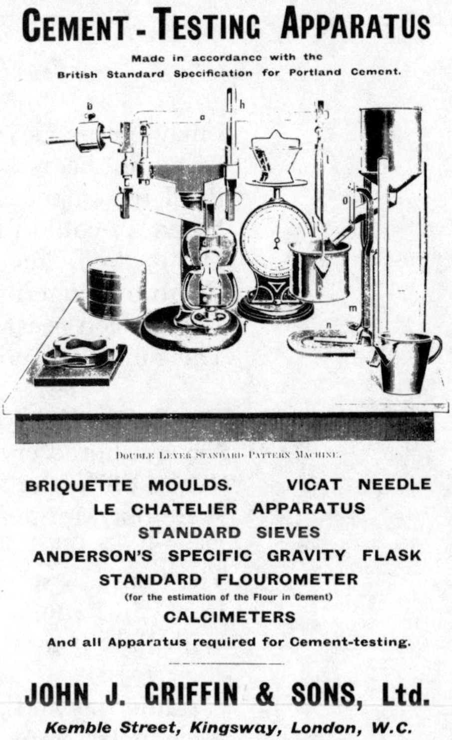

CEMENT-TESTING APPARATUS

Made in accordance with the
British Standard Specification for Portland Cement.

DOUBLE LEVER STANDARD PATTERN MACHINE.

BRIQUETTE MOULDS.   VICAT NEEDLE
LE CHATELIER APPARATUS
STANDARD SIEVES
ANDERSON'S SPECIFIC GRAVITY FLASK
STANDARD FLOUROMETER
(for the estimation of the Flour in Cement)
CALCIMETERS
And all Apparatus required for Cement-testing.

JOHN J. GRIFFIN & SONS, Ltd.
Kemble Street, Kingsway, London, W.C.

Fig. 45. Laboratory testing equipment.

The end of the war meant another turning-point in Ernie's career, when he was appointed foreman and assistant production manager, and in 1950 he was able to buy his first car, a Standard '8'. There was now more time for him to become involved with community life, with the parish council and the school board. There was also the annual Flower Show – in Ernie's view one of his most difficult jobs was to avoid hurting any exhibitor's feelings, even when it was common knowledge that some prize-winning entries had never been seen growing in their owner's gardens!

Although Ernie never abandoned all his boyhood hobbies and interests, there were some new ones to add. With a good camera, important village events could be recorded and re-lived through slide shows, and his tape recorder enabled the sound of the early birds at Washford Pits or Shipton to be heard at any time of day. With his deep love of the countryside, it was only natural that his interests should include village history and customs, and a wide range of folk music, whilst his friendship with several retired 'boat people' from the Oxford Canal gave him an insight into their special way of life. Even when they went on holiday, whilst Winnie looked forward to a day on the beach, Ernie usually found time to browse in bookshops, or on market stalls, and made plans to visit a nearby museum or traction engine rally.

During the 1960s the couple moved to a new home in Kidlington, and a few years later their son Ivor got married. With the arrival of the grandchildren – Ben and

Anna – there were always treats to be planned, but Winnie and Ernie noticed a sharp difference from their young days in the contents of a Christmas stocking!

* * *

Village Childhood Memories

I may not be as young as some,
I may not be as wise,
But I remember days of summer sun
When we could idly lie
Out in the fields of tall yellow corn,
Camp in hedgerows oh so green –
The dew on mushrooms in early morn,
The sunset so serene.

The days so long and free of care,
Never a bored cry was heard,
'We're off to the Mill' – 'Well don't wet yer 'air'
Were our Mother's parting words,
Over Back-field gate, through Pearsons fields,
The footpath so often trod,
Into Mill Lane, past quarry still,
With light hearts and a fishing rod.

A tiddler jar and a chocolate bar,
If y'r lucky, some lemonade –
Long-legged shorts, or gingham skirt,
Short socks and ribboned braid.
We never seemed to fear the stranger,
Our parents worried not –
Through village life we saw no danger,
The prowler was the fox.

The harvest time, flying chaff, red baler, rhythmic hum,
Old Stanley's shout – 'Get orf them bales –
Or else I'll tell yer Mum'.
We ran like 'ell when Charlie Bartlett
Chased us out of her barn –
But once over the fence we turned and yelled,
And then spun such a yarn.

Tall tales we told of doings brave,
To those who were not there –
Made them gape like battered ruins,
Until they said 'Oh yeh!'
'Tell us another' – 'Betcha didn't!' – 'oo cares any'ow' –
'Come on, let's go down second park –

Betcha can't ride a cow!'
Those days of easy pleasure,
Those days of peace of mind,
Are almost gone forever,
Only memories are left behind.

Angie Quartermaine

CHAPTER NINETEEN

'My Village' by the Children of Kirtlington

Although I have been extremely fortunate in obtaining so much oral history from older residents, I thought it would be interesting to take this a little further, and find out what today's children think of their village. Miss Mary Viner and Miss Katherine Hunter were kind enough to act as judges with me for an essay competition advertised through the *Village News*. Prizes of book-tokens were presented at a tea-party, and in between mouthfuls of chocolate cake, the winning essays sparked off lively discussions between young and old. I hope the readers of this book will be equally entertained.

The Eel Trap by Lucy Briscoe

My favourite place? Well, it must be the eel trap. If you do not know what an eel trap is I will describe it for you. It is a small bridge over the river at a confluence (where a river splits in two), the water rushes through the eel trap leaving any eels or debris contained in its flow. It is let through by two old stone sluice gates; some water flows through into the main river and on, other water runs down a small channel and into a large concrete box. The latter has a small grill in the side to let out the water, however, any unfortunate eels remain trapped in the box.

You can stand and lean on the rails of the bridge, but I prefer to climb around them and sit on the box sheltered by the willows. Here you can contemplate the timelessness of the atmosphere. All your thoughts are drowned in the tumultuous crash of the crazied froth of the water beneath you. The noise is immense, you would not hear if anyone was there to talk to you. Some days the river is very full and the froth and the bubbles roar at an incredible pace and reach high above the water level. Then the foam rages in your ears and crashes against itself like thunder, and then you could be anyone, anywhere, anytime.

On quieter days you can as it were contemplate your surroundings. To your right you can just see the tiny bridge over a small stream and the path on into the field beyond, away over two bridges there, into the track that leads towards Tackley. To your left is the small path back over a tiny bridge past the mill and the old pub to the lock. In front of you stretches the tumbling waters of the river. A few yards ahead is a small ridgeway of raised stones – all that remains of the ford. Amid the crash of the spurting water it is easy to hear the wheels of wagons and carts crashing over the river in years gone by, maybe going up to the mill or the pub or on business from Tackley to the village.

This is the air of timelessness that flows with the water around the eel trap. You sit there for an unknown length of time, lost in your thoughts as they foam and swirl, rushing through your head, as the waves through the sluice gates, to join the main stream of thoughts bubbling on as one.

Then when realism creeps back around you and you get up and look at the web of your thoughts, you slowly walk back along the well-trodden path and the rushing, tearing, raging of the water lessens in your ears, it becomes quieter, quieter, like a gentle waterfall until it dwindles and fades. Only a whisper quivers in the air, the faint rhythm of the eel trap.

Lucy Briscoe
Age 15
The Barnhouse, Kirtlington

The Park by Anna Kennedy

I really like the park and we are lucky enough to live opposite it. I often go for walks there. I have a friend called Roy who takes his dogs for walks in the park; I sometimes go with him. On our walks we have seen quite a few interesting things. We have seen a grey squirrel, some rabbits and pheasants. We have picked conkers which aren't quite ripe so I ripen them off on our garden wall. There are cows in the park and I often stroke the little bump in between their ears. Number 64 came quite a lot to the fence where we stopped and had a little rest. In the paddock by the park gates used to live a pony called Honey. My friend Roy used to exercise her up and down the park but she died a couple of years ago. Now there is a brown bay horse called Polly living in that paddock. She is my favourite thing in the park. Just before Christmas she went up to South Farm to have her foal in February. Me and Roy can't wait for Polly and her foal to come back to the paddock. My friend Isobelle wants Polly to have her foal on her birthday which is in February. Farther across the fields Polo goes on every Saturday or Sunday. Last summer Prince 'Charles' came to play polo on our pitch. Once every year Mr. Buxton (the owner of the park) closes the gates. My dad says that he does it just to show that it belongs to him. Right down in the heart of the park, there is a lovely lake. On one of our family walks we thought we saw an Otter. A lovely surprise once was a great crested grebe with its chicks. Sometimes there is a hunt. We saw a man dragging a piece of cloth. It was the scent for the hounds to follow.

I have really enjoyed going for walks in the park and now I have written this piece I hope you will enjoy going for walks too and get as much out of it as I do.

Anna Kennedy
Age 10
The Cottage, Heyford Road, Kirtlington

The Pond by Tom Kennedy

I like the Pond because the baby moorhens are there in the Summer. I like to see the moorhens go up to their island.

I think my toys go to the Pond at mid night.

I think a Witch has cast a spell on the wall because it falls down in the same Place each winter. I think the Witch Lives in the crooked tree on South Green.

Part two.

Perhaps the Witch has Planted a Spell on the daffodils to make them come up each year. Mathew wickson my dad and I and other men helped to clear a lot of ducweed. I suppose the Witch could Live under the weeping willow. My dad used to be in charge of the Pond. When I am old I will see if the wall Falls down each year Still.

Tom Kennedy
Age 7
The Cottage, Heyford Road, Kirtlington

APPENDIX ONE

The Old Folks at Home

Extracts from a letter-poem by Maggie May Kirtland

Just take old Suet and his daughter Dot,
She would like to have married old Johnny Scott,
Then poor old Pudden, who used to get tight,
And call at our house to wish us good night.
Old Tommy Young whose nickname was 'Nobble'
Would have been sorry to see me shut in the hovel.

There was Muffle, Shant Gate, and our old dog Toby,
And our mother who said 'you're quite welcome Joby'
When he got up from the table and said 'Thank you Mam'
After having a plate of our good home-cured ham.
Chitto his brother had killed many a pig,
There was Buttery, old Ducan, and my dear old Jig.

Let's get back to the old folk who lived near the Green,
A handsomer lot, I'm sure never was seen,
Old Coleman who went to the pits to dig stones,
And with Mrs. Hawkes lived her sister Miss Jones.
Can't you hear my old Jig singing 'Hoe the Corn Hoe'?
'Tis true that he sang from night until morn,
But I've never yet known him to go hoeing corn.

There was old Billy Scarsbrook and his brother Tom,
Our Babe's God Dad and God Ma were people called Long.
We had no Tom Thumb and we had no Miss Muffett,
But we had old Jack Pearman and old Daddy Puffett.
Now old Plumper Welch was a man who was blind.
Lived next to Will Collett and his family of nine.

And Danky and Satty they made quite a pack,
All lived in the village quite near to each other,
So if you knew one, of course you knew t'other.
Annie Simons and Henry, and Bess who was lame,
And old Ninky Tims who lived down the lane.

The Kirtland family were all very jolly,
The eldest one married a girl called Polly,
They were brought up together, and are still very clanny,
Les the other boy married a girl called Annie,
There was Annie and Nellie, Mag, Jess and Flor,
Then along came Millie, and she made one more.

135

When I read out these verses before going to bed,
Bob said, 'Silly thing, you're going soft in the head'.
I had a good laugh, but he doesn't see the joke quite,
He didn't know Kate Herbert and her old brother Mike
Who went every morning to work out at Wesson'
We shall have to go for him and teach him a lesson.

He doesn't improve, and he says 'Well who cares'.
I tell him I'll go down and fetch Policeman Ayres,
Who lived in our village a long time ago,
And must have heard Jig singing 'Hoe the corn hoe'.
I'm sure Nancy Biffett his aunt heard him sing,
As he tripped down the Causeway with a beautiful swing.

Down on the Green there lived old Charlie Badger,
A funnier man it would have been hard to find,
And at bed time he never would pull down the blind.
The kiddies would watch Charlie get into bed,
And often would shout 'Put your cap on your head'.
He wore a night cap and he looked such a fright,
When the kids shouted 'Badger!' he would put out the light.

Now Carter Stratford for Farmer Edgington worked,
If you rode in his waggon you would find that it jerked,
When the farm was for sale Carter Stratford felt sad,
And when selling the horses he said to our Dad,
'He can't sell old Bonny, she's such an old thing,
I'd as soon see her dead as put in the ring'.
Then Farmer Edgington came along where they stood,
'You'll not sell her Gaffer to you she's been good'.
Poor old Carter Stratford he looked very grave,
But his words to his master, old Bonny had saved,
The horse seemed to know when the sale was all past,
That she would stay with her master right up to the last.

Now the other morning a letter arrived,
The postmark was Bletchingdon on the outside,
It's from Auntie Millie our Rob said to me,
Then I tore it open and read it with glee,
I laughed when I read it, and thought it was sport,
I didn't know Jimmy Enser had an old horse called Short.

For me to write more is out of the question,
So while you are reading I hope you'll keep grave,
And when you have finished, please send to our Babe,
There's a number of verses I'm sure you'll agree.
And to write them again would about tire me.
I can just hear you laughing as I'm sure she would do.
With love from us all here to Theo and you.

Maggie May Kirtland was born in Kirtlington on 12 July 1883. When she was 15 she left school and went into service as a kitchen-maid, which meant leaving home. Four years later, she was working as a cook. She later married Robert L. Dollar, the 'Bob' of the poem. In 1925 she became a member of the St. Pancras Board of Guardians, and was also a member of the London County Council. Between 1928 and 1961, she served on the committees of three London hospitals – two of them as chairman. Perhaps her finest achievement was her appointment as a justice of the peace in 1934, a position she maintained until 1958. She was also on the boards of governors of several schools and, during the Second World War, worked for two years at the B.B.C. This remarkable lady died on 26 April 1980, at the age of ninety-six.

APPENDIX TWO

The Folk Tradition in Kirtlington

The Lamb Ale Festival

Fig. 46. William Kemp dances to the pipe and tabor.

The festival may have originated in the village's earliest Christian days, for it was the practice of missionaries then to permit their converts to celebrate the establishment of the new church with a feast and entertainment. Although we have no record of it for centuries, it seems certain that it had been long-established by the time Sir Robert Dashwood noted in his account book in 1732 - 'Gave 5s 0d Kirtling Morris at the Lamb Ale'.

It was customary for the lord of the manor to provide a piece of land for the Lamb Ale, and this area is shown on the 1811 Enclosure Map, apparently corresponding to the present allotments in Crow Castle Lane. The feast was held in the 'Lord's Hall' nearby, and older residents remember a path which led up from Mill Lane in this direction, past the *Six Bells* ale house.

Henry Taunt, who compiled a unique photographic record of Oxfordshire in the 1890s and 1900s, also wrote a short history of Kirtlington. He gives a description of the Lamb Ale, including references from Thomas Hearne's *Diary* and Blount's *Tenures*.

At Kirtlington, many years ago, tradition says 'a piece of land was set apart for the Lamb Ale, on one part of which wheat was grown to make the cake, and on the other barley to make the beer. There is no record of this now. Afterwards the Lord of the Manor annually gave £2.12s. in lieu of the land, but that, too, dropped when the Lamb Ale was discontinued ... The Lamb Ale was first held at Easter or Whitsuntide, but the date was afterwards changed to Trinity Monday [which is still kept as the date today]. Hearne, in his dairy, mentions 'Lamb-day' at 'Kirtleton', and goes on to say 'It seems on Monday after Whitsun week there is a fat live lamb provided, and the maids of the town having their thumbs tied behind them, run after it, and she that with her mouth takes, and holds, this lamb, is declared 'Lady of the lamb', which being dressed with the skin hanging on it is carried on a long pole before the Lady and her Companions to the green, attended with music and a Morrice dance of men, and another of women, where the rest of the day is spent in dancing, mirth and jollity. The next day the lamb is part baked, part boyled and roast, for the Lady's feast, where she sits majestically (and much respect is shown her) at the upper end of the table, and her companions with her with musick and other attendants, which ends the solemnity ... I am told 'tis on account of the inhabitants being toll free in Oxford and other places'...

Taunt noted that the form of the feast had changed somewhat in later years:

One of the barns, called the Lord's Hall, which stood just behind the gravel pit, was cleared out and dressed up with greenery and banners, and when the dray with the load of ale was due ... the Morrice dancers met it at Bletchingdon and escorted it to the village. Previously, one of the prettiest maids of the village was engaged at a fee of 25s. for three days, and a lamb being procured was dressed up with blue ribbons, and carried round on one of the men's shoulders to the different farmhouses and those of the tradesmen in the village; and at each place, after a dance, beer and money was given to the dancers, and that helped to pay for the feast. The lamb was then shut up till the Wednesday, and then killed, and boiled, and roasted the same day, and served the next in the Lord's Hall. The dancers consisted of a Lord ... two sword bearers who carried the Lamb Ale cake on staves ... six Morrice dancers proper ... These were attended by a Clown, and by one musician with a pipe and a tabor, and later by another with a violin ... After all expenses were paid, the balance (if any) was divided amongst the performers. The greatest deference was paid to the Lady ... only a modest and good girl was chosen for this important office. The lamb was not killed of later years, but grew so tame with being carried about and fed by hand, that he would follow the man like a dog.

The character of the Lamb Ale was considerably altered by the involvement of the Oddfellows and Box Club Friendly Societies in the later 19th century, and the effects of this involvement lasted until the 1920s. The Societies held their annual festivities on Trinity Monday, and included a church service, a dinner, a band, and the provision of fairground amusements. The Morris dancers were disbanded, and the special nature of the Lamb Ale was almost forgotten. George Dew, the relieving officer for the district, wrote in his diary on 12 June 1876:

There are two Benefit or Friendly Societies at Kirtlington, both of which hold their annual holiday today. There were many people there, and numbers of stalls and places of amusements, as well as an electrical machine, and the drunkeness as I rode through this afternoon was most disgraceful. This is the day I am told on which was formerly kept the 'Lamb Ale' in which a lamb was carried round in procession.

The children looked forward to the fair's coming all year. For those who had to work or go to school on Trinity Monday, a sudden attack of 'Lamb Ale Fever' was the solution – an illness for which the only cure was an immediate removal of the patient to the fairground!

In the 1920s there was a national revival of interest in England's folk tradition, and at this time morris dancers reappeared in Kirtlington. The true revival of the specifically Kirtlington morris, however, is the achievement of Len and Barbara Berry. They discovered a mass of information at Cecil Sharp House in London, the 'headquarters' of the folklore movement. Meanwhile in Yorkshire a dedicated Morris man called Paul Davenport had discovered two Kirtlington dances – 'Trunkles' and 'Old Woman Tossed Up'. He contacted the Berrys, and a new morris team was formed, to perform Kirtlington's own dances for the first time in over a century. The steps are complicated and dancers need to be fit and active. It takes at least six months to achieve competence, and practice sessions take place in the old indoor tennis court at Kirtlington Park.

Fig. 47.   Morris dancer.

The next problem was discovering what the correct costume should be. The Oxford Museum records that the Dashwood colours of pink and turquoise were used around 1800. The outfit consisted of an ornate grey and white striped waistcoat, moleskin trousers, a loose-sleeved white cotton shirt, baldricks or cross-bands over the legs decorated with rosettes, and a top-hat. The dancers were followed by two men with the 'Forest Feathers', a fertility symbol, being stout clubs decorated with rushes, flowers and ribbons. Apparently, young girls danced with the 'Feathers' at the end of the festival. Barbara and Len have created a costume based on this information. Paul Davenport designed 'Elmo', the morris's mascot, a griffon carved from elmwood, taken from the Dashwood coat of arms. The new Kirtlington Morris Dancers made their first appearance at the 1980 Lamb Ale Festival.

Besides the morris dancers, there are the 'Cyrtla dancers', young girls for whom Barbara has designed and made attractive white dresses, worn with pink sashes. Paul Davenport arranged a special dance for this group, in honour of the Berry's silver wedding!

The Berrys have also researched and reconstructed the old Lamb Ale procession. They had to remake the mace from an old illustration, as the original had been sold to Cecil Sharp House, where it was destroyed by a bomb during the last war. Barbara has adapted an old recipe for the Lamb Pie, containing rosemary and potatoes, as well as the meat.

Besides the folklore part of the festivities, however, there are other aspects to today's Lamb Ale festival. The fair is still a popular attraction for the young (and young-in-heart); the Lamb Ale Committee plan the feast and the amusements as far ahead as January. Edna Edgington, a member of the committee for many years, has the final word:

> The Lamb Ale in Kirtlington is still going strong – we are the only village to keep up the tradition. We have a good day here with dancing and ale. Sometimes the University Morris men come. The Merton Mayflies play us at cricket – there's a two-day Fair; it is our day, our feast, a jealously-guarded event, and treasured by all. This feeling even comes out in the younger generation.

Let us hope that the young people of the village will in their turn keep this fascinating traditional festival alive.

The Mummers of Kirtlington

Kirtlington can boast three mummers' plays, but they only came to light a few years ago. In the early part of this century, an American folklore enthusiast visited England to collect songs and plays. After some time, it was decided to return his mass of material to England, and it has remained ever since in the vaults of Cecil Sharp House. Here the three plays were discovered by a friend of Barbara and Len Berry. The material included notes about a play recalled by the late Robert Pearman of Kirtlington, and this is the one usually performed in the village today, augmented somewhat by material from the other plays.

* * *

MOLLY: (*besom in hand, comes in sweeping*)
            Good masters and good mistresses,
            I hope y'er all within.
            I come this merry Christmas time
            To catch you on the wing,
            Make room for me and my brave boys,
            And if you won't believe all that I say,
            Step in King George, and clear the way,
            Come in King George.
KING GEORGE: In comes I, King George,
            The man of courage bold.
            With my sword in hand,
            I won ten thousand pounds in gold,
            And men 'henters this door,
            I'll cut 'im down with my created hand.
            I'll cut 'im small as dust,
            Send him to make pie crust –
            Come in Jolly Frenchman.
JOLLY FRENCHMAN: In come I, the Jolly Frenchman,
            Where is that man that bid me stand,
            Said he'd cut me with his created hand.
            So an I'm come to face my foe,
            To give this man the created blow,
            So cock up your sword, and keep guard on your eye,
            Else down in this house you'll very soon lie.
(*They fight with wooden swords. The Jolly Frenchmen knocks King George down.*)
JOLLY FRENCHMAN: W'ur's the Doctor?
DOCTOR: 'Yure he is.
(*Doctor comes in riding on the back of Jack Spinney, who throws him off.*)
JOLLY FRENCHMAN: Doctor, Doctor, do they part,
            King George is 'oonded through the heart.
            Once at ant, and once at
            Ten pounds I'll freely give to thee.
DOCTOR: Who killed this man?
JOLLY FRENCHMAN: You did, for I didn't.

DOCTOR: I'm not one o' those quick quick doctors.

    I go about the country to cure not kill.

    Any old dummon is dead an' laid in her grave

    She was to take one o' my pills.

    I'm bound to cure 'er

    An' if this man an't too far gone,

    I can cure him too.

JOLLY FRENCHMAN: Cure 'en then.

(*Doctor has a tin box with peas in it, shakes and pretends to give wounded man one.*)

DOCTOR: Take one of my pills, as round as a vall,

    To cure his back, belly, stomach and all,

    Goes down his throat like soapsuds down a sinkhole,

    Comes out like a threshing machine.

(*pretends to give pill*)

    Now is the case as it was before;

    Rise up King George and fight once more.

(*King George gets up and fights the Jolly Frenchman again, who pushes him out at the end of his sword.*)

JOLLY FRENCHMAN: Wur's the doctor?

DOCTOR: 'Yure he is.

JOLLY FRENCHMAN: My old dummon was took very bad last night.

    How much do you charge to cure her?

DOCTOR: Ten pound!

JOLLY FRENCHMAN: Ten pound? I can't afford to give you ten pound,

    I pore man – I'll give you fifteen!

DOCTOR: Fetch 'er in, and let's have a look at 'er.

(*Jolly Frenchman and King George fetch Molly back, who is shaking and trembling all the while. They pretend to seat her in a chair and suddenly snatch from under her, so she falls on the floor. Then she gets into it. Doctor catches her by both hands, and pulls her about.*)

DOCTOR: Poor old crater, I think, she takes snuff,

    otherwise she chews tobacco. I think she's got the belly ache.

    I think she's got the toothache.

KING GEORGE: Well, draw it then!

(*Doctor gets a pair of pincers, and a large horse's tooth, puts it into the pincers, puts it up to her mouth. Two men get behind. As he draws, they push her head forward. He holds up tooth in pincers.*)

DOCTOR: Well enough, the pore old crater might suffer – look at the tooth!

MUMMERS: Come in Beelzebub!

BEELZEBUB: In comes I, old Father Beelzebub am I,

    On my shoulder I carries my club,

    And in my hand a drippin' pan,

    Don't you think I'm a merry old man?

    I had three sons come home last night,

    Hawking' and spawking' and spittin' about the house.

    I bred 'em all three up in a sawpit;

    As I was a gwine a broad narrow lane

    I met a pigsty tied to an eldern bush,

    I knocked at the maid,

And out comes the door.
Her ast' me if I could drink a crust of bread and cheese,
And eat half a pint of beer.
I said 'no thank you', but meant 'yes please'!

MUMMERS: Come in Jack Spinney!
JACK SPINNEY: (*outside*)
My name y'ent Jack Spinney,
My name's 'Mister Spinney'.
In comes I as 'ant been it,
With my great head and little wit,
My head's so big, my wit's so small,
I've brought a fiddle to plaze 'e all.

(*Plays on fiddle stick strung with wire.*)
(*The Play closes with the last two lines of song:*)
So all bonny lassies, fill up y'er glasses,
Let's have a little bit of a jig.

Bibliography

Alexander, Henry, *The Place Names of Oxfordshire*, Clarendon Press, 1912.

Alexander, Michael, *Beowulf*, trs., Penguin Classics, 1980.

Beazley, Michael, *Encyclopaedia of Prehistoric Life*, Rodney Steel & Anthony P. Harvey, 1979.

Bede, *A History of the English Church and People*, Penguin Classics, 1982.

Branston, Brian, *The Lost Gods of England*, Thames & Hudson, 1974.

Brown, Rev. W. L., *Plan of Alchester*, 1841.

Buchanan, R. A., *Industrial Archaeology in Britain*, Penguin, 1977.

Budgett, Hubert, *Hunting by Scent* (private circulation).

Chaucer, Geoffrey, *The Canterbury Tales*, Penguin Classics.

Clare, John, *The Shepherd's Calendar*, OUP, 1973.

Compton, Hugh J., *The Oxford Canal*, David & Charles, 1976.

Cox, Barry, *Prehistoric Animals*, Hamlyn, 1969.

Cunliffe, Barry, *Iron Age Communities in Britain*, Routledge, 1974.

Curling, Bill, *Derby Double*, William Luscombe, 1977.

Dawson, Keith, *The Industrial Revolution*, Pan Books.

Dodsworth, Charles, *The Early Years of the Cement Industry*.

Forrester, C. S., *Hornblower and the Atropos*, Sphere, 1980.

Fussell, G. E. and K. R., *The English Countryman*, Orbis Publication Co.

Garmonsway, G. N., *Translation of the Anglo Saxon Chronicle*, J. M. Dent, London, reprinted 1982.

Hadfield, Charles, *British Canals*, David & Charles, 1979.

Halstead, I. B. and Jenny, *Dinosaurs*, Blandford Press, 1981.

Hansen, Harry, *Canal People*, David & Charles, 1978.

Hansen, Harry, *The Canal Boatman, 1760-1914*, Manchester University Press, 1975.

Hartley, Dorothy, *The Land of England*, McDonald General Books.

Hoskins, W. G., *The Making of the English Landscape*, Pelham.

Hodges, Sid, *Bicester wuz a little town*, Sprint Print, 1968.

Horn, Pamela, *The Rural World, 1780-1850*, Hutchinson, 1980.

Jenkins, J. Geraint, *The English Farm Wagon*, David & Charles, 1981.

Kivall, E., *English River Names*, Clarendon Press.

Landsell, Avril, *The Clothes of the Cut*, British Waterways Board.

Leeson, R. A., *Travelling Brothers*, Paladin, 1980.

Malet, Hugh, *The Canal Duke*, David & Charles, 1961.

McKnight, Hugh, *Shell Book of Inland Waterways*.

McMaster, J., *History of Kirtlington, Oxfordshire*.

Mossman, Keith, *Shell Book of Rural Britain*, David & Charles, 1978.

Muir, Richard, *The English Village*, Thames & Hudson, 1981.

Parker, James, *The Early History of Oxford, 727-1100*, Oxford Historical Society, 1885.

Postan, M. M., *The Medieval Economy*, Pelican, 1981.

Plot, Robert, *The Natural History of Oxfordshire*, 1677.

Prior, Mary, *Fisher Row*, Clarendon Press, 1982.

Ransom, P. J. G. *The Archaeology of Canals*, Worlds Work, 1979.
Readers Digest *Field Guide to the Wild Flowers of Britain*.
Richardson, C., *Practical Farriery*, Pitman, 1973.
Rolleston, Margaret Ann, *An English History Note Book*, 1924.
Royal Agricultural Society Journal, Vol. 24, Part II, John Murray, 1863.
Samuel, Raphael, *Village Life and Labour*, History Workshop Series, 1975.
Searle, Alfred B., *The Natural History of Clay*, Cambridge University Press, 1912.
Sherwood, R. E. *Civil Strife in the Midlands*, Phillimore, 1974.
Smith, Donald J., *The Horse on the Cut*, Patrick Stephens, Cambridge, 1982.
Stenton, Doris Mary, *English Society in the Middle Ages*, Pelican, 1955.
Stukeley, W., *Itinerarium Curiosum*, 1776.
Tate Gallery Publication, *Constable: Paintings, Watercolours and Drawings*. Taunt, H. W., *Kirtlington, Oxfordshire*, 1905.
The Victoria County History of Oxfordshire, vols. 1-9.
Thomas, Leslie, *The Hidden Places of England*, 1981.
Townsend, James, M.A., *The Oxfordshire Dashwoods*, OUP, 1922 (private circulation).
Walker, E. D., *The Natural History of the Oxford District*, 1926.
Walton, Izaak, *The Compleat Angler*.
Wilson, J., *Roses and Castles*, Waterways Museum (booklet).
Young, Arthur, *General View of the Agriculture of Oxfordshire*, 1813.
Young, G. M., *Victorian England*, OUP, 1949.

Items in the Local History Collection, Oxford County Library

Oxfordshire Census Returns 1841-1881 (inclusive, all on microfilm).
18th and 19th-century Oxfordshire papers (some on microfilm).
Kirtlington Parish Magazine and The Village News.
Extensive Kirtlington ephemera and photographs.
The Victoria County History of Oxfordshire.

Magazines

The Waterways World (various).
The New Scientist, 17 May 1979.
Science, vol. 194, 3 December 1976.
Blue Circle Publications.
Oxford 1929-79 (booklet).
Circle Magazine (various).
Blue Circle News Sheets (various).
Bicester Hunt News
Country Life
Horse and Hound
Shooting Times
Farmers Weekly
The Countryman
The Ark

Manuscript Material

Dashwood, Sir James, 'A General Account of money expended on my new House and
the outworks about it, began 12th September 1741' East, Charles, 'The Bread
Book' 1850-1855.
Gile, Aubrey, 'A Soldier's Diary'
The account books of the Kirtland family, Blacksmiths and Farriers.
Notebooks of the late Ernest James King.

Newspapers

Jackson's Oxford Journal
Jackson's Oxford Journal Illustrated
Oxford Times

In the possession of the Bodleian Library

Blome Richard, *The Gentleman's Recreation*, 1686.
The 'John Johnson, and 'Douce' collection of printed ephemera (various).
Settlement certificates (various).
Griffiths, Matthew, 'An Oxfordshire Community, 1500-1750'. (Thesis) Ps.D.Phil.d.
6549.

In the possession of the County Record Office

Parish Registers
Gamekeepers' Deputations
Victuallers' Recognizances
Extensive Dashwood manuscripts and papers
19th-century Directories of Oxfordshire
Bicester Magistrates Records
Kirtlington Wills and Inventories
Parish Records

Index

Abingdon, pilgrimage to, 5
Agricultural Labourers Union, The National, 9, 94, 112
Akeman Spinney, 122
Akeman Street, 1
Alchester (Old Town), 1, 2
Anglo-Saxon: jewellery, 3; settlement, 2, 3; village dialect, 4
Apprentices (Kirtlington), 53
Arden, Anthony, 24, 70
Aulnay, Abbey of, 5
Aulnay, Lucy de, 5
Aves Ditch (Ash Bank or Wattle Bank), 2

Bede, 5
Bennett, the Revd. Reginald George, 11
Bennett, the Revd. Reginald Ward, 11, 52, 119
Beules, Alice, 13
Beules, Henry, 13
Bicester (Berncestre): 1, 13, 71; Magistrate's Court, 61, 88, 124; Medieval hospital, 13, 14; Priory, 14, 25; Workhouse, 56
Bicester and Warden Hill Hunt, 76, 77, 107
Birinus, St, 5
Blackamoor, Thomas the, 19
Black Death, 7, 15, 63
Blacklands Field, 2
Blacksmiths and farriers, 110, 112, 122, 123, 124
Blake, Edith, 51, 125
Blake, Frederick, 124-5
Blake, Winifred, 125, 129
Bletchingdon: 3, 28, 53, 76, 87, 96, 106, 127-8, 139; Manor House, 28; Park, 111
Blue Circle Industries p.l.c., 95
Bodsworth, Victor, 89
Bohun, Humphrey de, 14
Bohun, Joan de, 14
Bohun, Mary de, 14
Bordars, 12
Bowelles Manor, 13
Brindley, James, 82, 89 see also Oxford Canal
Brokenton, Thomas, 14, 75
Bronze Age (settlers), 1
Brown, Lancelot ('Capability'), 31, 40
Bryon, Richard, 22
Buckland, William, 96

Budgett: Alan, 41, 79, 80; Arthur, 71, 79, 80, 81, 117; Hazel, 23, 38, 40, 41, 51, 77, 80, 107; Heather, 81; Hubert, 23, 38, 40, 51, 77, 107, 125; James, 81
Bull, Betty, 24
Bull, Thomas, 24
Buxton, Christopher, 35, 40, 41, 42

Camville, Gerard de, 13
Carucates, 12
Cattle, 73, 111, 124, 126
Census returns (1841-1881), 61, 71, 86, 100, 101, 112
Chamberlain, Sir Thomas, 17, 19
Chandler, Mrs. Edith Georgina see Giles family
Chapel of St John the Baptist, 13
Charles I (king), 27
Charles II (king), 29
Cherwell, River, 1, 12
Chittenden, the Revd. Thomas, 9, 56, 73
Church of St Mary the Virgin: Attendances (18th century), 8; Bellringers, 9, 35, 120; Choir and music, 9, 101; Expenses (general), 8, 11, 27, 33; Furnishings and relics, 5, 7, 8, 11; Parish registers, 8, 27, 53; Parish Vestry, 60; Priests and clergy, 5, 6, 112; Recusants, 8; Saxon origins, 5; Tithes, 7, 68; Vandalism, 7
Civil War, 8, 27, 28
Cockes, John, 24
'College', the, 54, 56
Cooper, Fred, 52
Cottager, 16
Cromwell, Oliver, 28, 29
Crowcastle Lane, 2, 49
Cuthred, 3
Cyrtla's Brook, 3
Cyrtla's Gate, 3

Dashwood Arms, 61, 89, 126
Dashwood: Sir Robert (1st Bart), 8, 66, 75, 83, 138; Sir James (2nd Bart), 8, 22, 26, 30, 31, 32, 33, 36, 56, 66, 78, 99; Sir Henry Watkin (3rd Bart), 33, 61, 82, 83, 124; Sir George (4th Bart), 33; Sir Henry William (5th Bart), 8, 33, 90, 100, 123-4; Sir George Egerton (6th Bart), 23, 37, 47, 56, 61, 70, 88, 100;

Dashwood (cont.)
   Lady Mary, 11, 34; Charles, Lt.-Col., 46;
   Frederick Loftus, Major, 34, 71; Henry
   George Mayne, 33; Margaret Frances, 34;
   Muriel, 35, 36; Children, 19, 33, 35, 47;
   Expenditure, 19, 33; Family crest and
   motto, 19; Marriages, 30, 33, 34; Political
   Lye, 19, 32, 33, 34; Property Transactions,
   19, 23, 31, 56; Sports and pastimes, 19, 33,
   78
Deane, the Revd. James, 73, 103
Deed, Major, 80
Despenser, Hugh, 14
Dew, George James, 71, 91, 101, 139
Dillon, Major A. H., see Oxford Portland
   Cement Company
Dillon, Viscount, 34
Dinosaurs, 96
Dissenters, 9
Dolphin Inn, 8, 27
Domesday Survey, 12, 83
Dunstan, archbishop, 5
Duns Tew, Manor of, 30

East: Albert, 46, 110, 111; Algernon, 111;
   Aubrey, 111; Charles (sen.), 46, 100, 110,
   112, 115; Charles (jun.), 111; Dollie, 111;
   Ethel, 111; Frances, 110, 111; Jack, 111;
   Jessie, 111; Louie, 111; Luesa Ann Avenal,
   110; Percy, 111; Robert, 111; Walter, 110,
   111; William, 109
Edward I (king), 5, 12
Edward III (king), 13, 14
Edward IV (king), 15
Edwards, Lionel, 77
Eeley, James, 23, 118
Eeley, Joseph, 71
Emigration, 73
Enclosure Act (1811), 63, 66, 76, 83, 121, 138

Farming patterns (16th-18th-century), 58, 63,
   66, 68, 73
Faulkner, Mrs. Esmé, 119
Fishing, eel-trapping, 83, 89
Flight, Frances, 26
Flight's Mill, 28, 50, 70, 83, 88, 89, 94, 118
Football, 121, 124
Fox, Frises, 16
Fox, John, 16
Foxtownsend Farm, 115, 120
Freeman, Eric, 96
Friendly Societies, 57

Gamekeepers, poachers, 124
Gaunt, John of, 14
Gay, Jordon de, 5
Gay, Hilda de, 16

Gay, John de, 16
George II (king), 32, 58
George III (king), 33
George Inn, 19
George and Dragon Inn, 110
Gibbs, James, 40
Gibraltar, Rock of (inn), 86
Giles: Aubrey, 49, 89, 118, 119; Edith Georgina
   (later Chandler), 118; Laurence, 89, 94

Hall, Anthony, 26
Hardley Farm, 2
Harres, Thomas, 24
Harvesting, 71
Hawkes, John, 34, 53
Henry IV (king), 14
Henry VI (king), 15
Henry VIII (king), 14
Her Majesty the Queen, 81
Hermit see Jurdan
Heyford Camp, 51
Hides, 12
Hiring Fair, 71
Hoar Stone Spinney, 1
Horses: breeding, 78, 79; hunters and agricul-
   tural, 106, 108, 111, 115-16, 123
Horse racing (flat), 78, 79
Humez, Richard de, 5
Humez, William de, 12
Hundred Court, 13
Hunting, 75
Hunt Racing, 22, 76

Iron Age: pottery, 1; burials, 1

Jackson's Oxford Journal, 33, 34, 37, 38, 43,
   71, 73, 77, 128
Jackson's Oxford Journal (illustrated), 46
Jersey, the earl of, 70, 76, 79, 106
Johnson, Bill, 115
Johnson, Ada (née Hawtin), 115, 117
Johnson children, 116
Journeymen, 53, 54
Jurdan, Nicholas, 13

Kermack, Dr., 96
Kelly's Directory, 68
King: Beatrice, 126; Charlie, 46, 126; Emma,
   127; Ernie, 49, 52, 77, 83, 88, 90, 92, 93,
   96, 97, 105, 109, 125, 126, 127, 128, 130;
   Eva, 128; Harry, 46, 47, 126, 128; Ivor,
   129; Joe, 126; Thomas, 126; Winifred (née
   Blake), 130; great-grandchildren, 129
Kirtland: Arthur, 122, 123; Edwin, 122, 123;
   John, 70, 122; Leslie, 77, 122, 123, 124;
   Maggie May, 137; Marion, 122, 123, 124

Kirtlington Park and Oxford University Polo
   Club, 42, 51, 80, 81
Kirtlington Schools: Attendances and log book,
   101, 103; Dame Schools, 99; Entertainments,
   103, 119; Expenses and endowments, 99,
   100, 101; Fees, 100, 101; Lessons, 99;
   Pupils and prizes, 86, 87, 100, 103, 105;
   School rules and legislation, 99, 100, 103,
   105; School song, 96; Staff, 46, 98, 100,
   101, 105; Times of war, 46, 47, 103, 105
Kirtlington village; Administration, 58, 60, 61,
   62; Amenities, 38, 123; Building work, 26;
   Highways, 60, 61, 109; Land tenancy
   changes, 15, 24, 41, 64; Manor House, 14,
   15, 30, 90; Manor tenants, 12, 13, 14, 15;
   Market, 25, 27; Organisations and clubs, 34,
   38, 40, 57, 68, 117, 127, 139; Origin of
   name, 1, 3; Population, 52, 99; Slaughter-
   house, 25, 73, 74; Tolls and taxes, 24, 61;
   Tradesmen and craftsmen, 24, 25, 61, 68,
   73, 112, 127; Turnpike, 61; War Memorial,
   47, 52; Woodland and tree planting, 31, 58,
   62, 73
Kirtlington Park, 16, 22, 23, 26, 31, 32, 34, 35,
   37, 38, 40, 41, 51, 77
Kite's Pond, 14, 41
Knights and Knights' Fee, 12, 13

Lamb Ale Festival, 128, 138, 139, 140
Lands Improvement Company, 71
Lenthal, Sir John, 27
Leven and Melville, the earls of, 34, 37, 38, 46,
   47, 76
Leven and Melville, the dowager countess of,
   37, 38, 47

Market boats, 86
Mercia, king of, 3
'Mercurius Aulicus', 27
Mermaid Tavern, 26
Methodist chapel, 9, 119
Middleton Stoney, 13, 70, 106, 109
Militia, the, 43
Miller, Sam, 71
Monkey Room, 32 see also Kirtlington Park
Morris Dancing, 139-40
Mummers Play, 141-3
'My Village', essays by Kirtlington children,
   132-4

Napoleonic wars, 43
Northbrook, manor of; Bridge, 22; Chapel, 16;
   Dovecot, 23; Farming, 16, 17, 22, 52, 63;
   Field names, 16, 23; Fishing, 16; Furnish-
   ings, 32; Inhabitants, 16, 17, 23, 30, 75;
   Tenants, 12, 16, 22, 23

Oldburie field, 1, 24
Osiers, 83
Oxford Agricultural shows, 70, 71, 92
Oxford Arms (Kirtlington), 92, 110
Oxford and Bucks Light Infantry, 46
Oxford Canal: Acts of Parliament, legislation,
   86, 88, 89; Animals, 83, 87, 88; Boatmen
   and their families, 83, 86, 87, 88; Boats
   and cargoes, 70, 83, 86, 88; Building and
   construction costs, 82; Company and work-
   force, 83, 95; Flora, 89; Pigeon Lock, 83, 88,
   89, 109, 118; Preliminaries and shareholders,
   82, 83; Tolls and income, 83, 86, 87, 88;
   Wharves and bridges, 22, 83
Oxford Flying Weekly (journal), 33
Oxford Portland Cement Company: Dillon,
   Major A. H., 90, 94, 121; Foundation
   and management of, 90, 95; Horses, 91;
   Machinery, 94; Raw materials and manufacturing processes, 90, 91, 92; Wages,
   costs, 92, 93; Workboats, 88, 91, 95;
   Workforce, 91, 92, 93, 105
Oxford and Shipton Cement Company, 94, 95,
   109
Oxford Times, 73
Oxfordshire Yeomanry, 43, 46, 71

Park Farm, 116, 117
Park, Keeper of, 14
Peninsular War, 46
Pigeon Lock see Oxford Canal
Pigeon shooting, 125
Pigs, pig farming, 68, 117, 121, 123
Plot, Robert, 96
Ploughley Hundred, 13
Police and lawbreakers, 25, 58, 60, 61, 63, 66,
   68, 125, 126
Portway House, 14, 78
Portway, The, 1, 2
Poverty and charity, 53, 54, 56, 60, 71, 75, 124
Powys, Mrs. Libby see Kirtlington Park
Prince Philip, His Royal Highness, 81

Queen's Own Oxfordshire Hussars Yeomanry,
   47
Queen Victoria, 34, 58

Rainald, 16
Railways (local), 70, 86, 88
Rawlins, Ralph, 22, 75
Reliance Dance Band, 108-9, 129
Rogers, Thomas, 26
Roman: coins, 2; road building, 1, 2;
   settlements, 1, 2, 94; villas, 2
Rook shooting, 125

Sandford, John, 8, 98
Saxon: barrow, 13; invaders, 2; settlers, 3

Scarrott: Jack, 120; Martha, 51, 120; Sybil,
    119; Will, 119
Serfs, 12
Settlement certificates, 54
Shepherds and sheep farming, 24, 63, 65, 70,
    71, 108, 109, 115, 121, 123, 126
Shipton-on-Cherwell, 94
Sideman, bishop, 5
Six Bells Inn, 61, 68
Slade Farm, 2, 51, 52
St Anne's, vicars of, 7
St John's College, 7
Strikes and unions, 73
Stukeley, W., 2, 13

Tackley, 3, 28, 49, 52, 87
Talbot: Alf, 108; David, 109; Edwell Walter,
    108; Ellen (née Woodley), 109; Jack, 108,
    109, 128, 129
Taunt, Henry, 138, 139
Temperance Society, The Church of England,
    34, 103
Thorman, Phillip, 73, 74
Thrupp, 89
Three Pigeons Alehouse, 83, 87, 88
Tooley, Herbert, 91
Tournaments, 13
Travellers and vagrants, 127
Tugwood: Adelaide, 106-7; Henry, 106-7; May,
    106-7; Victor, 106-7, 125

University College (London), 96
University Museum (Oxford), 96

Valentia (Viscount), 33, 34, 46, 76, 77, 127
Village News, 52, 132
Villeins, 12
Viner: Bob, 121; Edith, 121, 122; Henry, 115,
    116, 122; Mary, 73, 120, 121, 122
Virgates, 12
'Vitruvius Britannicus', 31

Wales, H.R.H. the Prince of, 42
Wales, H.R.H. the Princess of, 42
Wakefield's Bakery, 26
Walpole, Horace, 31
Washford Pits, 24, 88, 89, 94, 95, 96, 106
Waterways Board, 89
Waterways World, 91
Wetherby, Matthew, 8, 27
Whicker, Adrian, 8
Whicker, John, 8
Wickson family, 4, 87, 88
Wildreidge, Mr. Tindall, 1, 95
Wills and Inventories, 17, 22, 25, 66
Windebank, Lt. Col. Francis, 28
Witanagemot, The, 5
Weston-on-the-Green, 76
Woodstock, 98, 99
World War I, 46-9, 94, 126
World War II, 51-2, 80, 95, 105-6, 116, 120,
    129

Yardlands, 12

List of Subscribers

Mr. and Mrs. T. R. Abernethy
Frank and Doreen Attwood
Austin, Debbie and Robbie
Mrs. P. A. Baker
Amelia and Hannah Banks
N. S. and B. Barfoot
Wendy Basker
Mr. and Mrs. I. Bates
Lady Beach
The Belton Family
Margaret Bennett
Rev. R. G. Bennett
Reg Binning
Professor and Mrs. A. H. De Bono
Helen Bradley
Barbara Bramwell
Lucy Briscoe
Kathleen Burgin
Marjorie Butler
Lucy Calcutt
Joan Cannings (née Kirtland)
B. E. Carlo
Aubrey Cherry
Brian Cherry
Joan Cock
Peter Collett
B. D. Cooke
Frederick J. Cooper
Charles and Julie Courtney
A. D. M. Cox
J. W. M. Crisp
Brian and Alice Duncan
Mrs. Alice East
N. J. Eeley
Mr. and Mrs. Julian Eeley
J. A. Eldred
D. W. Enser
J. R. Enser (Jnr.)
J. R. and E. B. Enser
Peter R. T. Enser
A. Everett
S. K. Finesilver
Captain Nevill de Rouen Forth, T. D.
Eric F. Freeman
Mrs. S. Gee
J. N. and S. Gibbens
Bill Giles
Dorothy Giles
Mark Giles
Gerald J. Gracey-Cox
Roy M. Green
Mrs. G. E. Griffin

Lilian Griffin
B. H. Guy
Mr. and Mrs. E. W. Guy
Roy W. Halliwell
Margaret Harris
Richard G. and Janet Harwell
Celia Hawkesworth
Christopher Hawkesworth
Dorothy L. Hawkins
J. D. Hayes
John Hayward
Caroll A. Henderson
B. Hensman
Renée K. Hill (née May)
Miss J. R. Hilton
Dr. and Mrs. T. D. Hobbs
Doreen Hodgson
Christian G. Hunter
John Hunter
W. E. Isaacs
Miss Betty Jane Jalley
Stephanie James
G. A. and S. M. Jannetta
Eustace Jones
Brian C. Keys
Kay King
Mr. and Mrs. John Kirtland
Ron Kirtland
Kirtlington C. E. School
N. L. Lawrence
C. H. Lawton
David and Rosemary Marriott
Carolyn Mikula
Benjamin Moody
Freda Morgan
Dr. and Mrs. A. G. Mowat
Mrs. Frances Mussett
Ethel Needham
Philip and Emma Oldcorn
Oliver and Helen
Mr. and Mrs. N. L. Orchard
Oxfordshire County Libraries
David James Parrott
Mr. and Mrs. James Henry Parrott
B. P. and G. E. Pattemore
Clare A. Pearce-Boby
Mr. and Mrs. D. B. D. Petrie
Marguerita Pickles
Carol and Alan Ponsford
Alexander Postan
H. P. Powell

Neil S. Rawlins
Andrew and Melanie Read
Claud and Elizabeth Regnard
W. A. Rogers
W. K. Rose
Mrs. Sarah Rowe
L. J. Scarsbrook
Christopher Shapland
Ray Simmonds
Jean, Chris and Peter Simpson
A. G. Skinner
Verna and James Slack
Hazel Frances Smith
D. R. P. and J. M. Sprake
Anne and Mark Stallard
Mrs. P. A. Staveley
D. C. Strong
Elisabeth D. Svendsen, M. B. E.
Rupert Thorneloe
Francis and Muriel Toombs
A. W. Townsend
Mrs. M. H. Trafford
Michael and Sarah Traynor
J. H. Turnbull
John Tylor
Mrs. Alice Tyrrell
Edith Tyrrell
Frank Tyrrell
Mrs. J. W. Tyrrell (née Giles)
William F. Tyrrell
Barry Vickers
Steven Vickers
Miss M. Viner
A. Ward
Bill Warland
Daphne Warren
D. J. Watts, M.Phil.
Jan E. Westbrook
Julia Elizabeth White
Mr. and Mrs. Whitley
Leslie Wickson
M. W. J. Wickson
Roger Wickson
W. D. ('Bill') Wickson
Cynthia Wiernik
George Wiernik
Sonia Wiernik
Revd. David Wilcox
T. A. and J. C. Wilkins
Brian C. Wing
Nora Wooldridge